P9-BYG-523

Insatiable Appetite

Exploring World History
Series Editors
John McNeill, Georgetown University
Jerry Bentley, University of Hawai'i

As the world grows ever more closely linked, students and general readers alike are appreciating the need to become internationally aware. World history offers the crucial connection to understanding past global links and how they influence the present. The series will expand that awareness by offering clear, concise supplemental texts for the undergraduate classroom, as well as trade books that advance world history scholarship.

The series will be open to books taking a thematic approach—exploring commodities such as sugar, cotton, and petroleum; technologies, diseases, and the like—or a regional one—for example, Islam in Southeast Asia or east Africa, the Indian Ocean, or the Ottoman Empire. The series sees regions not simply as fixed geographical entities but as evolving spatial frameworks that have reflected and shaped the movement of people, ideas, goods, capital, institutions, and information. Thus, regional books would move beyond traditional borders to consider the flows that have characterized the global system.

Edited by two of the leading historians in the field, this series will work to synthesize world history for students, engage general readers, and expand the boundaries for scholars.

Insatiable Appetite: The United States and the Ecological Degradation of the Tropical World by Richard P. Tucker

Insatiable Appetite

The United States and the Ecological Degradation of the Tropical World

RICHARD P. TUCKER

Concise Revised Edition

ROWMAN & LITTLEFIELD PUBLISHERS, INC.
Lanham • Boulder • New York • Toronto • Plymouth, UK

Rowman & Littlefield Publishers, Inc.

Published in the United States of America
by Rowman & Littlefield Publishers, Inc.
A wholly owned subsidary of The Rowman & Littlefield Publishing Group, Inc.
4501 Forbes Boulevard, Suite 200, Lanham, Maryland 20706
www.rowmanlittlefield.com

Estover Road, Plymouth PL6 7PY, United Kingdom

Copyright © 2007 by Rowman & Littlefield Publishers, Inc.
All rights reserved. No part of this publication may be reproduced, stored in a
retrieval system, or transmitted in any form or by any means, electronic, mechanical,
photocopying, recording, or otherwise, without the prior permission of the publisher.

British Library Cataloguing in Publication Information Available

Library of Congress Cataloging-in-Publication Data

Tucker, Richard P., 1938-
  Insatiable appetite : the United States and the ecological degradation of the tropical
world / Richard P. Tucker. — Concise rev. ed.
     p. cm. — (Exploring world history)
  Includes bibliographical references and index.
  ISBN-13: 978-0-7425-5365-1 (pbk. : alk. paper)
  ISBN-10: 0-7425-5365-5 (pbk. : alk. paper)
  1. Tropical crops—Economic aspects—History—20th century. 2. Tropical crops—
Environmental aspects—History—20th century. 3. Investments, American—Tropics—
History—20th century. 4. Environmental degradation—Tropics—History—20th
century. I. Title.
  HD1417.T83 2007
  333.70913—dc22

                                                                        2006101556

Printed in the United States of America

♾ ™The paper used in this publication meets the minimum requirements of American
National Standard for Information Sciences—Permanence of Paper for Printed Library
Materials, ANSI/NISO Z39.48-1992.

Contents

List of Maps   vii

Preface and Acknowledgments   ix

Introduction: America's Global Environmental Reach   1

1   America's Sweet Tooth: Cane Sugar Transforms
Tropical Lowlands   7

2   Banana Republics: Yankee Fruit Companies and the
Tropical American Lowlands   43

3   The Last Drop: The American Coffee Market and the
Hill Regions of South America   81

4   The Tropical Cost of the Automotive Age: Corporate
Rubber Empires and the Rainforest   113

5   The Crop on Hooves: American Cattle Ranching in
Latin America   151

6   Unsustainable Yield: American Loggers and Foresters
in the Tropics   185

Conclusion: Consuming Appetites   217

Notes   223

Selected Bibliography   251

Index   255

About the Author   269

Maps

1.1	West Indies	13
1.2	Hawaiian Islands	26
1.3	Philippine Islands	29
2.1	Central America	45
2.2	Ecuador, Venezuela, and Colombia	66
3.1	Brazil, Uruguay, and Argentina	85
4.1	Southeast Asia	120
4.2	Liberia	129
5.1	Mexico	154

Preface and Acknowledgments

Insatiable Appetite was originally published in 2000 by the University of California Press. This new edition is a condensation of the original text; each chapter is also updated with material from more recent publications. In addition, it includes both a new Introduction and new Conclusions. The original bibliography has been replaced by a Selected Bibliography that points readers to major writings on global and regional environmental history and the ecological changes resulting from tropical export economies. Readers can refer to the original edition for the full bibliography, as well as for additional details on the subject of each chapter.

I owe enthusiastic thanks to colleagues and readers for their critical support. In addition to the many who are mentioned in the acknowledgements for the first edition, the new edition has especially benefited from help from several colleagues, including Kurk Dorsey, Roger Levine, Michael Lewis, David Painter, Ravi Rajan, Mart Stewart, and John Soluri, in part reflecting their students' experience with the work. Jerry Bentley and John McNeill, general editors of the new Rowman & Littlefield World History Series, have been steadfastly supportive of this project. At Rowman & Littlefield, Susan McEachern and Sarah Wood have heartily expedited the complex process of revision and production. Patty Mitchell has worked overtime copyediting the manuscript with perception and rigor.

Introduction: America's Global Environmental Reach

The global impact of American power is currently under constant debate, both in the United States and around the world. Vast amounts of information are available on the reach of American political and strategic power. Most Americans understand far less about the social and economic consequences of American penetration of developing countries. A third dimension of America's impact has been almost totally ignored: the changes in the world's ecosystems that have contributed to American affluence.

The American "ecological empire" has many precedents. Throughout history, empires have expanded into remote territories and seas to exploit the natural resources of militarily conquered or economically dominated regions. But until the twentieth century the overall limits to ecological reduction in the tropics were limited by the technological limits of the early industrial revolution. In the nineteenth century, the early industrial stage of ecological globalization was led by the British Empire, with other European colonial powers following in more limited geographical spheres.

The twentieth-century American empire, though it has been more an economic and technological than political one, has surpassed all others in its grasp of Nature's global resources and thus in its worldwide ecological impacts. The world is shrinking not only politically but environmentally, as well. As Americans consume steadily more of the planet's resources, we have an increasing stake in the natural resources of formerly distant countries and, with that, a greater responsibility to know what has happened.[1]

This book explores the many American roles in the domestication and decline of forest and grassland ecosystems of the tropical world. In North America's temperate climate, forest cover is actually increasing.[2] But in the tropics, the home of the world's greatest biodiversity, forest cover has been rapidly declining for the past century. *Insatiable Appetite* traces America's leading role in these changes through the first six decades of the twentieth century.

The United States has been involved in the tropics since well before its own independence. But it rose to a preeminent international position after the war against Spain in 1898. In the early twentieth century, aggressive American expansion down the Atlantic and Pacific displaced European hegemony in colonial and postcolonial economies. Until the 1950s, American corporations had virtually free rein in any area of the tropics where investment promised to be profitable. They shipped tropical crops northward from the Caribbean and Latin America, northeastward across the Pacific from Hawaii and Southeast Asia, and even across the Atlantic from West Africa, to feed the American economy's ever expanding appetite. American consumers thus participated in the domestication and depletion of a wide range of ecological zones.[3]

Insatiable Appetite studies the era of unrestrained American capital investment and its partner, fast expanding consumer purchasing power in the United States. The narrative ends in the 1960s, when processes of global ecological deterioration became more complex as European and Japanese competition for tropical resources re-emerged, tropical governments became stronger, and international institutions became important players in managing global resources. *Insatiable Appetite* probes these processes by surveying six products of the tropical world that attracted large-scale U.S. investment, technical skills, and managerial drive, and were bought by American consumers: cane sugar, bananas, coffee, natural rubber, beef, and hardwoods harvested from tropical forests.[4]

Shortly after 1900, Americans began consuming large amounts of sugar derived from sugarcane grown in the fields of Cuba. To be sure, identical sugar came from sugar beets grown in many states within the United States. But Americans' craving for sucrose was so great that the market absorbed all it could find, whether it came from domestic beets or cane grown in the Deep South, Cuba, Hawaii, and even our new colony, the Philippines. In the same years, bananas became the first tropical fruit to appear on American tables. Until the 1960s, Americans consumed far more bananas than any other country of the temperate world. Bananas could not be grown anywhere in the United States, so the ecological changes resulting from banana production happened in tropical Latin America and the Caribbean on large American-owned and managed plantations.

Coffee was the third great American import crop that could be grown nowhere in the United States. But the story of coffee was different in several crucial ways from that of cane sugar and bananas. In the two regions of South America that became by far the largest coffee producers for American markets—southern Brazil and Colombia—local men of wealth, not Americans or Europeans (with very few exceptions), owned and managed the plantations. The Northerners' role was limited to buying and shipping coffee from the coastal cities of Brazil and Colombia. Hence, Europeans and Americans had almost no direct role in managing the land or the resulting environmental impacts. Second, coffee has been grown competitively by both large estate owners and small farmers; thus the social patterns reflected in coffee production and its environmental effects have been more variable than for sugar and bananas. Third, unlike these two crops, coffee grows in a wide range of ecological settings, in the hill regions of the tropical and subtropical world, where slopes are steeper than in the lowlands and soil erosion is a constant menace. So the impact of coffee production has added another ecological range to the moist tropical lowlands, in the overall catalogue of tropical forest reduction.

The fourth crop in this account is natural rubber, the tropics' contribution to the global demands of the automotive age. Most great rubber plantations were established in Southeast Asia, where American companies worked under the umbrella of Dutch and British colonial regimes until after World War II. Rubber, like cane and bananas, was a one-crop ecosystem that displaced Nature's biodiversity. But unlike sugar, bananas, and coffee, plantation rubber became one of the strategically vital resources for the military and economic power of the American empire, along with strategic minerals that were unavailable in the United States—indeed, the only tropical crop on the strategic list. For reasons of strategic security, the U.S. government cooperated unusually closely with the rubber baron Harvey Firestone to establish the world's largest rubber plantation in Liberia, the only major American agribusiness in Africa in the twentieth century. During World War II, natural rubber was supplemented by synthetic rubber, derived industrially from petroleum, which soon supplied half the world's demand for rubber. No other tropical crop has this sort of substitute.

In spite of steadily growing global demand, the acreage of former forest or small farms planted as a tree monocrop has expanded only slowly in the past half century.

The fifth "crop," beef, is not a vegetative crop. But cattle, too, have caused severe depletion of tropical vegetation systems, both as adjuncts to the other crops and as beef herds, a grassland monocrop in their own right. Both Yankee ranchers and Yankee meat processors invested in the Latin American cattle complex, from Mexico to Argentina. Their work transformed both forests and grasslands into pastures.

Finally, *Insatiable Appetite* considers tropical hardwood timber; it studies American loggers who felled mahogany and other timber for American markets, thus depleting the remaining tropical forests. Pioneer planters of sugarcane, bananas, coffee, and rubber rarely harvested hardwoods, simply clearing the great trees from the land, burning them or letting them rot. But some hardwoods had markets in Europe and North America as early as the sixteenth century, if they could be cut and transported to markets, which was no simple task before railroads and steam power appeared in the nineteenth century. As the technological means of harvesting valuable hardwoods from tropical forests became available, corporations investing in the products of tropical soils began exporting the timber, turning the forest itself into a valuable commodity in South-to-North trade. From the perspective of the forests, this presented yet another threat but it also became an opportunity to manage them for their own economic value. Cut-and-run logging led to professional forest management. A handful of American foresters were among the first to study the forests of tropical America and Southeast Asia in detail. Working in cooperation with logging firms and agribusinesses such as United Fruit, tropical foresters began to make progress toward sustainable harvesting of tropical hardwoods. By the 1950s they became the first articulate voices for sustainable use of tropical forests.

In the first five chapters, *Insatiable Appetite* traces briefly the rise of tropical agronomy, a science that (like forestry) gave promise of managing production sustainably. But since the fundamental concern of this narrative is changes in tropical lands, it centers on the locations where these commodities were produced, the locations where the domestication and decline of natural systems resulted from American appetites. The populations and ecosystems where Americans invested their effort, both being alien and poorly understood by the

Northerners, experienced the American presence in ways that corresponded to their own social, political, and environmental realities. The fortunes and impacts of American enterprises in the tropics depended on complex and shifting interactions between the Yankees and the landed and political elites of host countries: sometimes cooperative, sometimes competitive.

The environmental impacts were shaped most directly by workers on the plantations and in the forests. Whether they were slaves, indentured laborers, or free men and women, they made up the social history of environmental change. Some were massed together on plantations, often far from their homes, dependent on their employers or bosses for food and provisions. Others were nominally independent peasants, though more often than not they sold their products to exporters at prices dictated by the buyers. Their work, passing through many links, bound their lives to those of American consumers.

1

America's Sweet Tooth: Cane Sugar Transforms Tropical Lowlands

Sugar was the first tropical plantation crop grown on a large scale for European consumption. Sugar linked land and vegetation systems of the tropical Americas directly with the global economic web of the mercantilist empires. It was the first plantation crop to arrive with the Europeans; it was associated with one of the most ruthless of all labor systems, African slavery; and it has been the most widespread crop in replacing tropical lowland rainforests. Only bananas can rival sugar as a dominant monocrop, and that has been only in the twentieth century.

Americans began consuming tropical sugar from the Caribbean as early as the 1650s. Buyers of molasses and rum on the wharves of Boston, New York, Baltimore, and Savannah helped strengthen the slave sugar system. The ultimate consumers had no direct responsibility for the social costs of cane and virtually no awareness of its ecological costs, but they were players nonetheless. By the last years of the 1800s, Yankee investors and engineers became the largest scale players in the game. Protected by the U.S. flag, they achieved an unprecedented scale of industrialized agriculture in the cane fields of Cuba, the first flowering of American ecological imperialism. Cuba was the world's largest producer of sugar and its American estates were inheritors of four centuries of European imperial power.

The international environmental impacts of sugar monocropping have been massive. In many locations primary forest was cleared expressly so as to

plant cane. In other instances cane displaced previous field crops and pastures. Where cane grew, the cornucopia of flora and fauna was eliminated,
replaced by wide acreage of only one species. In many locations the higher
slopes above the cane fields were gradually stripped of timber for boiling the
raw cane juice and cooking the workers' food. Moreover, the field workers'
need for food and fiber led plantation owners to import those materials from
great distances. More than any other crop, cane sugar drew on the social and
ecological resources of temperate as well as tropical lands, as sources of food,
clothing, shelter, and labor. Beyond even this, the transport systems built to
take cane to the refineries and from there to worldwide markets opened to
domestication whole natural regions that had previously been inaccessible
to international capital.[1]

Cane sugar evolved originally in the islands of the Pacific, where several
species of tall grasses produced sucrose in their moisture-laden stems.[2]
Throughout the human history of the Pacific, islanders have enjoyed the
moderate sweetness of natural cane. Hybridization to produce more intense
sucrose began many centuries ago. Migrating slowly westward, domesticated
sugar was enjoyed in northern India by at least 500 B.C. It was used for medic-
inal purposes in Persia and Byzantium and reached the eastern Mediterranean
by the eighth century A.D. Arab traders took it westward from the Levant
through the Mediterranean, to Sicily and Spain. French Crusaders discovered
it in Syria in the late 1200s. They conveyed the new craving back with them to
Europe. By the late 1500s northern Europeans, led by the Dutch and English,
began aggressively looking for a way to circumvent their Catholic and Muslim
suppliers of Oriental goods. In the early 1600s sugar became a major item in
the East India Companies' imports from Asia.[3]

The driving force behind these investments was an expanding market in
Europe, where sugar became one of the aristocracy's luxury items in the sixteenth century, complementing honey as a source of sweetening in the Northerners' diet.[4] But it remained available in such limited quantities through the
eighteenth century that common people could still only dream of tasting it
regularly. A truly mass market developed during the industrial era of the nineteenth century.[5] By 1800 England consumed 150,000 tons annually, much of
it to accompany its new addiction, tea. Sugar consumption on this scale would
not have been possible without massive supply zones in tropical America, nor
would it have been possible without one of history's most brutal systems of

human exploitation, the use of African slaves to clear lands in the New World for plantations.[6]

THE NEW YORK SUGAR TRUST AND THE DOMESTICATION OF NATURE IN CUBA

The drama of American capital, entrepreneurship and engineering in transforming tropical lands began in the sugar industry of Cuba. Even in colonial times, from the mid-1600s onward, ship owners from Boston and other New England coastal towns competed with their European rivals to import Nature's products from the Caribbean. These men were the forerunners of the speculative entrepreneurs who brought industrial capitalism to the sugar industry of the islands.

By 1700 the North Atlantic maritime trade produced complex exchanges between the temperate and tropical Atlantic bioregions. The Triangular Trade, fatefully linked to the African slave trade, provided New England, New York, Philadelphia, and Baltimore with sugar's major by-products, molasses and the rum that was distilled from molasses. There was only a small market for refined sugar, for that was an expensive luxury. Poor people used molasses as their sweetener.

Through the eighteenth century, both continental North America and the Caribbean islands were still frontiers of European capitalist and industrial expansion. They linked with each other in a two-way trade largely consisting of primary products of land and sea. This trade between the temperate and tropical climate zones of the New World had momentous ecological consequences. The West Indian economy demanded timber from northern New England and the maritime provinces of Canada. Colonial ports and sugar plantations needed pine for construction; Havana and lesser ports needed naval stores (such as pine pitch and resin for shipbuilding) and some hardwoods.[7]

Equally important for the trade between ecological zones, the West Indies desired codfish from the teeming spawning grounds of the Grand Banks off Newfoundland. Caribbean slave owners looking for protein to keep their chattel working, found it in salt cod, which they purchased in massive amounts from Northern shippers who, in turn, had bought it from an international fishing fleet that competed in an endless free-for-all, in unregulated international waters, for a seemingly bottomless source of profit.[8]

In the years immediately following America's independence, its commercial and political relations with the European powers were so unsettled that Yankee traders' fortunes in the Caribbean were never secure. But their links with Havana from all the major ports on the Atlantic coast became steadily stronger. Their own hinterlands provided a wide range of natural and agricultural resources that paid for sugar products purchases, linking the clearing of forest lands in eastern North America with the decline of mahogany forests in the Caribbean. For example, Philadelphia found a major market for its goods in the West Indies. From about 1770 onward, Cuban farms made little attempt to provide adequate wheat for Havana's urban population. In any case, Havana's bakers preferred Philadelphia's flour, made from wheat grown on the farms of eastern Pennsylvania. In the 1790s, Havana was able to shift its rural acreage into sugar production, in part thanks to Pennsylvania's wheat farmers.

American investments in Cuba were highly speculative and risky; by the definitions of Spanish colonial law, the North Americans were smugglers and pirates. But Spain's weakened power led Madrid to gradually tolerate other traders, including the North Americans. Financiers usually chose to make limited annual investments or, at most, short-term business partnerships. For the most part, they stopped only briefly in port to load and unload cargo; few Yankees settled permanently in Cuba.

By the 1740s Havana was the most important port for Yankee traders in a network that stretched around the Caribbean's shores to Vera Cruz and Cartagena, and even as far along South America's Atlantic seaboard as Buenos Aires. As Richard Van Alstyne puts it, "Every mainland port and nearly every mainland merchant had ties in the West Indies. The West Indian trade permeated all parts of the mainland economy and contributed substantially to the wealth of the seaboard merchants."[9] The strategic rivalries of the North Atlantic did not end when the United States became independent. Yankee ambitions were not tied to commercial interests alone; a more vast vision of imperial leadership in the future of the Americas was emerging, as intense maritime competition between the British and Yankee merchant marines continued.

American investment in the Cuban sugar industry expanded rapidly after the War of 1812. New York became the dominant player in the game because its aggressive development of trade connections with Europe enabled Manhattan's merchants and bankers to offer Cubans an entire range of trade and financial services. By the 1830s, numerous New Yorkers were investing in Cuban sugar. However, the eastern seaboard was not the only region involved. New Orleans drew on the resources of the entire Mississippi valley for its trade with the West Indies. By the mid-nineteenth century its cotton, grain, and cattle exports made it second only to New York in its foreign trade. By mid-century the great valley's new railroad system linked New Orleans efficiently with the great economic magnet, Chicago. The Illinois Central Railroad traded wheat and pork for Cuban sugar.

Cuba held a strategic location: whoever held Havana could neutralize other nations throughout the western Caribbean. The aggressive empire to the north might turn it into an American lake. Between 1840 and 1860, U.S. imports expanded fourfold; by 1860, the United States was importing more sugar from Cuba than was Spain, Cuba's nominal colonial overlord. Businessmen in New York and New Orleans with sugar connections in Havana joined southern slaveholders to accelerate the long-standing campaign to annex Cuba and its slave economy, as the next step in the march of Manifest Destiny to turn the Caribbean into an American lake.[10] The annexation movement failed; the northern states' antislavery opposition to the annexation effectively postponed a U.S. invasion until 1898. Nonetheless, a pattern was being set: Yankee capital penetration followed by political and military support from Washington to guarantee American access to land and resources to the south. By the mid-1800s an additional complication arose, when beet sugar grown in the northern United States became an important market factor. Sugar is the only major tropical crop on world markets that can also be produced far northward into the zone of cold winters, because sugar can be economically derived from two different plant sources: cane and beets.

In 1747 the German chemist Markgraff isolated sugar from beets. Sugar beets were cultivated on a large scale in northern Europe during the Napoleonic wars, when France's loss of its Haitian supplies and then the British naval blockade of France forced the French to provide home-grown substitutes for many of their habitual imports. In the years after Napoleon's defeat, first north German and then Austrian, Polish, and Russian farmers moved into large-scale sugar beet production. The United States was not far behind. Beet sugar refining was introduced into Northampton, Massachusetts, in the 1830s by men who learned the technique in Paris. Soon Philadelphia joined the industry, and from there it spread rapidly westward as more states were settled by white farmers. In the 1860s, German immigrants in Ohio, Illinois, Michigan, and Wisconsin began to grow sugar beets. From there the cultivation leaped the plains states to Colorado, Utah, and, finally, California. The result was a revolution in world sugar production. In 1853 only 14 percent of the world's sugar was produced from beets but by 1884 the percentage rose to 53 percent. Consequently, international prices fell rapidly and the Cuban sugar-producing elite began to experience the unpredictable price variations that have haunted developing world commodity production ever since.

By the 1870s the Cuban economy was weakened by an internal upheaval known as the Ten Years War. In 1868 a patriotic revolution broke out, led by discontented cattlemen and coffee growers in eastern Cuba who had been losing status against the prospering sugar planters. In campaigns of attrition, government forces destroyed their ranches and crippled coffee production in the rebellious region. Thereafter, eastern Cuba was in decline for decades, land clearance there nearly halted in the resulting depression, and control of the economy lay with the sugar interests farther west.[11] In the doldrums that followed the rebellion, inexpensive land was available throughout Cuba. Many small U.S. investors moved in, buying coffee, sugar, cocoa, tobacco, and cattle properties. Yankee ship owners, traders, and bankers arrived with them, building a growing role in the export trade. One American had already built the first Cuban railroad in 1837, penetrating inland from Havana; another had designed steam-engine machinery that made sugar processing more efficient. Yankee engineers were contributing to Yankee control of the island.

Cuban sugar exporters faced a U.S. market whose price levels fell steadily after the 1870s. The average price for duty-paid raw sugar in the New York market fell from 11 cents per pound in 1877 to a low of 3.2 cents ten years later. Consequently, heavy competition developed for efficient, low-cost production. Moreover, consumer tastes in the industrial countries were shifting decisively from coarse brown muscovado sugar to refined white sugar. In order to survive, sugar entrepreneurs adopted fundamental changes in sugar refining. In the late nineteenth century, new refining technology transformed the scale of both investment capital and machinery. By improving the purity of the refined sugar, this technology drove semirefined sugar and small-scale production out of international markets. Most of the new machinery was designed by Americans: hydraulic pressure regulation, vacuum pan and centrifugal apparatus to purge and crystallize sugar from juice, and steam power

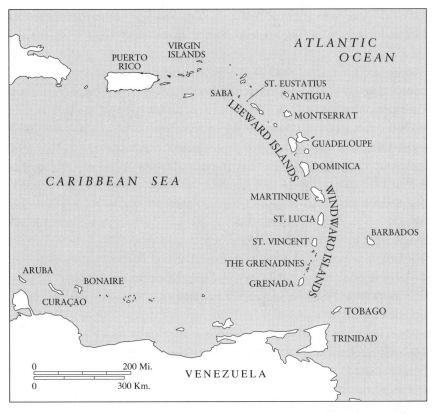

West Indies

to replace open fires in the more modern refineries. In 1885 there were some two hundred engineers and machinists in the refineries from the Boston area alone. As a result, by the 1890s the scale of competitive sugar refining increased exponentially and large investors centered in New York increasingly dominated the process.

The new sugar refineries, called *centrals,* were major industrial operations. Centrals required large amounts of cane, which had to be squeezed within hours of cutting or it rapidly lost its sugar content. New railroads financed by the centrals' owners greatly extended the distance it was possible to move freshly cut cane from field to factory. In the process, more than one thousand small Cuban mills closed; after 1898 there were fewer than two hundred.

The workforce in the cane fields was also transformed in the same period, with major ecological impacts. In 1886 Spain belatedly abolished slavery in Cuba and the work force became nominally free labor.[12] In the Matanzas plains of central Cuba, which had become the heartland of sugar plantation, many estates collapsed and their lands reverted to scrub pasture or subsistence plots. The workers, or *colonos*, were hardly better off than before: if they could locate a nearby central, they contracted to plant an agreed acreage in sugar, with advances from the central for their cultivation costs. This forced workers to take on most of the risk of poor harvests or low export prices and placed them in permanent debt to the centrals. Furthermore, the owners of the centrals made little effort to intensify production; their interest was restricted to the technology of refining. Workers thus escaped slavery but not hunger and, in the years after 1884, many fled to the hills of eastern Oriente province, becoming squatters in forest refuges and joining the ranks of the dispossessed that ultimately fought with Fidel Castro in the 1950s.[13] Marginal hill forests would now be degraded by frontier colonizers as a direct result of capitalist export agriculture.

THE YANKEE DOMESTICATION OF THE CUBAN LANDSCAPE

Many American investors were partners of Cubans and Spaniards. The most prosperous planters were already loosely formed into the "Club de la Habana," a landed elite whose culture and ostentation matched the most elegant anywhere in Latin America. They were almost as much at home in New York as in Havana. This helped their American partners cross language and cultural boundaries to work in the same business. Thus the elite that controlled the island until 1959 was a binational, closely intertwined network. The model of cooperation between American and Americanized indigenous interests, it was paralleled later in other Central American countries, and even more in the Philippine islands.

One of the earliest and most powerful Yankee operations was run by the Atkins family of Boston, whose long trading connections with Havana took them deeply into the sugar lands and a romance with rural Cuba. The Atkins story, as told in Edwin Atkins's autobiography,[14] shows how Yankee interests worked with changing conditions in Cuba through the 1800s, drawn more and more deeply into the fortunes of an agrarian economy transformed by the end of slavery and Spanish rule. The Atkins family had long been prominent in Boston's maritime trade. By the mid-1800s they were in banking as well as commission business with Cuba. Edwin Atkins settled in as manager of his father's Havana office. In 1884 they bought Soledad Estate, which they had been financing for years and entered the life of the planter class.

Soledad was upriver from the small port of Cienfuegos on the central south coast of Cuba. The estate specialized in intensive sugar production in its low-lying land and maintained forested hills above. It was a bucolic tropical paradise. After an early visit from Boston, Atkins's wife wrote enthusiastically, "The sail is delightful, the river is so still and the banks very pretty. Crabs and long-legged birds seem to be abundant on the shores."[15] She was entering the romantic life of the wealthy expatriate, presiding over the great house there for many years.

Cultured and philanthropic, Atkins established Harvard Garden on his estate, which became one of the outstanding botanical gardens and research centers in Latin America. In 1908 the Harvard biologist Thomas Barbour began a long working connection there. Barbour praised the Atkins home at Soledad effusively. "The great thick walls, the thirty-foot ceilings, the high barred windows and prodigious doors, produce the sensation of being cool, even when the temperature outside is pretty high."[16] The graciousness and antique charm of the planter's surroundings complemented his managerial acumen.

Underlying Atkins's love for the neocolonial life and his enthusiasm for natural history lay his firm belief in the virtue of free trade and modern industrial methods, freed from Spanish bureaucratic regulations and official corruption. His correspondence criticizes Spanish and U.S. high tariffs for choking off Cuba's economic development. Atkins was in a position to do something about American policy, for his family had influence in the highest circles in Washington. His father was one of several Boston bankers who had financed the Union Pacific Railroad; the senior Atkins was its financial vice president. He and Secretary of State James G. Blaine also had joint railroad interests. So the younger Atkins could catch the secretary's ear and argue with him the strategic value of lowering American sugar duties by casting reciprocal agreements with Spain.

By 1890 Atkins was one of the two most powerful American investors in Cuba, along with Horace Havemeyer of New York. Between them they ultimately held the key to the Cuban sugar economy. Atkins alone controlled

12,000 acres, including 5,000 in cane, and twenty-three miles of narrow-gauge railway. These sugar lands were already planted when he arrived, but other investors had to clear forest or grassland to plant the new cane. Havemeyer, the most aggressive Yankee investor of all, combined nineteen refineries into one operation in 1888, including Atkins's interests, which Havemeyer succeeded in purchasing. In 1890 Havemeyer's budding empire became the American Sugar Refining Company or, more simply and ominously, the Sugar Trust.

Sugar refining in the United States had begun in the late eighteenth century in New York, then spread to other east coast cities. Monopoly efforts or the "trust movement," began in 1881, when Havemeyer and the Brooklyn Sugar Refining Company reached an agreement to reduce production so as to drive up prices. Under Havemeyer's lead in 1887, eight companies combined into the Sugar Refineries Company, to coordinate their marketing strategies. When they closed ten of their twenty plants, greater efficiency meant rising production.

There were some feeble governmental efforts to control the Sugar Trust. In 1889 the Supreme Court dissolved the Trust but it quickly reorganized under a more permissive law. Then the five major independent sugar producers, plus the San Francisco magnate Claus Spreckels (who bought a competing refinery in Philadelphia), launched a rate war. The Trust won, by buying out its competitors. Havemeyer and his dependents soon controlled 90 percent of U.S. production. The extent and pace of Cuba's land clearance for sugar now depended on political wars in the halls of the U.S. Congress. Havemeyer's success was built on congressional guarantees of duty free imports from Cuba. If the beet sugar lobby could persuade Congress to set an import tax on cane sugar not only would the cane sugar importers suffer but a major impetus to cut down tropical forests in Cuba and elsewhere would be inhibited.

In the years around 1890 the U.S. government was basking in a period of budget surpluses. Hence, when Congress passed a new tariff law that year, the Cuban-American sugar lobby had little trouble in gaining a clause totally exempting its product from any duty. Cuban sugar production immediately boomed; in 1893 it passed one million tons for the first time. But the victory was short-lived. The U.S. beet sugar lobby retaliated; the 1894 Wilson Tariff set a new duty on raw cane sugar. Until then the Sugar Trust had been refining its raw sugar within the United States, guaranteeing it a more uniform and highly refined quality than sugar refined in the Cuban ingenios, and incidentally forcing Cuban exporters to market their sugar through Havemeyer.

Washington's tariff powers thus enabled American business to dominate marketing and, therefore, production of the crop that, in turn, dominated Cuba's lands. In 1894 Cubans reopened their war of independence against Spain, frustrated by Spain's restrictive tariff policies. Nationalist armies once again laid waste to sugar production.[17] At that point few American investors actually owned and managed Cuban sugar estates. That step followed when the United States replaced Spain in 1898 as Cuba's overlord.

In 1898 the U.S. Navy intervened in the war, sweeping Spain off the island. Cuba was under American military domination for the following four years. A treaty resolved Cuba's status in 1902, declaring it independent. But Congress, fearing European intervention or further disorder in the Cuban countryside, added the Platt Amendment in 1903, which arrogated for the United States "the right to intervene for the preservation of Cuban independence, [and] the maintenance of a government adequate for the protection of life, property, and individual liberty."[18] Thus unilaterally, Congress assured American investors that their government was prepared to send its army back onto the island in order to guarantee the safety of their capital. The proviso was to have profound consequences for Cuba's landscape, for it placed the full potential force of the American military behind the investors who came to dominate Cuba's economy in the following years. The way was now paved for American-financed clearing of the remaining rich lowland soils of central and eastern Cuba.[19] As long as virgin soil remained available, high-price levels for primary commodities on world markets immediately resulted in deforestation unrestrained by any government regulations.

No sugar central could function without efficient transport facilities. American engineers moved rapidly into the Cuban hinterland after 1902, demonstrating that the U.S. role in building the infrastructure of economic development had at least as important long-range environmental consequences as did investment in the land itself. The key to opening eastern Cuba to world sugar markets was a west-to-east railroad across the country. William Van Horne, who in his earlier years had built the Canadian Pacific Railroad and then speculated in Guatemalan railroad construction, assigned himself the task. Impatient with slow-moving governments, he waited for no franchise, right of way, government subsidy, or declarations of eminent domain but began purchasing properties in 1900 and building his line, completing it several years later into Oriente Province. His tracks made possible a vast expansion of large American-owned estates into the lowlands and hills of Camaguey and Oriente, which transformed poverty-stricken but free peasants into plantation laborers.

Ironically, Van Horne saw himself as a champion of the small farmer, intending that his line would give free campesinos access to wider markets for their produce and result in a conservative and prosperous small capitalist class. As he remarked at the time, "The country can only reach its highest prosperity and greatest stability of government through the widest possible ownership of the lands by the people who cultivate them. In countries where the percentage of individuals holding real estate is greatest, conservatism prevails and insurrections are unknown."[20] Washington, prodded by the Havana—New York coalition, continued to maintain favorable tariff levels for Cuban sugar, paving the way for its greatest boom during and after World War I. The war brought devastation to Europe's sugar beet production, which dropped from 8 million tons in 1913 to 2.6 million tons by 1919. War on the sea also disrupted shipment of New World sugar to Europe. In the wartime emergency, Allied governments abandoned free-trade principles, beginning an era of coordinated intergovernmental planning of international markets, which triggered massive forest clearance.

In 1917, Great Britain established the International Sugar Board, which the United States joined. Complementing that action, as the United States entered the war, Congress passed the Lever Act, giving the president power to control production and marketing of foods for the duration of the war. Faced with intense competition between American beet sugar growers and Cuban cane sugar, Washington set up the Sugar Equalization Board the following year. This guaranteed both Cuban and Yankee growers high profit levels, so they continued felling the forests eastward in Cuba. It was also a major opportunity for American banks and importers to achieve their long-imagined goal of displacing European capital in the Caribbean economies. Yankee protection during the war was a bonanza for Cuba. Cuba's production spiraled upward; by 1919 it surpassed 4 million tons for the first time. In 1909 Cuba had produced 10 percent of the world's sugar; ten years later it produced 25 percent. Sugar was also now overwhelming the rest of Cuba's economy. By 1919 it provided 89 percent of Cuba's exports.

By the end of 1918 an unprecedented speculative race was on, popularly dubbed the "Dance of the Millions." New York banks lent millions to Cuban growers, and even Havana's bankers committed all the capital they could command. As historian Leland Jenks noted acidly, "There developed in Cuba between 1917 and 1920 most of the phenomena of speculation, industrial combination, price-fixing, bank manipulation, pyramiding of credits, and over-capitalization, which we are accustomed to regard as the peculiar gift of the highly civilized Anglo-Saxons."[21] In order to achieve this production boom, growers brought great new areas of land under sugar production; they still did not attempt to increase the efficiency of growing and harvesting sugar. Engineers preferred innovating with machines to improving the working conditions of the campesinos. The result was a further attack on the natural landscape. By 1920 many areas of marginal hill forest in Camaguey and Oriente were put into sugar by eager speculators, in locations where soils could not grow sugar competitively except in times of inflated international prices. When price levels collapsed shortly after 1920, some of these lands reverted to degraded scrub forest or were taken over by squatters.

In 1921, as European beet sugar production recovered, global prices crashed, in a classic extreme price-supply cycle. Many Cuban sugar barons defaulted on their loans from New York banks and control of the industry shifted decisively to the United States. In New York the National City Bank alone took control of fifty mills in the summer of 1921. The Cuban government, under the weak new president Alfredo Zetas, drifted toward bankruptcy. Its fiscal affairs were turned over to the American president's personal envoy, Enoch Crowder, who saved it from collapse only by arranging a massive new loan from J. P. Morgan. International prices recovered after two years and were strong again through the mid-1920s. By 1927 Cuba produced 6 million tons, 62 percent of which was now directly under U.S. control. Atkins and Havemeyer, in particular, raised new capital from around New England and Pennsylvania, combined into a new corporation named Lowry & Company, and prospered.

Making the most of the international boom in sugar prices, the estate owners scrambled to clear additional forest land or plow old cattle pasture in Camaguey and northern Oriente, even though slopes were progressively steeper and soils increasingly marginal. They simply cut and burned large tracts of forest and scub growth. This large-scale slash and burn method was essentially identical to the technique being used around the tropics to make way for coffee, bananas, rubber, cotton, and other market crops. Many species of trees went up in smoke, dashing any hope of developing a modern timber industry in the Cuban hardwood forests.[22] Except for sites near the coast, it was simply not worth the investment and labor to haul the trees to a river or coastline for shipment to distant markets.

Harry Franck, an American businessman and traveler, wandered through Oriente in 1920. He recorded a frenzy of land clearing and its impact on the natural ecosystem.

> Here vast stretches of virgin forest, often three to five thousand acres in extent, are turned into cane fields in a few months' time. With machetes and axes which to the Northerner would seem extremely crude—though nearly all of them come from our own State of Connecticut—the [woodsmen] attack the immense and seemingly impenetrable wilderness. The underbrush and saplings fall first under the slashing machetes. Next the big trees—and some of these are indeed giants of the forest—succumb before the heavy axes and, denuded of their larger branches, are left where they lie. . . . When at last the fires are set and sweep across the immense region with all the fury of the element, fuel sufficient to keep an entire Northern city warm during the whole winter is swept away in a single day.[23]

Franck caught the fuller significance of what was happening to the land. He concluded by warning, "The time is near . . . when the Cubans must regulate this wholesale destruction of their forests or see the island suffer from one of those changes of climate which has been the partial ruination of their mother-land, Spain."[24] Yet, in a significant oversight, he made no mention of the Yankee capital that was largely responsible for the Cuban workers' efforts.

The Dance of the Millions was responsible for that particular maelstrom in the forest. But the brief, giddy postwar boom was part of a quarter-century of massive land clearances. Between 1905 and 1921, sixteen new processing factories were built in central and western Camaguey, so as to attract cane planting to forests and former grazing lands. Six more went up in eastern Camaguey and twenty-four in Oriente.[25]

The reality of these transformations on the land was illustrated by the new Manatí central and its adjacent lands on Manatí Bay, on the north coast of Oriente. Some natural forest still stood in that area, a mixture of mahogany forest and coastal palm woodlands. Interspersed with the forests were savannas, which grew on well-drained but sandy soil and had formerly been used to run cattle. The forest soils were richer in organic matter than adjacent savannas and were, therefore, more interesting to sugar planters. The local coastal town, Victoria de las Tunas, had exported cattle and timber long back into colonial times.[26]

In 1911 Manuel Rionda y Polledo, a Cuban living in New York, joined with Yankee investment partners to purchase a huge tract of 150 square miles of land near Victoria for $1,500,000. They built a new central and began burning the forest. Within two years they cleared 15,000 acres with a workforce of three thousand and had 10,000 acres in sugar production. During the wartime boom they expanded production to 43,000 acres, 25,000 of which the company owned directly. By 1923 the Manatí Sugar Company produced almost 90,000 tons of semirefined sugar.

But trouble was in store for Cuba's sugar industry with the onset of global depression in October 1929. By early 1930, consumer demand in the United States and all other industrial economies began to fall precipitously, leaving one-crop export economies like Cuba desperate. The world sugar price, which had stood at 2.78 cents per pound in 1927, plunged to .78 cents in 1932, returning to the 1927 level only as World War II ended in 1945. Cuban sugar production fell by nearly one-half in the early 1930s. Cuban estate owners' income, which had risen from $100 million in 1920 to $200 million in 1929, collapsed to $40 million in 1932.

The effects on Cuban land use would have been even greater but for the political power of the American importers in their manipulation of import tariffs. In 1930 Congress passed its most restrictive tariff law, the Smoot-Hawley Tariff, building in a high sugar tariff for Cuba and its Caribbean neighbors. By 1934, as the worst began to pass in the United States, Congress established the first guaranteed minimum quota for Cuban sugar imports. This resulted from such intensive pressure from the importers that Secretary of Agriculture Henry Wallace called their lobbying "one of the most astounding exhibitions I have ever seen."[27]

A new system for American imports of tropical crops was emerging from the Depression, building in a more dominant role for governments and, therefore, for lobbyists. In primary producing countries of the Third World, economic collapse during the Depression made land use patterns and their environmental consequences depend heavily on the relations among a country's elite, its rural work force, and those who controlled its exports. The financial disaster of the Depression brought intense political and social pressures to Cuba, which had been ruled by Gerardo Machado, one of its most brutal dictators, since 1925. American control of the sugar economy rested directly on his regime.

Machado's style of governing has been characterized as "brutal but businesslike. . . . Machado's methods were those of a small-scale Mussolini. They included imprisonments without trial, torture of prisoners, and political assassinations."[28] For a time he succeeded in controlling the plantation labor force and his American friends continued to visit Havana comfortably. But social and political upheaval was inevitable in the battered one-crop economy. In 1933 a coup eliminated Machado and brought to power a young army officer, Fulgencio Batista. From then, until his overthrow in 1959, Batista was the kingpin of Cuban politics and economics. Washington gave its pliant junior partner full support. From 1933 onward President Franklin Roosevelt pursued Good Neighbor diplomacy, working to maintain Yankee hegemony through local regimes whose controlling elites were closely and profitably tied to the American economy. Batista and his friends were a classic example of that strategy.[29]

The impact of the Depression years on Cuba's lands was dramatic. Export markets in the 1930s were so reduced that no one opened new land to produce export crops. Indeed, the trend was toward deserting sugar production in eastern Cuba, where marginal hill lands had recently come under sugar cultivation. Many small sugar farmers reverted to planting maize and beans in order to avoid starvation. In a perverse way, agricultural production in Cuba moved back toward a balance between subsistence and export cropping. Other fields reverted to secondary woodland or scrub cattle pasture, usually resulting in soil erosion and depletion. And when World War II demanded increased sugar production from Cuba, it was at last achieved through greater efficiency of production, not additional acreage under cane.

By the late 1940s American owners began divesting their direct holdings in Cuban estates, by selling their lands to their Cuban counterparts and partners, though they maintained their massive marketing investments. They saw the dangers of political instability and the headaches of direct management of land and labor. Cubans, who had owned only 28 percent of the mills in 1939, owned 45 percent of them by 1946, and 59 percent in 1955.[30] By the mid-1950s all but seven of the fifty mills in central Cuba were owned by Cuban companies, and only four by Americans. Most were absentee owners, living in palatial homes in Havana and New York, close to the power intrigues of Batista and his gringo supporters. The effect was a drift back toward the pattern of the late 1800s, when the original Sugar Trust in New York controlled production in Cuba by controlling its international markets but exercised no responsibility for social or environmental conditions on the land.

Other American investors remained in Cuba. Hershey Chocolate had held lands and centrals in northeastern Habana province since early in the century. Between 1948 and 1952 Central Hershey, the twelfth largest mill in Cuba, produced nearly 600,000 sacks of sugar. Farther east in Camaguey, the major region of Yankee investment in the 1920s, the Americans also held on, controlling sixteen centrals in 1956, in contrast with nine owned by Cubans. Farthest east, in the more marginal sugar region of the Oriente mountains, twenty-five were American-owned and thirteen had Cuban owners.

By 1956, Fidel Castro was organizing a challenge to the regime from the eastern hills, using the same guerrilla base as his predecessors had since the 1860s. He gained support from rising numbers of sugar workers around the country. In the early years of the Cold War, both the Truman and Eisenhower governments staunchly supported Batista's regime. This eliminated any possibility of economic reform in the industry that might have averted revolutionary upheaval. When Castro and his supporters entered Havana in 1959, the end of a half-century of American dominance in Cuba was at hand.

The Eisenhower government's response to the new regime was to declare a total embargo on trade with Cuba in early 1960. The next chapter of Cuba's environmental history would be shaped by the sudden extinction of the American market and the Soviet movement into the resulting vacuum. Once again, ecological and political history were fatefully linked. The Caribbean historian Eric Williams points out that when Castro came to power, "82 percent of Cuba's total land area was farm land, but only 22 percent of that was cultivated. . . . American sugar companies controlled about 75 percent of Cuba's arable land."[31] But it proved extremely difficult to move out of the old pattern of one-crop exploitation. Moreover, the new regime was still in the same ecological orientation toward the natural resources of the land as its predecessors. Castro's policy was to continue the domestication of the natural ecosystems of the island, an ideology that replaced the capitalist version of the social control and domestication of Nature with the Marxist version, though with far greater concern for the needs of Cuba's population.

Castro's planners were determined to put idle land and labor to work. In 1961 they adopted a policy of diversifying production on the sugar lands, devoting some acreage to soybeans, peanuts, and cattle, in addition to growing additional food for local consumption.[32] A revival of cattle ranching in particular seemed worthwhile, to provide more meat and leather for Cuban consumption as well as for expanded exports. Large private farmers cultivated previously idle land to avoid expropriation. And on previously unexploited land, Cubans organized a major campaign to drain marshy lands, especially along the coasts. By 1962 up to 440,000 acres of "new land" were cleared of forest or replanted on previous fallows.[33]

Cuban farm managers took some land out of sugar entirely, and production fell severely on other sugar soils, as worker hours were reduced and repairs of refinery machinery began to run behind. Weeding and irrigation were neglected; the replantings needed in 1959 and 1960 were ignored; and in 1962–63 droughts hit the island. In 1960, the United States had cut off all equipment shipments, which had been Cuba's source of farm machinery and parts, fertilizer, pesticides, and even seeds. Once again Cuba's economy was haunted by its perennial food deficits. Food imports, coming from Europe and the Soviet Union, were running at $125—$150 million annually, requiring massive export sales to finance them. In 1962 a crisis in the balance of payments descended on a country that had been cut off from its near-monopoly sugar buyer: Cuba faced a $170 million deficit for the year. There was no choice but to re-emphasize sugar production, and to sell to Soviet buyers.

Through the 1960s Cuban sugar production rose again, this time with the stress on intensifying cultivation and expanding sugar acreage. Fortunately for the effort, there was no major disease epidemic in the cane, unlike in the fruit industry of Central America at the time. In a major irony, by 1982 cane covered 75 percent of all cultivated land, in comparison to 60 percent in 1958.[34] In sum, Cuba's century-long experience as the world's greatest producer of the oldest colonial monocrop left it with continued reliance on that crop. Ironically, this kept the country tied politically to its major buyer, though the buyer had changed. Cuba was linked with the Soviet Union in a variant of the dependency that characterized many colonial systems. The pattern of land use changed only marginally until the collapse of the Soviet market after 1990. That jolt, combined with the continuing U.S. embargo, forced Cuban agriculture into a shift from chemical-intensive export sugar to organic multicropping. In the 1990s, Cuba became the hemisphere's leader in genuinely sustainable agriculture.[35]

As long as American political alliances in the 1960s and 1970s remained tied to landlord regimes, U.S. policy could not consistently support environmentally sound resource management, for those regimes perpetuated a range of damaging land use practices. Moreover, as long as American policy refused to deal with any inter-American organization that recognized the Cuban government, it was crippled in contributing to environmentally sound planning for the Caribbean basin.[36] Within that overall picture, was sugar cane production moving toward becoming a stable agroecological system?[37] Cane sugar production is less susceptible to epidemic disease than crops such as bananas, and less punishing to soil nutrients than tobacco and cotton. But sustainability depends on far more than the biological potential of a single crop. To what extent sugar monocropping could be integrated into a balanced agroecological system varied from one location to another. It depended on a perpetually slippery equation of international prices, national political economies, and local ecological realities. In other parts of the tropical world, such as the cane producing areas of the Pacific, the variations could be startling.

SUGAR ESTATES AND ENVIRONMENTAL DEGRADATION IN THE PACIFIC

While Caribbean cane supplied the eastern and central United States, Americans west of the Continental Divide looked to the Pacific for sugar, especially during the years between the gold rush and the opening of the Panama Canal. Sugar entrepreneurs went first to the Hawaiian kingdom and then beyond to the Philippine islands. In Hawaii in the 1830s, the first planters found fertile volcanic soils at elevations above the coastal lowlands where native Hawaiians raised most of their food. Much of the land that ultimately became vast sugar plantations was arid, covered by a drought-resistant complex of trees and shrubs, with dense forest on higher mountain slopes above. The challenge to fledgling sugar barons was to drain massive flows of water across high slopes to fertile but dry acreage on leeward sides of the islands, away from the prevailing northeast trade winds.

But in Hawaii, as elsewhere, capitalist enterprise presupposed that land be defined as property not communally shared space. In 1850 the Hawaiian king declared the islands' land to be owned, in a Western sense, and sold great

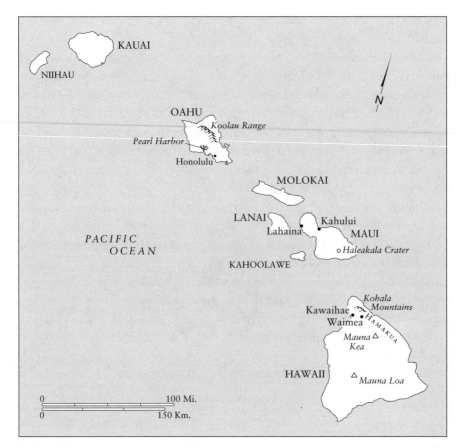

Hawaiian Islands

parcels to American investors.[38] Before long, five great corporations came to dominate Hawaii's sugar economy, just at the time when the gold rush in California brought booming profits and markets to San Francisco and the Bay Area.

In the following generation, the most powerful sugar magnate was Claus Spreckels of San Francisco, who outflanked the New York Sugar Trust in the race to share the market of the western states with beet sugar producers. Under his influence the Hawaiian king signed the Reciprocity Treaty with the United States in 1875, which allowed all Hawaiian sugar into the United States duty free. Spreckels immediately purchased 40,000 acres of land on Maui, "a dreary expanse of sand and shifting sandhills, with a dismal growth in some places of thornless thistles and indigo," according to one commercial observer who knew little about the ecology of that land.[39]

Spreckels had dreams of a sugar empire crossing the Pacific, from Hawaii to the Philippines and beyond.[40] But he also had rivals. In the century that followed, the Hawaiian economy was dominated by the Big Five sugar conglomerates, which engineered the coup that overthrew the monarchy in 1892 and turned the islands into an American territory. They imported an endlessly expanding indentured labor force of marginal peasants from China, Japan, and the Philippines. The Big Five organized the Hawaiian Sugar Planters Association (HSPA), financing agronomic research that rivaled the most advanced anywhere. HSPA promoted studies of cane diseases, biological controls, and soil productivity, which cooperated closely with the Territorial Forest Department to protect the upland forests, so as to provide a reliable flow of water to the plantations.

But the planters failed to control the workers' efforts to unionize in defense of their pay and working conditions. By the time Hawaii became a state in 1958, its sugar workers were the most productive and highly paid in the world. By the 1970s Hawaiian sugar was being priced out of national and world markets, and by the 1990s almost all the old estates had closed. Even in the twenty-first century, more diversified use of the former sugar lands is still a matter of experimental planting with other tree and annual crops.

Sugar history in Hawaii presented a striking contrast to sugar across the Pacific, but it also was a stepping stone for magnates like Spreckels to wider reaches of the wet tropics. By the early 1800s, sugar plantations spread throughout the colonial Pacific, on European-controlled islands and on Dutch-controlled Java. Early colonists set up small-scale plantations, producing semi-refined brown sugar. After 1815, markets in Europe and East Asia grew rapidly. Chinese traders who had been spreading throughout the southern Pacific and Southeast Asia stimulated much expansion of sugar acreage for Chinese markets. Europeans were not the only economic and ecological imperialists.

American control of Hawaii was a step toward the Philippines, where American entrepreneurs entered a system of social and ecological exploitation rooted in Spanish colonial times. The American impact there was to be based less on direct exploitation of the land than on the power of U.S. capital and markets to support Filipino landlords. Americans therefore had little sense of direct responsibility for their impact on the land. In 1898, the U.S. Navy seized the Philippines from Spain, along with Cuba and Puerto Rico; all three territories became major sugar producers for American markets. But for a century before that, Yankee trading firms had been gaining a foothold in Manila, where Americans began doing business in the 1790s, as a link in the Canton trade. There they coexisted with Spaniards, Englishmen, and other Europeans, as well as the long-standing Chinese trading community.

In that intense competition, the New England firms established close ties with Filipino exporters, setting a pattern of American partnership with the Filipino landed and commercial elite that was never challenged under American rule of the islands from 1898 to 1946, and indeed shapes land and resource use to the landlords' interests even now.[41] Americans provided the capital, technology, and marketing networks but rarely managed the land directly. Thus they remained one step removed from the environmental consequences of what they made possible.

Long before the first Spanish galleons appeared in Manila Bay, the Filipino people chewed the sweet juice from ripe natural sugar cane of the islands. In the late sixteenth century, Spanish adventurers began the gradual conquest of the islands, centering their attention on Luzon, the northernmost island. Establishing their colonial capital at Manila, they penetrated northward into the central lowlands. Missionaries or friars representing several monastic orders began developing rural estates in central Luzon in the early 1600s. Colonial exploitation of land and labor in the lowlands of central Luzon relied on a tenancy system dating long back into pre-colonial times. Central Luzon was dotted with rural communities of subsistence rice farmers controlled by large landowners, or *caciques*, whose power on the land the Spanish conquerors never undermined.

American whalers sailing to Java and Canton first purchased sugar in Manila around 1815. Sugar moved onto global markets in quantity in the 1850s and it was among the important crops of the early Philippine plantations, centering on the alluvial plains of the Pampanga River.[42] By 1870 it became the islands' most valuable export item, and it remained usually the first until the 1960s. Pampanga's sandy loam had long supported a dense population. These agricultural lands, specializing in rice production, did not need to be cleared of the primary forest that blanketed many other parts of the

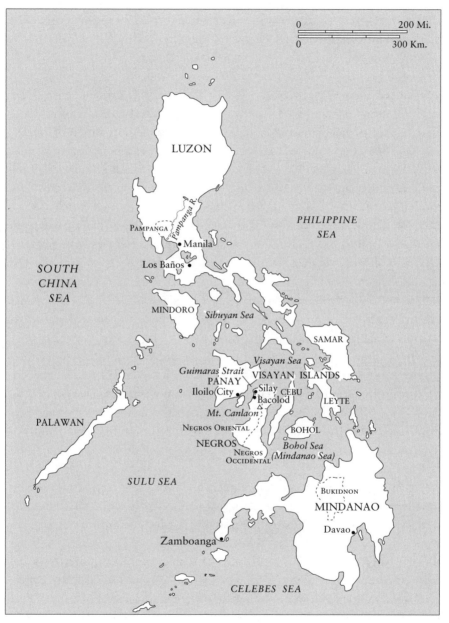

0   200 Mi.

0   300 Km.

LUZON

*PHILIPPINE
SEA*

PAMPANGA

Pampanga R.

• Manila

Los Baños •

*SOUTH
CHINA
SEA*

MINDORO   *Sibuyan Sea*

SAMAR

Visayan Sea

Guimaras Strait

VISAYAN ISLANDS

PANAY

Iloilo City •

Silay •
CEBU

Bacolod

LEYTE

PALAWAN

Mt. Canlaon

NEGROS ORIENTAL

BOHOL

NEGROS

*Bohol Sea
(Mindanao Sea)*

NEGROS
OCCIDENTAL

SULU SEA

BUKIDNON

MINDANAO

Davao •

Zamboanga •

CELEBES SEA

Philippine Islands

islands. Until the 1870s there was usually a rice surplus for export. After 1870, as more land was converted to sugar production on large estates, rice had to be imported from Cochin China, Burma, and Thailand.[43]

In the late 1800s, Philippine sugar exports were financed primarily by British and American investors. Rising international demand encouraged sugar estates to expand from densely populated central Luzon to other much more lightly populated islands, initiating large-scale deforestation of Negros, an island 300 miles south of Manila. Negros was mountainous, lushly forested but lightly populated. Its 150-mile-long mountain spine was dominated by volcanic Mount Canlaon in mid-island. Rivers cut many channels down the mountains into the sea but alluvial lowlands favorable for paddy rice or sugar were found only along the west coast, extending in a narrow strip around to the northeast. In the higher mountains survived a still thinner population of non-Christian shifting-agriculture tribal people who had been on the defensive against lowlanders, there as throughout Southeast Asia, for several centuries.[44] Before the mid-nineteenth century, small patches in the Negros forest had been cleared by rice-growing peasants closely related to peasants and urban weavers of Panay Island. The northwest coast of Negros lies only thirty miles across the strait from Iloilo City on Panay, the only well-protected port in the region. Americans arrived on the scene when Russell and Sturgis, the largest Yankee firm in Manila, opened the first American warehouse in Iloilo in 1863. Thus a pattern of dual ownership of Negros sugar lands grew up, in which power was shared between foreign investor-exporters and Filipino landlords. This resulted in more indirect metropolitan control of the land than on Hawaii or Cuba.

On the haciendas of Negros, foreigners had little or no direct responsibility for management of the land or its social and environmental outcomes. But they were vital to the transformation of sugar production into the forms of rural industrial capitalism. In the years that followed, sugar plantations transformed Negros's lowland moist forest to monocrop agriculture, on a belt approximately eighty miles long by thirty miles wide. Under the rugged cordillera, the rich volcanic soils and steady, typhoon-free climate were even more favorable than Luzon for sugar production. The little plantation communities were the advance guard of the attack on the forest ecosystem. In 1900, a visiting American military officer wrote, "Each hacienda was a community in itself—a feudal community of which the hacendero was the overlord. The hacendero's house, like a baron's fortress of the Middle Ages, stood in the centre of the buildings and dependants' huts. Many miles of almost uninhabited country might separate one hacienda from the next."[45]

On the early plantations milling was done in the traditional way, producing low-profit, semirefined muscovado, still laced with molasses.[46] The boiling process was fueled primarily by wood until the late 1800s, when severe forest depletion in the vicinity of sugar fields forced a gradual shift to using bagasse (dried crushed cane) as fuel. The same years saw a shift to more modern iron milling, using machinery imported from England.

Sugar exports from Negros began to expand in the 1860s. By 1880, 200,000 tons left the island, and the population of the sugar-producing region grew from 35,000 in 1845 to 150,000. The landlords' future seemed rosy until well into the 1880s.[47] But then a serious downturn in the market and the rise of violent resistance among the displaced lowland rice farmers and upland tribal swidden communities threatened to make the sugar era short-lived on Negros.

Mountain tribals resisted these incursions by settlers and land speculators. In response, the Spanish governor launched pacification campaigns, slaughtering many tribal people in the hills, in a bloody example of what was happening in many mountainous locations in the tropics. By the mid-1890s, scattered resistance against Spanish rule escalated into guerrilla warfare on all the major islands. On Negros the class and ethnic violence took the form of Papa Isio's revolt on the western slopes of Mount Canlaon in 1896, led by an immigrant from Iloilo who had lost his farm to a powerful planter. Isio had worked on a plantation until he tried to kill its owner. When that attempt failed, he fled to the mountains, where he was joined by other sugar laborers. The guerrillas fought a series of indecisive actions against Spanish military units until the collapse of the Spanish regime in 1898. From then on the fate of the sugar aristocracy, their tenant and tribal opponents, and the land itself would rest in American hands.[48] On Luzon, the rebellion centered on the sugar estates run by Catholic friars. By 1898, when Admiral Dewey summarily annihilated the ancient Spanish gunboats in Manila Bay, the ecclesiastical landlords were on their way back to Spain, and the future of the rich lands that they had turned from food production to export sugar was entirely uncertain.

The American business community had little enthusiasm for a colony on the far side of the Pacific. A striking exception was the cane sugar cartel centered in New York. Horace Havemeyer, Edward Atkins, and the Sugar Trust, struggling against the beet interests of Midwest and Western states, were closely associated with Governor Theodore Roosevelt in the circle of Republican expansionists around President McKinley. From early 1898 they pressed for annexation of the Philippines, for they had their eyes on the sugar lands of Luzon and Negros.[49]

The sugar magnates expected little opposition to the liberation from the Filipinos themselves. But they were grossly mistaken. The American takeover of rural areas was a protracted and bloody process, lasting six years and involving as many as 250,000 American troops in the fighting. Wide-ranging nationalist guerrilla forces resisted the American army's counterinsurgency, a far more tenacious opposition than the Spaniards had offered.

At the Philippine end of the process, the annexationists attempted to nurture Filipino allies wherever they could find men of similar self-interest. McKinley set up a martial law regime in 1900 and moved quickly to turn it into a civilian government. He convinced William Howard Taft, a federal judge in Ohio (and future President), to head the protocolonial administration, though Taft knew nothing about the islands. Taft needed Filipino allies to appoint to new civilian administrative posts and looked to the sugar gentry. On Negros, the landlord class was intact, though badly shaken by the depressed sugar market and the guerrilla campaign. Taft had little respect for the Negros landlords, writing bluntly to Secretary of State Elihu Root that they

> are generally lacking in moral character; are with some notable exceptions prone to yield to any pecuniary considerations, and are difficult persons out of whom to make an honest government. We shall have to do the best we can with them. They are born politicians; are as ambitious as Satan and as jealous as possible of each other's preferment.[50]

But he saw little alternative, since no other social class on any of the islands had any common interest with the Americans. It was not difficult to convince the planter class, however, of the advantages of the American alliance. The first and foremost advantage was military protection. The U.S. Army replaced the Spaniards in organizing pacification campaigns, finally defeating Papa Isio's scattered force in 1907. The planters' dominance was once again assured by a sympathetic regime.

The decade-long military campaigns had resulted in severe disruption of sugar production on the estates. But with a return of calm to the countryside,

Filipino and American sugar interests forged a new coalition much more dynamic than its Spanish predecessor. The Iloilo landlords were well familiar by then with the English speakers. Widespread Washington opposition to formal colonialism prevented American investors from taking over the friar estates on Luzon. The colonial constitution, the Organic Act of 1902, was a compromise, restrained by the Democratic Party's hostility to direct control of Philippine estates. It placed a 2,500 acre (1,024 hectare) limit on American companies' purchase of lands. Under the acreage limitation, American investors were reluctant to undertake direct management of land. By 1938 Americans owned only 171,330 hectares of agricultural land throughout the islands, only 2 percent of all land in private hands.[51]

American links to the Negros sugar lands contrasted with Hawaii, where there was no preexisting landlord class, and sugar estates had to be constructed from scratch. Furthermore, the takeover did not lead Yankee sugar barons to buy and directly manage the old estates, as they were doing at the same time in Cuba. Nor did they protect the watershed forests on the mountainsides above, as they did in Hawaii. American investors in Negros sugar had a more tempting alternative. Wary of the entanglements of direct land ownership, they could combine with local landlords. American interests thus perpetuated the social and economic polarization that had long existed in the Philippines.[52]

American sugar investors gained powerful backing from Congress and the colonial administration, despite opposition from the U.S. sugar beet lobby. The 1913 Underwood-Simons Tariff removed all limitations on the amount of sugar imported, the only Philippine product so favored. This brought Philippine sugar into the protected U.S. market, tying it tightly to the American economy. It remained there until the entire global system of import quotas was dismantled in 1974. The colonial administration went still further, establishing a national sugar board in 1915, with legal authority to aid new centrals. A year later, the Philippine National Bank was incorporated to provide finance capital for new centrals for a few Filipino owners, as well as crop loans to the sugar planters.[53]

There was room for them all in a production and export boom. The opening of the Panama Canal in 1914 made it feasible for Philippine sugar to compete on east coast markets. Rapid expansion followed during World War I, when Europe's sugar beet production left the international market. By 1920 there were twenty modern centrals in the islands, nearly all U.S.-owned, including fifteen on Negros. Expansion was the theme throughout the 1920s, even though world prices were volatile. And the greatest harvest ever was 1934, at the height of the international Depression.

Technical support and the first systematic information about the sugar industry came quickly from the colonial government. In 1908 the U.S. Department of Interior's Bureau of Science designated its top soil chemist, Herbert Walker, to do a systematic study of Negros. His report gave potential investors a close-up of the situation and revealed an authoritative American scientist's view of how to modernize sugar technology and transform primary forest into a marketable commodity. In the process it also documented the engineer's attitudes toward the social and ecological systems that would be the vehicle of that transformation.

Walker described the Negros sugar belt as rich in fine volcanic soils. But "all of this land is by no means suitable for growing cane. Much of it along the coast is covered by [mangrove] swamps, and the soil in the inland toward the mountains is often rocky and nearly barren." In contrast, south of the existing plantation belt "there is a large extent of forest land, mostly hilly, but containing several level plains where . . . sugar cane may be as profitably grown as in any other portion of the island." The planters were either Spanish mestizos or local caciques. Walker was cautiously impressed with some of them but noted that "the average yield for the island is greatly reduced by the comparatively large number of small growers who lack either the resources or the ability properly to care for their cane."

Efficiency and modernization, Walker believed, and ultimately the capacity to compete on volatile international markets, would come only from large haciendas. Walker was sanguine about the benefits of mechanization and systematic soil management. If a planter sold fresh cane to a central, this would raise the quality of sugar to internationally competitive levels, raise profit levels, and allow the planter to concentrate on better management of the land. As an important consequence, planters could then put more land under cultivation. This process would improve labor conditions, since it would raise workers' wages and benefits and allow nearly all of them to work the fields. At that time much sugar land was planted with no soil enrichment, so it inexorably declined. It could be fallowed, growing another crop in rotation, especially legumes, "yet there is still considerable virgin forest land as yet undeveloped"; and much low land previously planted only in rice could also be used.[54]

The American sugar barons moved aggressively in the Philippines, led by men from New York, California, and Hawaii, who brought capital and technology on an unprecedented scale. Within a few years they built the new generation of the Philippines' sugar centrals to international standards, thereby controlling the industry nationwide. The first to arrive was Horace Havemeyer in 1909. His American Sugar Refining Company, working with Philippine Commissioner Dean Worcester, reached out beyond his already massive Cuban holdings, purchasing that year the 58,000-acre San José friar estate on Mindoro Island, using Filipino politicians' help in setting aside the acreage limitation. Claus Spreckels and the San Francisco interests were not far behind. In 1912 Spreckels's associates organized the San Carlos central on Negros. By 1934 production at that refinery drew cane from 5,266 hectares of prime soil and achieved the highest yield per hectare in the Philippines. The San Carlos central milled nearly all sugar produced in one district for thirty years.

In 1918 the San Carlos combine opened its second Negros central through the Hawaiian-Philippine Company (HPC), which was run by Theo H. Davies & Co., one of Hawaii's Big Five companies.[55] Its strategy was to use Filipino laborers locally rather than incur the costs of sending them to the Hawaiian islands. HPC built a new central on Negros, which was a great financial success, paying its shareholders handsome dividends even in the early Depression. Its efficiency of sucrose extraction matched Hawaii, Java, Louisiana, and Cuba. HPC organized an association of its nearby grower-suppliers and maintained experimental facilities for hybrid types of sugar, technical advice, and access to fertilizers.

As a lobby, the Philippine interest was highly successful, maintaining privileged access to American markets through tariff preferences, even into the mid-Depression. The American sweet tooth assured steadily rising sugar production far away in the southwestern Pacific. In 1922, twenty-six American-owned refineries produced 233,770 tons of centrifugal sugar. By 1933–34, at the depth of the Depression, they produced a remarkable 998,123 tons, mostly by clearing the forest from additional land.

The scale of the centrifugal refineries was so great that U.S. owners had to draw cane from large tracts of land under consolidated ownership. The western

Negros plantations expanded their acreage by 44 percent in the 1920s. Land clearing continued rapidly onto marginal hill soils, in a process strikingly similar to the eastward extension of sugar production in Cuba in the same years. By 1938, 49 percent of Negros Occidental's arable land was in sugar, producing over half the total national sugar yield. Even the hardwood timber from some new clearings was marketed. Insular Lumber Company, owned in Seattle and the largest and most modern timber company in the Philippines, built its fortunes on large timber harvesting concessions in the Negros lowlands.

Severe conflict arose among mill owners, estate managers and laborers, adding to environmental damage. Thomas McHale, an American who knew the estates well, reminisced later,

> The new central mills clearly represented a quantum jump in technical and economic efficiency. Drawing cane from many sources and with no direct vested interest in the specific problems or prosperity of individual cane planters, however, the mills tended to be highly impersonal in their dealings with planters. As a result, planters began to complain that the contracts were onerous in that they required them to plant cane irrespective of weather cycles, disease infestations, price movements or other problems and that the mills had the right to take over management of their land if they didn't comply with their contract regardless of the reason.[56]

Small-scale hacenderos were often under capitalized and less able to compete with the big estates. They lacked skills or funds to improve irrigation, seed selection, fertilization, or mechanization. Many small owners fell into debt, even losing their properties. The land was rapidly being transformed into a factor of corporate industrial growth.

An extreme polarization developed between wealthy owners and poorly paid laborers. Hacienda owners were mostly Spanish-Filipino or Chinese-Filipino mestizos who had imigrated from Iloilo after the decline of the cloth industry there. These men were powerful on the land but dependent on foreign firms in Iloilo and Manila, which were extensions of the volatile New York and London sugar markets. As one observer noted, the plantation owners reveled in "almost unimaginable wealth. Mansions, servants, luxury cars, and round-the-world trips were commonplace for the owners of the large haciendas and the sugar mills." [57]

On the land, aside from a few American-linked plantations, production was never mechanized. Even more than in Cuba, expanded production meant additional removal of forest rather than more efficient production. The Negros landlords' power was so great that they could assure that the initial costs of opening new lands would be minimal. Few land titles were clear, and the planters' clearance strategies typically included fraudulently taking peasant farms by falsifying title deeds. The dispossessed peasants, both original locals and first-generation immigrants, had to retreat into the hills, where they began removing the forest cover from steep slopes in order to grow survival crops. Thus the plantations, like lowland monocrop systems throughout the tropics, were responsible for damage to watersheds far beyond the sugar acreage itself. The Negros plantations boomed in the 1920s, well able to compete with Hawaii for international markets, especially in the western United States. From 290,000 tons in 1921—half of which went to the United States—exports rose in eight years to over 670,000 tons in 1929, 94 percent of which was funneled into American kitchens.[58]

When the Depression descended on the islands after 1929, the Philippine sugar industry might have been expected to suffer as much as other producing areas but, ironically, the outcome was quite different. It rested on a new fight over tariff revisions in Washington, which would be the controlling factor in Negros sugar production and thus in its environmental impacts. Despite the best efforts of an American-Filipino joint sugar lobby, in 1934 U.S. beet producers and Caribbean cane growers won a major victory in the halls of Congress. The 1934 tariff overhaul set a quota of 1,015,185 tons for the Philippines; in effect, this became a ceiling on the expansion of acreage for American consumers. On the land in the Philippines, this led to a "quota race" because the new U.S. law stated that the Philippine quota should be allocated to producers on the basis of their recent performance. So every planter pushed to increase production. In a grim sequence, more forests fell while markets were frozen.

The turmoil of the 1930s was followed immediately by the disasters of World War II in the Pacific. Philippine plantations were badly damaged during the three years of Japanese occupation and many centrals were destroyed. By 1945 only twenty-six of the former forty-two remained in operation in the islands. During the war years, a large acreage reverted temporarily to food production, as tenant farmers struggled for survival, or reverted to tenaciously rooted, low value *cogon* grass. The 1945 crop year saw almost no cane harvests at all.

The Philippines became fully independent on July 4, 1946. But independence was tied to continuing subordination of the Philippine economy to American markets. That same year the Bell Trade Act, which regulated the new relationship of the two sovereign states, established a figure of 980,000 tons of sugar as the Philippines' duty-free quota for the American market, in a system that lasted until 1974. This guaranteed the sugar lords continued prosperity and power. Independence also caused a realignment of American involvement in the Philippine sugar economy. The shift in political power brought Filipino nationalism to the fore in all major economic sectors. In the pervasive corruption of the Philippines' public life, outsiders had to maneuver what political influence they could, especially in rural areas far from Manila. In 1957 U.S. direct private investment in Philippine agriculture was only $14 million, no more than 3 percent of total U.S. private investment in the Philippines.[59] Moreover, the flow of technical assistance from Hawaii stopped, further guaranteeing that the estates would continue to be managed along increasingly outdated lines. The Philippine estates were moving in the opposite direction from the Hawaiian sugar industry. More and more acreage was required in order to maintain the same level of output.

The Philippine lobby struggled to maintain its free access to the American market. The 1956 Laurel-Langley Tariff raised the quota slightly to 1,050,000 tons. But under pressure from rivals the act established a gradually rising duty for Philippine sugar, which reached 100 percent of other countries' duty by 1974, when the law lapsed and the era of international sugar quotas was ended. Another test of the Philippine lobby's influence in Washington came in 1961, when the United States cancelled Cuban imports and turned to other sources. Congress, while sharply raising the quotas of several Caribbean island countries, Mexico and Brazil kept the Philippine quota constant, a political defeat for Manila. Once again, the sugar barons responded to falling profits by expanding acreage under cane. From an average of just over 200,000 hectares in sugar in 1960, the national figure expanded to slightly over 500,000 hectares in 1974–75.

The highest stakes and worst abuses of plantation politics became evident only after Ferdinand Marcos became president in 1965. Marcos, who hailed from central Luzon, was determined to break up the old sugar elite in favor of his friends. He lavishly rewarded his supporters, men like Roberto Benedicto, the new sugar king of Negros.[60] Marcos added twelve new refineries on several islands. Politics thus extended sugar acreage at the expense of food production and forest in many areas. The expansion onto marginal land meant that production dropped by about one-third.[61]

Until the mid-1970s, world sugar prices remained high. But when the U.S. Sugar Act lapsed in 1974, the resulting global price collapse hit the Philippines hard. By then sugar consumed 65 percent of Negros Occidental's arable land and accounted for 55 percent of the Philippines' total sugar production, employing 440,000 workers. Then the price plummeted by 90 percent, to half of the cost of producing sugar. The sugar industry was in general bankruptcy by 1985. Two hundred thousand workers were laid off, with no severance benefits. Many haciendas closed or became only marginally productive. The acreage in sugar steadily fell; on some of it poverty-stricken squatters raised food; much of it went fallow and reverted to secondary woodlands or cogon grass.

On Negros Occidental, where Benedicto had taken over the estates of old guard politicians, severe malnutrition emerged. By 1978 food riots broke out among the desperate urban poor in the festering port of Bacolod. At the same time, the National Federation of Sugarcane Workers organized communes on leased lands but the owners suppressed them ruthlessly. The hinterland of Bacolod became a center of the New People's Army in the mid-1980s, recruiting many thousands of unemployed sugar workers. This threatened to create the very socioeconomic revolution that the United States had always identified as strategically intolerable.[62]

Social chaos translated into environmental devastation in the region around the plantations. Both the lowland sugar estates and the upland forest lands reeled under the conflict. No rational land management was possible; watershed forests sustained endless blows and erosion accelerated throughout natural as well as social systems. Politically outspoken priests reported a region of "treeless hills covered with brown cogon grass, eroded gullies, and isolated, bamboo-stilt houses clinging to the slopes."[63] Many migrants moved up from the lowlands, forced off their plots by the sugar barons, and left stranded on land incapable of sustaining them or even sustaining itself under the pressure of their desperation.

CONCLUSION: PLANTATION SUGAR AND ECOLOGICAL DECLINE

In Hawaii, the planters imported hundreds of thousands of laborers over a century-long period. Many of them and their descendants (especially the Chinese and Japanese) ultimately prospered, moving into the middle class and off the land into towns and cities. As urban consumers they put pressure on the limited food resources of the islands. The large-scale Filipino immigration from Luzon to Hawaii has done less well, remaining mostly tied to the plantations and recently facing massive layoffs. But the Filipinos in Hawaii have generally fared better than their counterparts at home in the Philippines.

The plantations of Negros, a thinly populated forest frontier in the early sugar era, faced a severe labor shortage, but surplus populations were nearby on other islands. The planters there were able to import thousands of seasonal laborers, but these sacadas only shared the misery of local year-round labor in the hinterland of Bacolod under the power of an ostentatiously wealthy aristocracy. As in other areas of the tropics where social polarization has created a landless labor class, their marginalization put increasing pressure on forest ecosystems, where some of them attempted to create an extra-legal squatter society. U.S. financial interests and consumer markets provided key elements of that marginalization. Americans' consumption of Pacific sugar replaced indigenous cultures with proletarian concentrations of ethnically uprooted laborers.

Even though these were not slave systems, like the earlier Caribbean and Brazilian sugar lands, the environmental costs of such systems were similar. A diverse range of natural ecosystems were replaced by sugar. On the Hawaiian islands, the previous vegetation varied from dry land scrub on slopes facing away from the northeast trade winds to the lush grasslands and forests of the windward slopes. On Negros, cane plantations replaced some subsistence rice paddy lands, but mostly they cleared virgin rainforest. Sugar corporations centralized control of vast acreages of land. In Hawaii, this entailed modernized management of estates under intense market competition. In their long-run interest the planters invested heavily in agronomic research, which for many years emphasized the search for biological controls of sugar pests. In sharp contrast, on Negros the Americans remained offshore, tolerating the severe social and ecological damage that local sugar barons perpetrated.

Were cane plantations, as managed ecosystems, biologically sustainable? As with any monocrop, sugarcane grown as a large-scale monocrop invited invasions of pathogens. In sugar cane's ancestral home, parasites attacked some varieties when they were grown on a large scale. But sugar cane did not suffer devastating disease attacks, as did Gros Michel bananas or Brazilian rubber, as we shall see. Sugar research centers overcame disease challenges effectively but ultimately only by increasing applications of commercial fertilizers and pesticides. The impact of intensive chemical use on soil and water regimes depended largely on local circumstances, since sugar cane in itself does not deplete soil nutrients as severely as several other tropical monocrops. So the long-term ecological viability of cane plantations remains problematic.

Banana Republics: Yankee Fruit Companies and the Tropical American Lowlands

The steadily increasing appetite of North Americans and Europeans for tropical fruit, especially bananas, produced impacts in the tropics similar to those in the cane sugar belt, doubling plantation agriculture's transformation of lowland rainforests. Several Latin American countries' economies—and patterns of ecological change on their lands—were radically shaped from the 1890s onward by North American corporations and markets. In 1970, Latin America exported 3 million tons of bananas, worth about $200 million, mostly from small countries of Central America and northern South America; this represented a high percentage of their export earnings. A generation earlier, even in the Depression years of the mid-1930s, 2.4 million tons were exported annually from Central America alone. In those days, Americans themselves consumed more than half of that. By the mid-1950s bananas were the world's fourth largest fruit crop—40 percent of all fruit in international trade. In the United States they were 10 percent of fresh produce sales.[1] The history of Northern consumption of this fragile tropical fruit is the most conflicted and widely debated story in the annals of export monocropping and expatriate corporate power in Latin America.

THE CONQUEST OF THE CENTRAL AMERICAN RAINFOREST, 1872–1945

In the late nineteenth century, on the Caribbean coastal lowlands of Central America, there were great stretches of forest for the taking. Seventy percent of

Central American water, from Belize through Honduras, Nicaragua and Costa Rica to Panama, drains into the Caribbean; its five most extensive river systems all flow eastward, carrying abundant year-round water supplies. The largest segment is the north coast lowlands of Honduras. From there the forest turns southward through the Miskito Coast of eastern Nicaragua, and across Costa Rica and Panama.

This is a broad plain cut by a series of short rivers that plunge from the interior mountains to the flat lowlands, where they slow to a meander and release rich alluvium on wide terraces. Except for these terraces, the lowland soils are mostly heavy, nutrient-deficient clays that are quickly leached under the year-round rains brought by the trade winds. Near the coast extensive swamps are a variation on the rainforest ecosystem. The wetlands support a wide range of flora and fauna, including a spectacular variety of migratory birds that spend summers ranging throughout North America.

To capitalist adventurers in the late 1800s the Caribbean coastal lowlands presented all the difficulties of wet tropical frontiers anywhere. In sharp contrast to the hill region above, the lowland zone was hostile to human health. Diseases of the rainforest were daunting, especially malaria, yellow fever, and hookworm. The workforce for any industrial-scale agriculture would face these parasites, the legions of Nature in her primeval form. The economic cost to investors would be high, until modern tropical medicine began to win its victories. Just as with other tropical export crops, bananas spearheaded the trend toward centralization of control and vertical integration, industrialization of the land, and a powerful link between tropical rainforest and Northern consumers—linking an attack on the rainforest to remote consumers' tastes and volatile international prices.

The transformation of rainforest from natural vegetation with some of the planet's richest species diversity to one-species banana plantations was predominantly American work. Two powerful corporations, first the United Fruit Company and shortly thereafter the Standard Fruit Company, penetrated the rainforest on invitation from pliant local oligarchic governments. Together they opened for exploitation regions that were remote from the national capitals in the hills. No all-weather roads led down from the hills to the Caribbean coastal plain. Virtually the only transportation was along the meandering rivers. A few tiny ports dotted the coastal marshes and beaches, usually near the river mouths. But the fertile flood plains were ideal for grow-

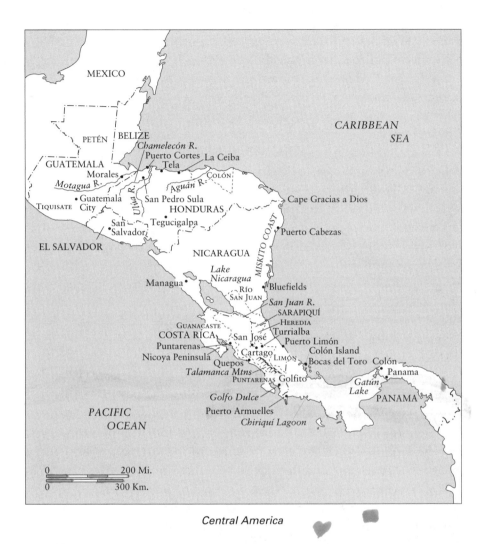

Central America

ing the demanding banana. Temperatures were high throughout the year, and
the annual rainfall was 80–120 inches. The dry season was so brief, usually
only a month, that bananas could be harvested year-round.[2]

Spanish colonial control had never effectively penetrated the Caribbean forest zone. Throughout the three centuries of rule from distant Madrid, the Ladinos or Spanish-speaking settlers stayed in the hills, avoiding the wet lowlands.
To the Iberian sensibility, the rainforest and its pre-Columbian inhabitants
were anathema. The hill estate owners had no administrative or technological

capacity to reach to the Caribbean lowlands. The coastal towns became refuges for losers in factional struggles and staging grounds for insurgents challenging upland regimes. Throughout the early decades of independence after the 1820s, Ladino governments were harassed by rebellions based on this remote coast. They dreamed of luring railroad builders and their financial resources from England and the United States, to help them consolidate their power.

The unstable regimes also had a financial motive for their efforts to settle the lowlands by attracting agricultural colonists. They used strategies similar to the U.S. government's effort to sell public lands. Searching for new capital by offering land, their chief form of wealth, they granted Europeans and Americans almost total independence in their operations until the 1930s.[3] Political instability and intrigue combined with Northerners' dreams of empire and fortune to attract a particular sort of reckless, highly individualistic gringo. Restlessly moving beyond the North American frontier, they were the same gambling stock as others in Kansas and Arizona. But the American presence was tenuous and dispersed until the high risks and formidable development problems of the rainforest frontier could be confronted by the superior resources and long-term staying power of large-scale corporations.

The first American banana entrepreneur was Captain Lorenzo Dow Baker of Boston, who put into Port Morant, Jamaica, in 1870 and discovered bananas and coconuts for sale on the wharves.[4] In a modest speculative move that launched an international industry, he bought 160 stems of bananas, selling them profitably on the New York market. Returning a year later, he bought 400 stems and sold them in Boston. Increasingly confident, in 1876 Baker launched the Standard Steam Navigation Company and the Boston Fruit Company. In 1877, he diversified his markets further, beginning regular shipments to New Orleans for the lower Mississippi regional market. Faced with British competition in Jamaica, Baker began to extend his sources in the late 1890s to include Central America, where land was far cheaper. By then his future partner was at work in Costa Rica.

During colonial times, Costa Rica had been a hinterland between the Panamanian interocean crossing and the Spanish regional capital in Guatemala. Costa Rica was always more lightly populated than many parts of Central America. It was a difficult challenge to travel to the Caribbean coast from San José, Costa Rica's capital in the central valley. The trip began with the climb across any of several passes through the volcanic cordillera. The struggle to cross the mountains was minor compared to the transit of the tropical low-lands, where there were no all-weather roads. The only possible routes before the railroad era were the rivers that drained the eastern slopes. Small boats taxied the occasional traveler down these streams.

After the 1820s the newly independent nation's government had encour-aged the growth of coffee plantations as the route to profit and progress, but that crop's only route to Europe from the central valley was by mule to the Pacific coast, and from there by boat around Cape Horn. By 1870 the govern-ment dreamed of building a rail line to Puerto Limon on the Caribbean coast. The elite of San José were adopting the international romance of the iron horse that seemed to be opening the frontiers of the entire world to settlement and prosperous agriculture.[5]

In 1871, just as Lorenzo Baker was beginning his operations in Jamaica, the Costa Rican government began courting Henry Meiggs, the American who was building Peru's first railroad. Meiggs was preoccupied in the Andes, so he sent his nephew, Minor Keith, to San José. The United Fruit Company's oper-ations in Costa Rica rose out of the railroad-building contract that they pro-duced. In return for building a railroad from San José over the hills and down through the lowland forest to Puerto Limon, the Costa Rican government gave Keith a ninety-nine-year lease on the proposed line, plus 800,000 acres of government land along its route or anywhere else within the country.[6]

When a land concession was designed as inducement for a company to build a railroad, the government granted only a provisional land title until the stipulated length of railroad was complete. This led to endless wrangling, but Keith moved ahead with construction. Coffee, a seasonal crop, could not bring business and profits to a railroad by itself. So Keith began to search for other goods, especially new export crops, which could be hauled on the same tracks throughout the year.

Most of the rainforest lands of Sarapiqui, the hinterland of Puerto Limon, were very thinly populated. Only the alluvial riverine terraces had supported cacao plantations in colonial times. By Keith's time, a tiny population of peas-ant farmers lived scattered through the forest. One of the products of their subsistence cropping was bananas. Later, under pressure from the railroad and fruit company, they increased their banana production for export, at prices dictated by the monopoly. In his railroad's first years, Keith bought and shipped bananas from many growers, both smallholders and private plantations run by Costa Ricans with Jamaican workers.[7]

Simultaneously, Baker and other Yankee commercial banana shippers had been surveying the entire arc of Caribbean coastal lowlands from Mexico to Colombia to diversify their supply areas away from hurricane-prone Jamaica. Baker's interest focused on the north coast of Panama, a virtually unpenetrated forest belt across the border from Costa Rica, where Minor Keith was also prospecting with tentative British partners. Both Baker and Keith preferred American partners, so in 1899 they united their interests and named the new corporation the United Fruit Company.

Their first joint venture was in Panama, around a cluster of islands in a semi-enclosed bay, some fifty by twenty miles in extent, called Bocas del Toro. Frederick Adams, the early chronicler of the United Fruit Company, sailed around the bay and its islands in 1914.

> The Chiriqui Lagoon is a mass of islands . . . several thousands of them—a perfect labyrinth of tropical islands in a setting which mocks description. Some of these islands rise in cliffs hundreds of feet sheer above the crystal waters which lave their bases. The crests of these heights are fringed with palms and with other tropical trees laden with huge flowers of flaunting colors. Ferns and clinging vines soften the lines of the cliffs. In places the passage between these precipitous islands is so narrow that there is barely room to float a canoe. Only the Indian guides can safely find a way in and out of this tropical wonderland.[8]

His lyrical description epitomized Northern adventurers' fascination with the overwhelming beauty of pristine tropical Nature. Yet they saw no contradiction between delight in wilderness and eagerness to domesticate it.

United Fruit built its Caribbean headquarters in the little town of Bocas del Toro. In 1900 the town was a swampy village, with a squatter population of English-speaking descendents of Jamaican slaves living in squalor and disease. The company built permanent houses and shops on higher ground, as well as a hospital that served its entire operations in western Panama and adjacent Costa Rica. By 1914 the company controlled 109,000 acres in Panama and Costa Rica, of which 40,000 acres were already in banana production, and employed nearly seven thousand workers. The infrastructure for that scale of operation was impressive: the company built 250 miles of railway spurs, all lined with plantations, through the former wilderness. Its interests were highly specialized but this infrastructure was beginning to open the entire region for general settlement and forest clearance.

United Fruit constructed an integrated operation from soil to railroad to shipping to wholesale markets in American ports. Keith lost money on most of his railroad contracts but his empire grew in related areas. The Costa Rican government relied on Keith to build the infrastructure of an entire modern economy; in the long run, this work probably had as great an impact as the banana operations in themselves. Within another few years, he added a $600,000 contract to build one municipal tram service for San José and another for the old colonial capital of Cartago nearby. He built a bank in San José, central markets for Cartago and Heredia, and an ice plant in Limon. No one else in the country could remotely compete with him for political influence and economic impact.

United Fruit's primary interest remained the profitability of the banana trade. In that pursuit it stretched its influence far beyond the borders of any Central American country. From the start it moved into international transport and marketing, building a totally integrated operation from plantation to consumer. By 1902 United's own fleet of banana boats, the famous "Great White Fleet," controlled most banana shipping to Europe, as well as to the United States. By 1912 it also controlled International Railways of Central America; a year later, it created the Tropical Radio Telegraph Company, Central America's first, to communicate with its jungle stations. United Fruit became a managerial and technological empire of its own, indispensable to the republics where it operated.

On this corporate basis, and with access to virtually unlimited amounts of land, United Fruit and its fledgling competitor, the Standard Fruit Company in Honduras, made the first third of the twentieth century the initial great era of banana culture and rainforest clearing in Central America. By 1930, United alone exported sixty-five million bunches of bananas to the United States, and owned 3,482,042 acres of lowland forest, equal to the area of Connecticut and Rhode Island combined. But 85 percent of that land was unused, maintained for future exploitation, or to keep it out of the hands of potential competitors.[9]

For its laborers, those anonymous men whose daily struggle was the actual point of confrontation between society and Nature, United relied upon the impoverished rural descendants of Jamaican ex-slaves. In the decades after emancipation, these workers were willing to go wherever wages were good. When the French were making their abortive attempt to build the Panama Canal, twenty-five thousand Jamaicans hired on. When the French failed in 1888, the unemployed workers looked for other wage labor around Central America. When the United States revived Canal work in 1904, nearly fifty thousand joined the massive crew, earning at least twice what they could have made at home. By 1910 Jamaicans also migrated to Costa Rica, Colombia, Nicaragua, and Honduras for banana plantation work, and to Cuba for sugar.

In Costa Rica, United Fruit hired migrant Jamaicans as the primary labor force on its 50,000 acres in Sarapiqui, preferring English-speakers. In 1911, forty thousand Jamaicans were working for United in Central America, not only as laborers but also as foremen, engineers, clerks, managers, and teachers. Though many of these workers were on temporary contracts, others remained as squatters on plantation fringes.[10] This pattern led to the growth of turbulent frontier communities in company towns. The uprooted men, bound only by industrial and cash structures, had no organic connection to the land.

In clearing forest for plantations, the company chose virgin alluvial soil on riverine terraces. The workers removed undergrowth, girdled high trees, and planted banana suckers immediately. Then they felled and burned the tall trees, leaving only native rubber trees standing. Bananas grew faster than weeds and natural second growth, smothering them. Long, rational ranks of a single species replaced the infinite, confusing variety of the natural forest.

In the early years, United purchased most of its bananas from small producers. But the economies of large-scale production were too efficient to ignore. The company soon decided to control 80 percent of production directly on its own plantations because of what it euphemistically called "tropical conditions and lack of respect for tropical contracts." The result was a classic enclave economy. In the corporate banana operations, the entire work force was controlled and managed like a great factory. The company built housing for managers and workers in a strictly hierarchical system. Companies built schools, hospitals, recreation facilities, and stores that carried only company-controlled goods. These outlets were virtually the only source of food for many plantation workers since the companies reserved the fertile alluvial terraces for the commercial crop or cattle pasture.

These enclaves radically reshaped the natural environment. In the jungle, the companies clear-cut forests, filled in low and swampy areas, and installed

sewage, drainage, and water systems. They transformed natural or spottily settled ecosystems into rational, orderly biofactories.[11] The society of the forest
region was changed from low-density farming and ranching, supporting
small market towns on the riverbanks, to an ordered industrial hierarchy with
a semiproletarian work force. There was little resident population in the rainforest. The main rivers and coastlines were lightly populated by forest Indians,
notably the Miskitos in the Honduran and Nicaraguan coastal lowlands.[12]
Entrepreneurs had to import labor for large plantations, for both the highland
Indians and Ladinos (people Hispanic in language and culture) resisted
migrating into the lowlands.

By 1913 United owned or leased 852,560 acres of rainforest land, including
221,837 acres under cultivation, in Jamaica, Santo Domingo, Cuba, Costa
Rica, Colombia, Nicaragua, and Honduras. The biggest prize of all turned out
to be the windward lowlands of Honduras, the largest segment of the
Caribbean rainforest belt. The government in Tegucigalpa was eager to have it
conquered, for the lowlands were more effectively cut off from that country's
centers of settlement in the hills than in Costa Rica. In colonial times, the
sparse Indian population had been nearly wiped out.[13] Spanish-speaking
Ladinos settled here and there along the riverbanks. Through the nineteenth
century, Honduras found no major export crop and achieved little economic
growth. By the 1890s its government fell deeply in debt. With an annual
income of around $1.6 million, it had contracted $124 million in loans from
private banks in London, a staggering debt ratio for the country. Great
Britain's fiscal control of Central American regimes was at its peak. Both the
Hondurans and the Americans were becoming determined to change that.

The Caribbean coastal rainforests might prove the source of wealth to lift
the country out of lethargy and foreign debt, but they would take massive new
investments to develop. Toward the coast there were many marshy areas and
shallow lakes. Along the coast, in brackish water, mangrove swamps alter-
nated with sandy beaches. The American writer O. Henry, describing a fic-
tional town on the adjacent Miskito coast of Nicaragua in 1912, caught the
note of dread and hostility in Yankee perceptions of the rainforest:

Between the sea and the foothills stretched the five miles breadth of alluvial
coast. Here was the flora of the tropics in its rankest and most prodigal growth.
Spaces here and there had been wrested from the jungle and planted with

bananas and cane and orange groves. The rest was a riot of wild vegetation, the home of monkeys, tapirs, jaguars, alligators and prodigious reptiles and insects. Where no road was cut a serpent could scarcely make its way through the tangle of vines and creepers. Across the treacherous mangrove swamps few things without wings could safely pass.[14]

The few settlements were cut off from the interior; indeed, there was no motorable road or railroad to the inland capital of Tegucigalpa until after 1950. This thwarted the national government's efforts to control its own tropical frontier, which began to develop separately from the interior hills. By the mid-twentieth century, the coastal zone had over 20 percent of the national population, half of the national export revenue, its entire railroad system, and most of its industry. This development was largely the work of the Yankee banana barons but they, in turn, built upon a previous generation of local entrepreneurship, ultimately overwhelming it.

When the first foreign banana purchasers dropped anchor off the north coast of Honduras in the late 1870s, the largest town was San Pedro Sula, near the mouth of the Ulua River, just east of the Guatemala border, where 1,200 people were settled. The local gentry were tentatively growing several crops, including coconuts, cacao, rubber, bananas, and citrus, for sale to steamship captains.[15] On acreage that had been cleared for crops and then degraded, they ran scrub Criollo cattle on the meager grass cover, in the traditional Iberian hacendero style.

Most of the banana growers were small-scale farmers; two-thirds of them cultivated less than ten acres of bananas along with their other crops. Yet fifteen thousand acres produced over one million stems for export, not a trivial amount for the local economy. These frontier farmers cultivated bananas by ancient methods of forest clearing. They cut down the brush and small trees, then burned the slash. Using wooden dibble sticks in the ashes, they planted bananas and related species of plantains. Weeding was done only once a year and was rough, just enough to inhibit fast-growing weed species from competing with the tall bananas until banana shade inhibited the weeds. This system minimized soil and nutrient loss; it contrasted sharply with techniques of European cultures in temperate climates, which insisted on clean weeding, both to eliminate competition for soil nutrients, and to be neat and esthetically satisfying to Northern eyes. The Northern system was labor intensive and it produced much more soil erosion than tropical techniques. But Europeans and North Americans were slow to understand the implications of such methods when they began to manage rainforest lands.

Local banana growers also converted some existing grazing land to export crops. The municipal governments that they controlled gave them additional public land, most of it still forested. They then had to confront severe problems of transport for marketing their crops. From 1887 onward they formed growers' associations to negotiate with purchasers and even attempted to set up steamship service to New Orleans. In the long run, all these local cooperatives failed, either because of internal dissension or because they were overwhelmed by the Yankees' corporate scale and market knowledge.

River transport was risky and unpredictable, so in the 1890s the commercial gentry turned their hopes to railroads. They lobbied the national government to grant land concessions to foreign railroad builders. An attentive ear was found in the Hondurans' governing elite, who were encouraging industrial technology and corporate investment, influenced by the doctrines of European Liberalism. One tenet of the Liberal ideology was "scientific agriculture," a term that assumed that agricultural expansion was the basis of a strong economy and that monoculture, efficiency and standard quality of product were the hallmarks of progress. By 1890 this ideology exercised a strong influence on government policies.

This influence provided opportunities for Yankee immigrants. A miscellaneous lot of Americans had already begun filtering southward into the region. As early as the 1870s there were three hundred of them in San Pedro Sula, making up one-fourth of the town's population, looking for land grants and commercial contracts. U.S. consulates had been involved in these commercial probes since the 1830s. Closely cooperating with the Commerce Department's International Office, they monitored commercial possibilities and sent many informative reports back to Washington.

By the 1870s numerous American steamships were stopping at all the coastal Honduran towns. In 1877 the Oteri and Brothers steamship line began service from New Orleans. Soon there were several competitors, primarily from New Orleans, some from New York; they were all irregular and unpredictable, much like the workers who drifted south. The sweltering docks of New Orleans sent men to work on the Honduran coast beginning in the 1890s. The Mississippi Delta was a major supplier of fruits and vegetables to urban markets around the American southern states, attracting many Italian and Sicilian immigrants to its intensive small-scale farming and marketing. Three brothers, Joseph, Luca, and Felix Vaccaro had been successful brokers of locally grown oranges until Louisiana citrus farming was wiped out in February 1899 by a cold wave that plunged temperatures to minus 7 degrees Fahrenheit, the coldest ever recorded that far south. With nothing left to lose, the Vaccaro brothers decided to turn their entrepreneurial talents to Honduras, where crops would never be touched by frost, and they could diversify into purchasing coconuts and bananas as well as oranges. The brothers founded the Standard Fruit Company, which became United Fruit's primary competitor in the American banana business, and more than its equal in southern U.S. markets.

A competitor of the Vaccaros, Samuel Zemurray, arrived in Honduras from New Orleans in 1905. By 1910 he leased 5,000 acres on the Cuyamel River and founded the Cuyamel Fruit Company. Shortly thereafter, Zemurray gambled with the future by buying 15,000 acres more, so as to outflank the Vaccaros. This triggered a corporate race to control Central America's largest rainforest. Great banana plantations arose around San Pedro Sula, which became the second largest city of Honduras. The foreign fruit companies looked to the efficiencies of large-scale production, processing and transport facilities, which would be viable only if they could be sure of major land leases and infrastructure concessions for long periods of time. They insisted on full legal support from the Honduran government. This led to intricate political maneuvering, in which the fruit companies had the full backing of the United States government.

The Honduran government wanted a share of the profits. In 1893 it established a 2 percent duty on the value of exported bananas. But this tax was collected quixotically, for the government had barely begun to develop a presence on the coast. More lucrative was its power to grant land concessions to foreign companies in return for building railroads. The government was desperately eager to establish fast, reliable transport from the capital to the coastal region. Following the international strategy of the time, it granted foreign construction firms extensive land rights in return for a commitment to build the lines not only into the areas that the companies wanted to open for banana production but all the way through the hills to Tegucigalpa.

The Honduran government was inconsistent regarding land sales to foreigners. An 1895 law guaranteed homesteaders alternate lots along railroads, so as to prevent the companies from completely dominating vast regions of rainforest. Moreover, an 1898 agrarian law prohibited public land sales within eight miles of the coast. In 1906, in a rising tide of anti-American feeling, this limit was extended to thirty miles from the coast. But the major companies could usually either evade the laws' restrictions or force their repeal. In many instances the companies bought alternating lots through intermediaries or from the individuals who owned them.

This went almost too far for nationalist elements in the Honduran Congress, where anti-American feeling remained strong. A new law promulgated in 1909 required the government to give only the temporary use of government lands, not grant full title. Facing severe factionalism and chronic political instability in Tegucigalpa, the companies fought fire with fire, financing rival contestants for power. Honduras' two political parties, locked in a protracted struggle between personal factions, both encouraged the banana barons' meddling behind the scenes. The companies insisted on favors in return.

In a particularly notorious instance, Zemurray cultivated close relations with President Manuel Bonilla. When Bonilla's forces overthrew his anti-American rival, Miguel Davila, in 1907, and the British demanded repayment of their loans, the U.S. State Department saw a strategic opportunity. Secretary of State Philander Knox, attempting to replace British banking throughout the Caribbean basin, worked with J. P. Morgan and other American private bankers to buy out the British. Not to be displaced, Zemurray financed a little army led by Bonilla and a New Orleans soldier of fortune named Lee Christmas, which invaded Honduras by a north coast landing in 1911. The U.S. Navy and the State Department withdrew their support from Davila and reinstalled Bonilla in his place. As a reward for his efforts, Christmas was appointed U.S. Consul for Honduras. In gratitude to Zemurray, President Bonilla had the land law revoked by his Congress, paving the way for large sales of land to the Northern speculators. As historian Walter LaFeber acidly concludes, "If Honduras was dependent on the fruit companies before 1912, it was virtually indistinguishable from them after 1912."[16]

There was simultaneous saber rattling in Nicaragua, where Wall Street and the State Department assisted a client, Adolfo Diaz, in overthrowing the anti-American President José Santos Zelaya in 1909. Once in office, Diaz refinanced the Nicaraguan government's debts on the basis of loans from New York banks, an early step in the process of displacing the British financial underpinnings of Central American regimes. The United Fruit Company was deeply entangled in these machinations from its base in the coastal town of Bluefields.[17]

This suited U.S. strategic interests well. In 1911 President Taft proclaimed, "It should be the policy of this Government, especially with respect to countries in geographical proximity to the Canal Zone, to give to them when requested all proper assistance . . . in the promotion of peace, in the development of their resources, and in a sound reorganization of their fiscal systems."[18] Strategic ambitions of the American imperium were forging an alliance with the corporate powers that were leading the conquest of the rainforest. A year later the Honduran government sold more forestlands to Sam Zemurray, who proceeded to make the town of Tela the center of his operations. The Vaccaros had gained only the use of alternating plots; Zemurray gained ownership of 500 hectares per kilometer, including his branch lines.

The two fruit companies were not to be trusted to uphold their side of the bargain in the railroad contracts. Between them they built one thousand miles of railroads to serve the region's fruit economy, but did not complete a connection to Tegucigalpa. They kept defaulting on the interior mileage through the hills, for it would bring them no profits, only greater government influence over their operations. This was only one aspect of the regulatory chaos in the region.

In the lowlands, land laws might be in place but little land was actually surveyed in detail, and local ownership and usufruct rights were rarely clear. Entrepreneurs eager to get on with their work did not bother to wait for the surveyors to arrive. Instead, they could use what was called a denouncement procedure, similar to the one used in U.S. homestead land sales administration. Anyone interested in a specified parcel of land could "denounce" it in public, and require an auction. As in the western United States, this procedure was open to many abuses by agents of either local or foreign speculators. The fruit companies were free to accelerate the process of forest clearance.

On the north coast, the fruit companies proceeded to transform land—mostly marshland and forests—into plantations. From the start they had to build transport infrastructure where little or none existed. They built railroads and port facilities. They straightened riverbeds, applying technology that the U.S. Army Corps of Engineers had been developing for a century in the eastern United States. Standard Fruit set about transforming the central north coast hinterland of La Ceiba. In 1913 it exported over 2.8 milli 1919 the figure rose to a spectacular 5.5 million stems, loaded directly from boxcars on the pier onto waiting steamers.

Meanwhile, Zemurray's crews attacked the forests on the rich soils of nearby lowlands. Zemurray imported construction materials duty free, and assembled five hundred workers. By 1921, they built two hundred miles of track, including both mainline and narrow-gauge feeder lines. Banana exports from Tela rose exponentially. In 1915 the tiny port shipped 1,203,500 stems; five years later that figure leaped upward to 4,576,500 stems. The north coast as a whole reached its maximum banana production in 1929–31, when thirty million bunches were exported from Honduras annually, a remarkable one-third of total world exports. Most of them were shipped directly to ports on the east and Gulf coasts of the United States.

Most of the farms that produced those millions of stems were created on newly cleared forestland, in valleys and bottom lands ranging from mangrove to palm to mixed hardwood and bamboo forests. The crews faced daunting problems with poorly drained, marshy lands, so Zemurray's workers began draining wide areas of wetlands.[19] Paul Standley, the leading American tropical biologist, surveyed the area in 1927–28 and produced the most incisive description of the transformation.

> Practically all the land within this area that is fit for the purpose is covered with banana plants, which, however beautiful when standing alone or in moderate quantities, become exceedingly monotonous when massed in plantations many miles in extent. Between banana plantations however are large areas unsuited for their cultivation. These consist, near the coast, of wide marshes and of densely wooded swamps which cannot or have not been drained. . . . Much swamp land has been ditched and planted. The most spectacular of these unused areas is the great Toloa Swamp, [which] is like many other swamps or marshes in Central America, a shallow lake with an abundance of aqautic plants, and such a profusion of water birds as one sees only in the tropics.[20]

Standley's report was a reminder that draining marshlands also reduced avian habitat, including that of migratory birds. The value that banana plantations extracted from natural systems entailed a threat to wildlife diversity, though that was never counted as an economic cost. By the 1920s Zemurray's company, steadily expanding its engineering works, also diverted silt-laden annual flood waters into lagoons, to build them up for banana production. By 1930 its system of drainage canals and dikes included ninety thousand feet of canals and forty-four thousand feet of dikes. The company's enormous extent of domesticated land enabled it to export over ten million stems of bananas that year. By then, although the upland forests on its concessions remained largely in their natural condition, in the valleys and river bottoms the species composition on the land had changed to monotony.

Traditional economic wisdom has it that the corporate enclaves of Central America were almost entirely self-contained, and contributed little to their respective national economies. Recent research has begun to show that this somewhat misses the point. As in any plantation system, workers were drawn from a wide area, thereby interacting with their home locations, and food had to be grown to feed them. The environmental consequences of a plantation complex were wide reaching, becoming more difficult to distinguish from other factors as they became more distant from the core areas.[21]

Throughout Central America the economic difficulties of the Depression intersected with a compound ecological crisis that hit the companies in the form of soil depletion and plant diseases. By the late 1920s the banana companies were forced into the major task of shifting their production bases from the Caribbean coast to the Pacific. The damage they had done in the Caribbean lowlands was about to be repeated—with the concurrence of all three national governments—on the other coast.

The corporate plantations were more precarious than any banana grower dreamed at the dawn of the banana era. Subsistence producers had always grown several varieties of bananas and plantains for their own and local consumption. But a large concentration of any single-species product virtually assured massive attack by some species of micropredator before long. Disaster struck in the form of a root mold, Fusarium, which attacked the Gros Michel, the only banana variety then in mass production. Discovered first in 1903 on a plantation in Panama, it was soon popularly called Panama Disease.

Panama Disease was carried in the soil. Propagation of the commercial banana, thousands of plants at a time, could be done only by dividing the root stock of existing plants, a process that transmitted the root mold with it; hence the planters could not interrupt the disease cycle, as propagation by seeds might have done. When Panama Disease struck, plantations usually lived only for eight to ten years before they shriveled. The first production declines were in 1913 and by the 1920s the epidemic was advancing rapidly through the entire Caribbean coastal region, threatening to destroy the entire industry. In Honduras, Zemurray began abandoning farms in the mid-1920s and sold out to United Fruit in 1929. As late as 1933 United controlled over 130,000 acres of national lands with rights to over 200,000 acres more. But the company renounced these additional lands, largely because of Panama Disease, and abandoned this great tract.

Operations as far flung as these, in which many millions of dollars were invested, had to be supported by agronomic research on a scale of botanical experimentation that no small producer could finance. Zemurray had the financial resources to hire the best available tropical botanists. He set up a research laboratory and experimental farm at Lancetilla, a short distance inland from Tela, which quickly became the finest tropical crop research center in Central America. In 1925 he hired Wilson Popenoe, the leading American tropical botanist of his time, to head the laboratory and experimental farm. Son of a mining engineer who had spent many years in Central and South America, Popenoe was a world authority on avocados and a soil expert. He had compiled years of experience as an agricultural explorer for the Division of Foreign Seed and Plant Introduction of the U.S. Department of Agriculture. He was the author of a standard book on tropical agronomy.[22]

Zemurray's idea was that if American crop and soil science could devise ways of producing massive amounts of export crops sustainably in Central America, Popenoe's team might make a major contribution. The Lancetilla center might mediate successfully between the forces of development and the ecological realities of the lowland ecosystem. But in United Fruit's chemical laboratory there, though plant pathologists worked feverishly to eradicate or at least control the disease they had no success, even after years of effort.[23]

To compound difficulties even further, in the 1920s a second epidemic appeared in the plantations, the Sigatoka Disease. First detected in the Fiji islands, Sigatoka was an airborne fungus, attacking the leaves of the banana plants, withering them as their fruit neared ripening. Sigatoka hit Central America hard, compounding the effect of Panama Disease. By the mid-1920s United's pathologists learned that Sigatoka could be controlled by spraying the plants with Bordeaux mixture, a copper sulfate or arsenic solution, though the treatment was expensive. Many small growers, who could not afford the additional expense, were ruined. By the mid-1930s Sigatoka infected 80 percent of

Honduras's crop, and its effects were almost as severe elsewhere. And still no remedy for Panama Disease was found. The diseases that the corporate system had brought into prominence helped to increase the corporations' monopoly of commercial production.

Two strategies were presented to possibly save the industry from total collapse. Growers could move the plantations to new soil every decade, clearing new forest each time. The alternative was to develop disease-resistant varieties of banana that would be acceptable to consumers in the United States and Europe. Those varieties, variants of the Giant Cavendish banana, were finally perfected only in the late 1950s. Until then the only available strategy was to continue moving every ten years or so, abandoning the plantations to other crops.

After removing everything of any money value, including rails, bridges, and telephones, United turned over some of its former banana lands to the Costa Rican government. It left other lands to its Jamaican workers, whom it was compelled to lay off because the government refused to allow Afro-Caribbeans on the Pacific coast. Workers' towns crumbled. Only a mixed population of Jamaicans, Ladinos, and Indians were left on and around the abandoned plantations, cultivating their varied food crops on small plots, while secondary woodlands grew up around them and weeds reclaimed the streets of sleepy towns.

The previously undeveloped Pacific coastal plain is far narrower than the Caribbean lowlands, lying against the steep slopes of the cordillera. Where the central mountain range is high enough to block the moisture-laden trade winds, the Pacific lowlands are seasonally dry during the cool months, from Mexico as far south as western Costa Rica. Along the rest of Costa Rica and Panama, and south along the Pacific through Colombia and Ecuador, lies a rainforest belt that is wet nearly all year. On the Central American peninsula the rain is brought from the northeast by Caribbean trade winds; along the northwestern coast of South America it is brought off the Pacific by the Humboldt Current. In the 1920s, this moisture supported a rainforest that was as biotically varied as the Caribbean forest. Rich volcanic soils collected in alluvial fans along the area's many short rivers.

In Costa Rica, United Fruit obtained 175,000 acres on the Pacific coast in 1920. In order to buy land cheaply at auction, United frequently used local intermediaries. In 1929 the U.S. Vice Consul in San José described United's rivalry with the Costa Rican government:

Although sub-rosa the company and the government endeavored to seek some satisfactory solution, on the surface neither appeared to be doing anything. The company maintained its exploring and investigating parties in different parts of the country and . . . acquired large tracts of land which had been bought by individuals who undoubtedly were using company money.[24]

By 1938 United completed shifting its Costa Rican operations entirely to the Pacific coast. In Panama its strategy was the same. United bought 17,000 acres of forest through an intermediary, and took thirty-year leases from the Panamanian government on two large parcels just east of the Costa Rica border. A year later the company abandoned its Bocas del Toro operations and moved to the new port of Puerto Armuelles. Panama's government paid for a thirty-four mile extension of its national railroad through the company's new region to the coast. United paid for the new wharf facilities that made Puerto Armuelles a viable deep water port. The company and a compliant local government thus opened that previously "neglected" section of Panama's rainforest region to general development.

BANANA POLITICS AND THE CONTROL OF NATURAL RESOURCES

Political conditions were beginning to shift in ways that would ultimately change the pattern of land management away from total domination by foreign corporations. By the 1930s the Yankee corporations' power was first challenged, both by governments determined to claim a larger share of the new wealth and workers determined to improve their pay scales and working conditions. By the end of the Depression years, the companies no longer had a totally free hand to operate as they wished. By the 1950s this shifting trend in power would lead the companies to sell most of their direct interests in Central American land and work instead through local subsidiaries or semi-independent producers. Thus American corporate managers could virtually eliminate any direct connection to the labor force or working conditions on the land and present a more elusive target for nationalist attacks. It became more difficult to define where responsibility lay for sustainable land management.

Neither the governments nor organized labor were yet consciously concerned about resource sustainability, for the rainforest was still just beginning to be penetrated on a large scale. New land on the tropical frontier, under economically unprofitable forest cover, was still abundant in every Central American country except El Salvador. It was a delicate balance between enticing the companies in and virtually giving away sovereignty. But once the companies were deeply committed, governments could begin harder bargaining.

The government of Costa Rica led the way in devising ways of holding the companies accountable for the terms of their contracts and the division of their profits. From as early as 1892 the Costa Rican Congress had made efforts to establish an export tax on bananas. For a long period it failed. The classic United contract was signed in 1900, allowing free export of all its bananas for ten years, even though local exporters had to pay a banana tax. In 1910 the Costa Rican Congress established an export tax of one cent per bunch, but United forced it to lock that trivial figure in place for twenty years in the contract.

In 1929, shortly before the Depression's onset, the Costa Rican government negotiated a new contract with United Fruit for another twenty years. The government's first proposal projected a tax of five cents per bunch for the first six million bunches per year, four cents for the next eight million, and three cents beyond that. Anticipating the multinationals' frequent tactic after 1945, in response United threatened to move its operations entirely out of Costa Rica to rival countries. This was no idle threat, for the company had been looking for new sites ever since the onset of banana diseases; it had hired some of the world's highest paid soil scientists to prospect for appropriate sites.

A compromise contract adopted in 1930 showed how little a local government could yet do against the giant and the benefits that it alone could promise. The contract established a tax of two cents on each bunch of bananas until 1950. It then allowed the company to expand its railroads wherever necessary for its crops, or remove or change lines even on public lands, after making an agreement with the minister of public works. Further, United gained the right to build a new port, Golfito, on the Golfo Dulce on the Pacific, in return for which the company agreed to give the government a trivial 5,300 acres of abandoned plantations to begin new agricultural colonies for local workers who had been left unemployed by the company's move to the Pacific coast. This agreement blatantly favored United Fruit; the company now could legally expand its operations to an entirely new region.

Anti-American nationalism arose in each country of Latin America almost as early as U.S. capital penetrated its frontiers. The emerging Latin American labor movement combined resistance to oligarchic governments with hostility toward gringo corporate imperialism. Naturally enough, nationalist fervor tended to focus on major corporations like United Fruit. In the first years of the century, confident Yankee executives and their defenders became accustomed to treating that sentiment as another routinely annoying hindrance to their work. As early as 1914 Samuel Crowther, apologist for United Fruit, wrote,

> There is a considerable amount of anti-American propaganda throughout the Caribbean countries. It is in part communistic and in part commercial and also it is mixed up with Pan-Latinism. . . . It is something for the intelligentsia to write about and it is a safe subject for orators. The communistic [movement] becomes important only when it is used for some ulterior purpose such as stirring up strikes on America.[25]

In fact, it was far more than that. Peasants who had been transformed into a concentrated wage labor force were in a position to organize collectively. The first major labor protest in Central America focused on the United Fruit Company in Honduras. In the early 1920s a series of strikes at its headquarters in Tela provided a precedent for conflict on the banana lands, and new patterns of incursions into the forest. The corporations were working in tandem with the expanding strategic interests of the American government, which was determined to maintain its hegemony over the region around the Panama Canal. That policy, encompassing the effort to displace British finance capital from the region during World War I, meant propping up any local regime that would work according to the political economy of American domination.

In the isolationist days of the 1920s, Washington moved gradually away from direct intervention in the Caribbean and Central America toward indirect forms of domination, with the implicit but clear support of Washington's diplomatic weight. But relations between the U.S. government and the corporations were not always smooth. Dana Munro, a top Central American specialist in the State Department throughout the 1920s, argued in retrospect that the Department of State "was interested in promoting trade and finding profitable opportunities for the investment of American capital abroad. Helping Americans who found themselves in difficulties in foreign countries was an important part of its work. . . . [Indeed,] the fruit companies in Central America often took care of their own interests in ways that the department strongly disapproved of."[26]

With the full backing of American power, Central American governments set about repressing labor resistance. In Nicaragua, Augusto Sandino raised a rebellion against the oligarchy in the late 1920s, organizing a guerrilla movement in the hills east of Managua. He focused his first protest against the United Fruit Company, demanding better working conditions and higher wages for the plantation workers. The movement demanded the dismantling of the latifundia, so that good soils would be available to peasants to grow their own subsistence crops. This would gradually begin to change management of the banana lands and surrounding forest areas. The regime in Managua ultimately suppressed Sandino's forces, but their memory surfaced again in the 1970s in the Sandinista movement.

The Depression accelerated the trend, as Americans and Europeans cut back on their consumption of such optional market-basket items as bananas. Both markets and production shrank drastically, unemployment was widespread, and worker desperation was rising against both companies and governments. The most intense Depression-triggered conflict occurred once again in Honduras, where a protest against United Fruit broke out in 1931, specifically over the issue of water rights. In a major consolidation two years earlier, United bought out Zemurray, and inherited his sophisticated irrigation system, which watered thousands of acres. United wanted to add twenty-four thousand acres more to the system and petitioned the Honduran Congress in 1931 for the water rights, using the usual array of pressure tactics. However, a 1927 law stipulated that irrigation water was to be delivered free to holdings less than twenty hectares; for any larger acreage a fee of $1 per hectare per year would be charged for using national waters. Public demonstrations demanded charging the company $10 per hectare.

Soon a rebellion broke out against the alliance between United and the Honduran government, one led by General Gregorio Ferrera, a full-blooded Indian, and based in the zone behind the fruit companies' ports. Government forces retaliated, and Ferrera was killed in June 1931. As the death toll rose, the revolution faded away and no further threat to the company's operations arose during the Depression years. In Costa Rica a more sustained labor protest movement developed. There the Communist Party was founded in 1931. Under its leadership a massive banana workers strike broke out in 1934. The Costa Rican government, less repressive than most Central American regimes, finally forced United to grant better working conditions. The days of totally unregulated Company control of its concessions were not going to last forever. But United and Standard faced more desperate challenges than that in the following years.

THE CAVENDISH ERA AND INTERNATIONAL EXPANSION

During World War II total exports from tropical America fell by over a half, as crop shipments to Europe were badly disrupted until 1945. The United States maintained production and imports from Central America closer to prewar levels, despite the difficulties with banana diseases and the diversion of much of United Fruit's Great White Fleet into wartime work. After 1945 the American fruit corporations continued to control the North American market. Within the United States banana consumption grew only slowly in the immediate postwar years. Though the American population grew rapidly during the baby boom, per capita consumption fell by about 20 percent by the mid-1960s. The economy's annual imports, which averaged 1,301,000 stems in 1934–38, rose only to 1,675,000 in the years 1962–64.[27]

The banana companies made a major genetic and commercial breakthrough in the 1950s, when they finally established that a different species of banana, the Giant Cavendish, did not carry Panama Disease. They began a long and complex process of changing production from the Gros Michel to varieties of Cavendish that they developed on their experimental farms. And they continued diversifying their source locations and the range of fruits and other export crops that they produced.

Major shifts in production locations took United and Standard into Colombia and Ecuador in northern South America, where the political economy of fruit production contrasted with Central America. The banana corporations never dominated these national governments, as they did in the smaller countries to the north. In the early 1900s United Fruit had organized some plantations in Colombia but both there and in neighboring Ecuador after World War II the companies worked largely through small holder producers, returning to a system reminiscent of the earliest operations in Central America. Yet in each variation of the political and agronomic system forests were cleared and new regions were opened to broader forces of colonization.

Ecuador was an entirely new frontier for the multinational banana industry in the 1940s. From its great belt of Pacific lowland rainforest it had previously exported a few stalks of bananas, but only down the coast to Peru and

Ecuador, Venezuela, and Colombia

Chile. However, lacking a concentrated production area, it was still free of Panama Disease, so the American fruit companies, this time led by Standard, moved massively to Ecuador. Largely because of them, by the mid-1950s Ecuador became the world's largest exporter of bananas and many patches of its hitherto largely intact rainforests were quickly cleared.[28]

United Fruit first explored Ecuador's possibilities during the Depression, as an extension of its interests along Central America's Pacific coast. As early as 1933 United purchased one former cacao plantation of ninety-six thousand acres at Tengel, but it only planted one-eighth of that land in bananas. Standard Fruit also prospected in Ecuador, since United had outflanked it in Colombia. But the shipping problems of World War II prevented either multinational from moving in until peace returned.

Major export production began in the Guayas lowlands of Ecuador in 1947, the hinterland of the ancient port of Guayaquil on the Gulf of Santa Clara. The production area then quickly spread inland toward Quevedo, a frontier town founded in the 1850s that had seen rubber, cacao, and balsa wood booms rise and collapse. In the 1950s banana production also expanded along the drier south coast, anchored by the new port, Puerto Bolivar, which was hacked out of mangrove marshes. There the fruit was grown on irrigated plantations on dry land. This was in sharp contrast to the wet north coast, upriver from the port of Esmeraldas, where over one hundred inches of rain falls annually and there is no dry season.[29] That rainforest region supported a unique biota with perhaps the greatest biodiversity on the planet, including many species found nowhere else. Some of its soils were rich fresh alluvium; others farther north were equally nutrient-rich volcanic soils.

Prior to the era of the multinationals, agricultural settlements in the area were sparse and the regional economy was sleepy. There were some old semi-disused cacao and coffee plantations; cacao hacienda owners lived elegantly in Guayaquil, Paris, and Madrid. Previously there had been only one railroad, from Guayaquil directly east into the highlands, then north to Quito. In the lowlands there was no railroad nor even any all-weather roads. Most of the region still supported virgin forest, which political planners and economic investors did not value for itself.

The Ecuadorean government, eager for rural development and foreign investment after 1945, built roads up the central valley to encourage small-holder migration inland; the new highways were largely financed by U.S. government aid and World Bank funds. Government forest was available for clearing in fifty-hectare plots, which could be purchased on easy terms. Between 1948 and 1951 smallholders cleared ten thousand hectares of primary forest for new plantations. These pioneers preferred clean weeding, to keep jungle growth under control until bananas were tall enough that their shade suppressed weed growth. The short-term consequence was sheet erosion, especially on hilly terrain. Previously this had already been a serious problem in Jamaica. As one commentator noted, "A similar prospect faces Ecuador, but the industry is as yet much too young and heady with optimism to have given any attention to such matters."[30]

In a country that the United States had never controlled politically, United Fruit never dominated the industry. Its local subsidiary grew or purchased only one-fifth of the country's export production. Ecuador's markets were rapidly diversifying to include Western Europe as well. By the late 1950s European exporters were equally strong. A Swedish firm operated the major plantations in the northern Esmeralda area; German, Belgian, and older Chilean interests were responsible for the rest of the great boom.

Above all, United had to face competition from Standard Fruit until Ecuadorean firms themselves entered the export market. The great majority of Ecuador's banana exports were grown by small-scale producers. The export firms set up contracts with individual growers; they did not manage the land themselves. Consequently, until the early 1960s increased production was achieved almost entirely from additional acreage taken from primary forest on many small holdings rather than by intensifying production on land already cleared.

United Fruit in particular provided information about cultivation and disease control to its growers. Nonetheless, though production was less centralized than where corporate plantations ruled the land, the two dread diseases became widespread in the course of the 1950s. Sigatoka became a far more severe threat than Panama Disease. It first appeared in 1949 and was widespread by 1952. Spraying with copper sulfate was an inefficient and costly process on small, hilly properties.

In Ecuador the era of expanding banana production at the expense of natural forest was explosively rapid but brief. By the 1960s Sigatoka made a major contribution to the end of expansion in Ecuador's banana industry. Production stabilized and acreage peaked by 1965, at about 120,000 hectares. During the 1970s the country's acreage under bananas fell by half, to just over 60,000 hectares in 1980. But productivity gradually rose, especially on the larger estates that sold directly to foreign firms; in the same decade, exports fell only from 1,364,000 tons to 1,318,000 tons. And as the expansion of European demand leveled off with the decline in growth of personal incomes there, the insatiable American market began to absorb a larger percentage of Ecuador's exports again in the 1970s.

By the late 1970s Standard Fruit had about 8,000 hectares of bananas under multiyear contract, which provided it with about one-third of Ecuador's exports. In contrast, United's local subsidiary controlled less than 10 percent of the market. And by the late 1970s the Ecuadorean consortium Noboa controlled nearly 40 percent of national exports. The era of domination by North

American companies had been fairly brief, and limited in its direct penetration, but crucial in its time.

In the overall picture, the international market could no longer support endlessly rising exports from Ecuador. But the environmental impacts of three decades of rapid expansion were permanent. By 1970 approximately half of the former forest was cleared. The entire lowland rainforest region of Ecuador had been opened to settlement and agriculture. Bananas were the spearhead of infrastructure development and, consequently, of immigration and the growth of towns and small farms. On the farms, soil erosion, severe in some places, resulted from the farmers' practice of clean weeding on hilly terrain. In a country where the foreign giants did not establish large plantations but bought the fruit from many smallholders, the acreage under bananas was more widespread and dispersed than in the concentrated plantation enclaves of Central America. Even in Ecuador, though, the cleared acreage was concentrated considerably in strips, along roads, rail lines, and rivers.

United and Standard had also achieved major new production in their old lands, in Central America in the 1960s, by planting varieties of the Cavendish banana. Panama Disease was fastidious; it had no taste for any roots except the Gros Michel. In one sense, the adoption of the Cavendish marked a return to the beginning, since by planting a genetically new type of banana the industry was able to shift back to the same Caribbean lowlands where corporate production had begun more than a half century earlier. But in other ways the further expansion of cultivated acreage in the banana belt of Central America was a qualitatively new chapter in the history of clearing rainforest for export fruit production. The maturation of the corporate agrochemical industry in the same years provided commercial fertilizers and pesticides that the more delicate Cavendish banana required in order to achieve its full potential. And the corporations were gradually learning to diversify not only their supply regions but their range of marketable crops as well.

In the Central American fiefs of the banana multinationals, there had been little overall increase in exports during the 1950s. The most dramatic events there were political, as the foreign multinationals and the host governments maneuvered for control of the banana wealth. After World War II, political conditions were shifting so sharply that they threatened the power of the landed oligarchies and their foreign supporters. Guatemala boasted the most turbulent banana politics of all the Central American countries in the decade after 1945. Events there showed the raw political power of the banana giants, especially United Fruit.

Across the border from United's north coast Honduran plantations, Guatemala was becoming a U.S. protectorate. Until the 1930s banana production in Guatemala centered in the Motagua River valley in the Caribbean lowlands, where Zemurray's operations expanded from Honduras. Between 1913 and 1929 Guatemala's banana exports to the United States rose by over 150 percent. In 1929, of the country's total $25 million exports, $17 million were coffee and $3 million were bananas; all the bananas were grown in the lower Motagua valley. Panama and Sigatoka diseases hit the valley's plantations in the late 1920s, so United shifted to the Tiquisate area on the Pacific lowlands.[31] Serious disadvantages faced them on the Pacific coast: there was no good harbor; communications with the interior had hardly begun to be constructed; and the area was drought prone. Yet by the late 1930s production there averaged 167,000 tons.

Under postwar presidents Juan José Arevalo and Jacobo Arbenz, Guatemala made the most determined land reform efforts of any Central American country.[32] The country was as socially and economically polarized as any in the region. Two percent of the population owned 72 percent of the land, while 50 percent of the people together owned 4 percent of the land. Rural per capita income was only about $90 per year. Malnutrition was widespread, and it worsened as coffee and banana lands expanded at the expense of food production. Arevalo, elected president in 1944, was determined to turn uncultivated lands into food production. As a first step in that direction, he designed the Law of Forced Rental, which required that oligarchs must rent unused land to farmers at low rates. In 1950 Arbenz succeeded Arevalo as president and went a step further in supporting peasant unions against the great landowners. In the same year, the National Peasant Union Federation was forged, unifying twenty-five regional peasants' unions. In 1952 Arbenz's government passed the more aggressive Agrarian Reform Law, designed to break up big estates and return land to food production. It nationalized unused lands, compensating owners with twenty-five-year bonds carrying 3 percent interest.

The greatest holder of uncultivated land in Guatemala was the United Fruit Company. United had previously rejected renegotiation of its contract with Arevalo, so in 1953 Arbenz announced the nationalization of 234,000 acres of United's uncultivated land. Using an assessment based on official tax records,

Arbenz offered the company $1 million in compensation. United Fruit, out-raged, demanded $16 million but verified that it was producing bananas on only about 5 percent of the vast lands it owned.

Arbenz was also planning a new electrical power system for the capital, independent of United's system that, until then, was the only source of power for Guatemala City. He also planned new roads and railroads independent of the company's systems. Clearly, the company would either have to begin to adjust to a reduced role in the country or retaliate. In 1953 the national labor federation forced the government's pace by organizing strikes in United's electric company and railroad, so the government nationalized them. This was going too far for the Americans, because by then the new American pres-ident was Eisenhower and the Cold War was fully entrenched in Washington. Secretary of State John Foster Dulles's New York law firm had represented United Fruit, and his brother Allen Dulles, the new head of the Central Intel-ligence Agency (CIA), was on United's Board of Directors.

The CIA organized an army under General Castillo Armas on a United Fruit banana plantation across the border in Honduras. In a military coup in 1954, Castillo Armas threw Arbenz out and took power. United recaptured a quarter of a million acres of land, though it agreed to raise the government's cut of profits from 10 percent to 30 percent, and gave up 100,000 acres for land reforms. It never would have made those concessions to Arevalo or Arbenz; under the new oligarchic regime, the promised land distribution was never implemented. The country remained safe for international corporate capital.[33]

Under its refurbished alliance with Guatemala's military and landed oli-garchy, United Fruit was assured of continuing control over the agricultural lowlands. In 1955 United planted 52 percent of Guatemala's banana lands and exported 75 percent of its bananas. A decade later it still accounted for 52 per-cent of the acreage under bananas. While United prospered, Castillo Armas and his successors maintained oligarchic control of the fertile lowlands, into the interminable decades of civil war against the campesinos and the Indian com-munities of the highlands whose poverty forced them to provide much of the labor on coffee, banana, and cotton lands below. (Guatemala's troubles were not entirely political. The weather itself occasionally cursed the land. In 1954–55 hurricanes caused widespread flood and wind damage; half of Guatemala's pro-duction was destroyed.) In 1964 United closed its production in Guatemala's Pacific lowlands, selling its territories there to private entrepreneurs who turned them into highly productive but heavily pesticided cotton farms. Poisoning of workers and water pollution downstream into estuarine and coastal ecosystems were the environmental consequences of those operations.[34]

By the late 1950s the multinational corporations finally had won the struggle against Panama Disease. Standard Fruit developed the Giant Cavendish banana, while United Fruit developed the genetically similar Valery. But the Giant Cavendish was a more delicate fruit than the Gros Michel, bruising more easily. The old system of shipping whole stems of fruit was not viable. Each hand of bananas had to be carefully cut from the stem and boxed for shipment. This required that the companies integrate into the packing operation at each plantation or collection point a steady flow of cardboard cartons. The first exports of boxed fruit left Central America in 1959, and the first from Ecuador were shipped in 1963. By 1965 nearly all Latin American banana exports were boxed. To complicate matters, the new varietal fruit was more susceptible to pests than its predecessor. It demanded more commercial fertilizer and pesticides in order to reach its full potential. This opened a new chapter in the history of Latin American export fruit production.[35] Intensified production ran escalating risks of soil and water pollution and workers' diseases.[36]

By growing the new banana varieties in Guatemala, the United Fruit Company was able to return to its pre-1930s lands on the Caribbean. Now intensifying its cultivation techniques, it soon raised production back to its record 1930 levels. Exports rose to 198,000 tons in 1960. This increase resulted almost entirely from an intensification of productivity, since the acreage planted in bananas from one year to the next did not vary greatly, averaging about sixteen thousand hectares from the mid-1950s well into the 1960s. Seemingly, this was a stabilization of land use and employment, in a far more sustainable agroeconomic system than previously under the Gros Michel banana. But the costs were high; intensification required ever-increasing amounts of commercial fertilizer and pesticides, which were supplied by American agrochemical giants led by Dow Chemical Company and Monsanto Chemicals. This produced a drain on the country's dollar reserves. And effects on the health of the work force and the health of the land and water were accumulating. The new system only seemed to be more sustainable than the old.

Next door to Guatemala was Honduras, the classic banana republic. The banana economy of the north coast gave Yankee corporations hegemony over the country's political and economic system. In the early 1950s American consumers continued to dominate Honduran foreign trade. Americans ate 75 percent of Honduras' banana exports and 50 percent of its coffee. In return, the United States provided two-thirds of Honduras' imports and 85 percent of its foreign investment. The two giants, United Fruit and Standard Fruit, controlled the entire commercial production and export of the country's bananas. After their sojourn on the Pacific they returned to the north coast to grow the Cavendish banana. Their plantations and railroads once again dominated the fertile alluvial river valleys. The area planted in bananas on the north coast rose dramatically from 70,000 acres in the mid-1950s to 170,000 acres in the early 1960s, much of it land that had produced Gros Michel bananas a generation before. Their port facilities and steamships supplied the major markets of North America and now also Europe with the delicate golden fruit.

In the 1950s the pattern of international markets for Central America's bananas was shifting away from the total American dominance of the previous decade. As Europe's consumer economy recovered, its banana purchases rose rapidly, while American consumption grew only slowly. If the giant American corporations were to maintain their position, they would want to expand their sales in Europe. By 1966, 75 percent of Guatemala's banana exports were going to Western Europe, mostly on United's ships. Honduran exports presented a similar picture. Production there remained relatively stable, but a rising percentage was diverted from North American to European markets. The rest of American consumption came largely from Ecuador.[37]

In Honduras the complicated triangular politics involving the companies, the labor force, and the government proved to be less violent than in Guatemala. For fifteen somnolent years between 1933 and 1948, President Tiburcio Carias did little to develop his country's economy. His successors in the 1950s made more energetic economic development efforts, and they tolerated a more active grassroots labor movement, which focused on the foreign banana companies. In 1954 forty thousand workers launched a spontaneous strike at the companies' docks at La Ceiba. They finally gained token concessions from Standard Fruit: 4–8 percent wage increases plus two-week annual vacations. The fruit companies had produced a concentration of plantation labor; thus they were the catalyst for the rise of the rural labor movement. But they had no intention of losing political control.

Costa Rica provided a sharp contrast, at least in the political relations between the government and the American corporations. Costa Rica evolved after 1945 into a stable, moderate political regime determined to manage its economic growth with some degree of equity. It might not have turned out that way, for the country's economy was heavily influenced by United Fruit and other foreign companies, and the Costa Rican Communist Party was the strongest in Central America, its strength centering among the banana workers. As Walter LaFeber comments,

> Costa Rica prided itself on its distribution of wealth, but the equality was remarkable only when compared with the grossly unequal distribution in the rest of Central America. In truth, key sectors of the society were foreign-controlled; the profits from its large amounts of exports rolled out of the country.... Large areas of the country were controlled by oligarchs who refused either to cultivate their land or allow others to do so.[38]

As early as 1943 President Rafael Calderon engineered social reform legislation that provided an eight-hour workday and a social security system, and guaranteed labor the rights to form unions, bargain collectively and strike. Calderon's regime declined into incompetence and corruption by the late 1940s, triggering opposition led by the charismatic Pepe Figueres. In 1948 the larger landlords openly opposed Calderon's land-reform coalition but were defeated by Figueres and his allies in a revolution of the moderates.

Figueres gained popularity when he denounced the power of United Fruit and other foreign companies. But he was a pragmatist; soon after he swept into office in 1953, he negotiated a new contract with United that both sides could support. It reiterated United's access to land and water resources, its ownership of harbor facilities in Limon, its railroads in the old banana lands outside Limon, and the right to build new lines. The contract also tripled Costa Rica's share of profits from the banana industry, enforced minimum wage laws on the company plantations, and turned a token five thousand hectares of company land back to the government.[39]

In 1955 United planted 58 percent of the country's total banana acreage and controlled 99 percent of Costa Rica's banana exports. In the late 1950s United returned to its old plantations on the Sarapiqui lowlands outside Puerto Limon, slowly closing down its Pacific lowlands plantations, or shifting them from bananas to African oil palm. The new corporate acreage came in part from newly cleared forest, but more from old Gros Michel lands returned to cultivation with Cavendish. The geographer Pierre Stouse assessed in the late 1960s that the larger-scale estates may have been more stable, economically and environmentally, than small private producers.[40]

In Costa Rica as a whole, the banana corporations began experimenting with new strategies for managing their lands. Beginning in the early 1950s both companies began selling or leasing their unused lands to local government or private producers.[41] In 1952 United launched an experiment in Costa Rica called the Higuerito Project, dividing large plantations into small parcels managed individually by its former workers. The company gave a ten-year lease at a nominal rate, then transferred title to the farmer; the company managed disease control and transport fruit; and the company kept exclusive purchase rights for the bananas produced, at its price. For United Fruit, this system reduced its costs and risks, but for the smallholders it was not a bonanza. Part of what they delivered to the company came at the expense of food production. In addition, smallholders who were attracted into the commercial banana system now faced the danger of price slumps. The new possibility of profits meant also higher risks on the volatile international market.

United's directly cultivated land was gradually reduced to about 17,500 acres in the mid-1970s, plus some 74,000 under associate producers. Standard Fruit maintained all its land under direct ownership until 1965. Then it began diversifying ownership; soon nearly half was worked by associate producers. By then the associate producers included former company employees, larger private companies and even several local cooperatives. Despite these major changes in the pattern of ownership of acreage under production, the companies still controlled the system. As one skeptical observer described the system years later, "The associate producers are under the administrative control of the superintendent . . . and they act according to the advice of the company; the infrastructure and the development expenses of production all are handled by the company, and they depend totally on the company for the sale of their fruit."[42] The company provided credit, technical advice, seeds, fertilizer, machines, chemicals, aerial spraying, irrigation equipment, and packaging. Advance guarantees of price were usually below 25 percent, often as interest-bearing loans. Producers thus bore the risk of plant diseases and hurricanes. In sum, the banana giants continued to thrive in the era of chemical-intensive production. Their political power was still formidable, and they were assured of U.S. government support. They were direct beneficiaries of the Cold War and Washington's determination to maintain economic control in Central America.

CROP DIVERSIFICATION

The corporations also increased their efforts at crop diversification, both the crops themselves and the locations where they were grown. Other crops besides bananas could still grow on the cleared alluvial lands of the river bottoms. United Fruit had remained on some abandoned plantations during the Depression, attempting a strategy of crop diversification. The most successful experiment involved intensifying planting of a tree crop, cacao, which had been introduced centuries earlier from its evolutionary birthplace in the lower reaches of the Andes. The cacao tree grew widely in the moist lowland forests from southern Mexico southward, dispersed through woodlands with many other species. The chocolate-producing beans, growing in large pods directly from the tree trunk, had been harvested and traded for centuries by the indigenous communities.[43] In the early 1900s the British had transplanted cacao to West Africa and successfully grew it in single-species plantations, replacing wide areas of natural moist forest especially in the Gold Coast, the present-day Ghana. The burgeoning chocolate industry of Europe (and the spurt in sugar production that accompanied it) was responsible for eliminating an area of African rainforest, by translocating a tree from the rainforests of the Americas.[44]

Cacao was a transitional crop in the decline of United's original Caribbean coastal operations. In 1932 United had 24,809 acres in Costa Rica and 14,277 acres in Panama, where, guided by English-speaking Jamaican foremen, its workers interplanted cacao trees with diseased banana trees. But the Central American climate was not as favorable for concentrated cacao plantings as the Gold Coast; it was too wet, and fungi prospered when their host was concentrated. Nonetheless, by 1966, cacao became Costa Rica's fourth largest export. Commercial crop diversification was gradually emerging, in response to both economic and ecological pressures against total reliance on one crop.

The botanical agenda of diversification specialized in tropical fruits, especially citrus and pineapple. Oranges had been a familiar item sold to boats trading along the Caribbean coast before they were elbowed away by bananas. They returned in escalating amounts, introduced to new countries on a commercial scale by the fruit multinationals after a series of corporate mergers that began in 1950s. For example, Dole Fruits (which had absorbed Standard) began to export fresh or processed pineapples from Honduras. But workers protested the heavy use of pesticides for pineapples there.[45] In the 1960s the fruit companies in Honduras and Costa Rica also began to grow oil palm, for margarine and salad oil, on former banana lands, importing the palm from its ancestral home in the wide delta of the Niger River in equatorial Africa. Globalization of tropical horticulture was in full swing.

By the 1970s the bananas that Americans peeled were still imported entirely from Latin America. Three American companies—United Fruit, Dole, and Del Monte—handled 78 percent of all imports. Del Monte began importing bananas only in 1969, but by 1984 it controlled 19 percent of the market.[46] Yet there was also more space for independent companies as well in the 1970s. They increased their share of the American market from 8 percent in 1971 to 22 percent in 1984; this share was dominated by Noboa, an Ecuadorean consortium, shipping to New York, and Turbana, a subsidiary of the Colombian consortium UNIBAN, which shipped to Miami.

Bananas arrived at twenty American ports. Over half entered through three ports: New York (21 percent in 1984) for eastern markets, Long Beach (17.5 percent) for the West Coast, and Gulfport/Mobile (15 percent) for the Mississippi basin. From there the leading companies maintained national sales networks, linked to jobbers and chain stores in the years after a 1958 court order forced United to divest its monopoly of ripening and marketing facilities.[47]

CONCLUSION: THE BANANA MULTINATIONALS' ENVIRONMENTAL LEGACY

Corporations alone did not drive the market for bananas or the use of land to meet the market demand. International consumption of the golden fruit shifted through these years, although the United States continued to provide the world's largest market, and in fact a steadily rising percentage of the global market. In the aggregate, American consumers behaved differently from Europeans and the Japanese. On those two continents consumption grew rapidly at an early stage of rising incomes then leveled off. But demand continued to grow steadily in the United States; even in the 1970s consumption rose faster in the United States than in Europe or Japan, rising from 26.5 percent of total global sales in 1973 to 36 percent in 1983.[48] Americans were eating nearly twenty-five pounds of bananas per person per year by the 1970s, higher than people anywhere in Europe or Japan. Ninety-five percent of all U.S. households purchased bananas. Because bananas had become such an automatic presence on American tables, any international production glut was dumped on the American market, even at depressed prices.

This enormous scale of concentrated corporate power had grave consequences for the ecological destinies of the region. In the seventy-five years that American fruit companies had dominated the Caribbean basin's tropical lowlands, the region had undergone several stages of environmental change. The first and most fundamental stage was the transformation from rainforest to plantations. Then, beginning in the 1920s, the early plantations underwent reversion to subsistence farming and secondary woodland. The 1950s ushered in an era of intensified, chemical-based banana production. Corporate agrocapitalism was the driving force of ecological change, both on its plantations and in the surrounding lands from which it drew both labor and resources.

Had the companies' management of land and resources improved as experience increased? Had their plantations become more or less sustainable? By the 1960s bananas grew on more stable acreage for longer periods than in the era of the Gros Michel banana and Panama Disease. But this was accomplished only with accelerating applications of chemical fertilizers and pesticides. When aerial spraying began in the 1950s, the toxic chemicals wandered far from the fields for which they were intended. This was a new era in the industry, with inexorably evolving consequences, in the form of serious damage to workers' health. Toxification of soils and downstream water was not monitored at all in the early years of intensive agrichemical use.

Crop diversification, another trend of those years, helped stabilize the region's agroecology and export economies, by moving away from reliance on a single crop species. But some major alternative cash crops, like oil palm, were also grown in massive, one-crop plantations. Export agroindustrial production also grew at the expense of food production for local needs. This drove campesinos onto marginal lands, mostly hill forests, or into cities, destabilizing societies and ecosystems.[49]

One by-product of the corporate agrosystem was settlement and land clearance throughout the lowlands, a process that then accelerated beyond the immediate range of the corporate economy. This transformation rested as much on consumer demand as on corporate resources. Consumers in the mass markets of the Northern world benefited from the pleasure and nutritional value of the banana, as the range of their diets expanded beyond what temperate climates could provide. Banana corporations represented the highest degree of American ecological imperialism, matched only by Firestone Rubber in Liberia in their capacity to control entire countries. Another perennial crop, coffee, played a similar role of forest clearance at higher elevations around the Caribbean and Latin America. Its economic scale was greater, and its consumers were more insistent. The dessert tables of Europe and the United States provided drink as well as food, caffeine as well as sugar and fruit. But in striking contrast to the banana plantations, Americans did not directly manage the coffee groves.

The Last Drop: The American Coffee Market and the Hill Regions of South America

COFFEE IN THE AMERICAS: COLONIAL TRADE AND CONSUMPTION

Of all tropical crops sold on world markets, coffee is the first in value and has the most varied social and environmental impacts in the lands where it is grown. By the 1960s, coffee had the second highest value of any internationally traded commodity, surpassed only by petroleum. It is grown across hill regions throughout the tropical and subtropical world—anywhere on the planet that has a moderate climate and does not suffer winter frosts. Coffee exploits ecological zones different than that of the lowland rainforest where sugar, bananas, and other export monocrops thrive. Coffee is versatile in its habits, growing in a wide range of natural settings and soils throughout the world's warm uplands, needing only moderate rainfall and temperatures above freezing in order to thrive. Unlike sugar and bananas, coffee is a perennial tree crop. Coffee groves can be grown on steep slopes where other cash crops cannot be easily sustained but the groves often cause heavy erosion or gradual depletion of soil nutrients. As a perennial, however, coffee presents economic difficulties, for a plantation cannot adjust its production annually to meet market demand. A tree begins to bear fruit in the third or fourth year; production rises for several years and then slowly falls for a useful life of twenty to forty years.

Coffee is grown on varying scales of operation and in many combinations with other crops. It is as economically competitive when harvested from peasants' small plots for a cash supplement to their subsistence crops as it is on

argument
gives jobs to poor people

large landed estates with slave, sharecropper, or wage labor. Hence, in contrast to sugar, coffee is not necessarily tied historically to slavery's radical disruption of social and subsistence systems, though in its most ecologically destructive form, in Brazil, that was the pattern.

origin
The coffee tree evolved as an understory tree in the hilly woodlands of Ethiopia in northeastern Africa. Early in its domestication it was planted in groves in Yemen; from there Arab traders introduced it to southern Europe in the thirteenth century. Market demand developed first in the Mediterranean countries, spreading from east to west, then northward through Europe, where large-scale consumption began during the Renaissance.[1] Eighteenth-century France, in particular, provided a thriving market. In the last decades of the Ancien Régime, the coffee house, in Paris and elsewhere, became a cultural institution as a public location where political debate was allowed to thrive uncensored. Marketing organizations grew up to supply the rising enthusiasm. Coffee culture was transferred to the North American colonies during the same period. In the 1700s, in towns along the eastern seaboard, a shared pot of coffee was an important middle-class convention, marking sociability and hospitality. The search for sources of coffee took North Atlantic consumer culture into tropical America.

While England was organizing its mania for tea through a vast expansion of imports from Asia, France experimented with coffee production on its Caribbean islands from the 1720s onward, reducing its reliance on sources from the Arab world. Europe was well on its way to dictating the ecological destinies of hill lands suited for growing mildly narcotic drinks, as well as lowlands suited for sugar, the great sweetener.[2] Colonial sugar plantations had rooted Western Europe's importers of tropical products firmly in the Americas. The hill regions of both the Caribbean islands and the Latin American mainland promised profitable results from coffee plantations in a climate zone above the sugar estates.

Coffee was chronologically the second major export crop produced by independent Caribbean basin regimes for European and North American consumers. Before 1800, coffee was grown in the Americas mostly on French-owned plantations in Saint-Domingue (Haiti), which used slaves as the labor force. Sugar plantations had already cleared Haiti's lowland vegetation; coffee farms cleared the higher hillsides and disrupted watersheds. Some 40 million pounds of coffee beans were grown in the colony and shipped to France in 1789, the final year of the Ancien Régime. Then, in the wake of the French Rev revolts erupted in Haiti in 1791. By 1800, the ex-slave Toussaint reigned and proceeded to dismantle the plantation economy. The dense populace reverted to subsistence farming and Haiti's hilly landscape continued its downward spiral toward becoming the Caribbean's most devastated environment.

During the Napoleonic wars continental European markets for goods brought in by sea were severely disrupted by the British Navy's tight blockade of the French coast. But after 1815 coffee consumption in Europe—and its cultural extension the United States—rose steadily throughout the century. American thirst generated the largest single market, reaching almost 750 million pounds by 1900, or over 13 pounds per year for every person.[3] As Northern coffee consumption increased, its sources of supply in the Americas multiplied. Ladino landed gentry and urban exporters together harvested a bonanza of hard currencies. In the twentieth century, coffee production has had an enormous impact on Latin America, covering the largest area of any plantation crop in the region. In 1960 it covered 7.3 million hectares (over 18 million acres), in contrast with 4.6 million hectares for sugar and only .7 million hectares for bananas. Among all crops, only wheat and maize covered a greater acreage.[4]

About two-thirds of Latin America's coffee production is currently exported to Europe and North America. During the mid-1960s, the United States consumed more than 40 percent of the world's international coffee trade, importing slightly more than all of Western Europe combined. Coffee now represents between 15 percent and 25 percent of Latin America's foreign exchange earnings each year, ranking behind only petroleum.

SOUTHERN BRAZIL: COFFEE PLANTERS DEVOUR THE FOREST

A survey of Latin America's coffee history must focus on southern Brazil, the world's dominant producer since the 1830s. Coffee built modern Brazil, in a symbiosis between the Portuguese-Brazilian landed elite and international market demand, led by the United States. Well before 1900, Americans were Brazil's dominant coffee purchasers, becoming indirectly responsible for destroying Indian populations, sustaining African slavery on the plantations, and then attracting more than one million European immigrants, as well as generating capital for the railroads and infrastructure that made Brazil Latin America's most powerful country.

In southern Brazil, American purchases were key to the extension of frontier zones, as coffee came to be grown on increasingly marginal land. Social and political conflicts, as well as ecological deterioration inexorably resulted. For a century, this wave rolled onward as long as more virgin land was available. A Brazilian plantocracy squeezed maximum short-term profits from the deforested land, driving African slaves until 1888 and a largely European immigrant labor force thereafter. Few foreigners ever owned these estates. Europeans and Americans only purchased the harvested coffee on the coast, so they felt no responsibility for the land. Indeed, they rarely paid much attention to the systemic effects of their investments or even knew much about the local settings of agrarian relations.

During this time, coffee trees were viable in a belt stretching inland beyond the coastal rainforest, where southern Brazil's landscape ranges from subtropical to temperate. The coastal rainforest reaches southwest beyond the colonial capital, Rio de Janeiro, which was built around one of the few fine harbors on that entire coastline. The vegetation gradually becomes less tropical as the coastline continues on toward São Paulo, the city that coffee built. Coffee *fazendas,* or slave estates, flourished from the 1820s onward in the Paraiba valley, Rio's hilly hinterland.[5] The upper Paraiba River has a moderate maritime climate and fertile soil of decomposed granite, with adequate rain for the growing season, followed by a dry season convenient for the harvest. But its hills are typically steep and unstable.

Through the mid-nineteenth century, plantations spread rapidly up the steep hillsides. Land was virtually free for purchase by any speculator with connections to the imperial court in Rio. Labor was the largest element of operating costs, even though the workers were slaves imported from Africa.[6] The early estates were highly risky ventures; many failed within a few years, when speculators with little knowledge of the land carved them out on poor soils.

Soil on the sloping hills rapidly eroded due to reliance on the conventional techniques of planting and tilling.[7] Coffee trees require well-drained soil, so bands of woodcutters felled forest trees straight down even steep slopes. Lianas grew among the trees' crowns, binding them together, so when a giant fell, it dragged many others down with it. Workers burned the jumble of felled trees and then planted coffee seeds or seedlings in rows between the large trunks to provide for good drainage in times of heavy rain. The fires often swept out of control, invading adjacent standing forest. Each August a pall of smoke hovered over the region, but the ashes provided nutrients for the

Brazil, Uruguay, and Argentina

seedlings for their first couple of years. In the scramble for quick profits, the fazendeiros paid little attention to quality of tree stock, planting clusters of whatever coffee berries they could obtain from their neighbors. Mulching and harvesting were done haphazardly by slaves who had no incentive to work efficiently. In consequence, soil fertility was neglected and many trees bore profitably for only twenty years or so.

By the 1850s, even in a time of prosperity, massive difficulties began to be evident on the fazendas of the Paraiba basin. Estate owners faced rising costs and unreliable profits on volatile international markets, as well as declining productivity from the first generation of coffee trees. The planters' early euphoria changed to worry and gloom over their prospects. A few planters began to acknowledge the devastation, but most paid no attention to the critics, for it was less expensive to move to new virgin territories available for almost nothing from a government eager to conquer the forest. The indomitable British traveler, Richard Burton, went through the Paraiba valley in 1867 and reported that it was "cleaned out for coffee. . . . The sluice-like rains following the annual fires have swept away the carboniferous humus from the cleared round hilltops into the narrow swampy bottoms. . . . Every stream is a sewer of liquid manure, coursing to the Atlantic, and the superficial soil is that of a brick-field."[8]

In the last years of the nineteenth century there was demoralization in the Paraiba coffee zone. The devastation of eroded plantations, with their aging trees, plus the end of slavery in 1888 and the impossibility of paying free labor competitive wages, led land owners to let most old plantations go to secondary growth of grasses fit only for cattle. Ranches gradually replaced fazendas. "Under the beating rains of summer and the annual rough harvests and weedings, defertilized and aged coffee bushes no longer produced fruit and were abandoned. Some were used for firewood, others were cut down, and the rest withered away."[9] Hundreds of thousands of old coffee trees were abandoned as planters migrated to new lands and began again the process of clearing forests for the humus and nutrients in their virgin soils. The familiar equation of free land, crude tilling methods, and rapid erosion of hillsides continued for another half-century.

From Rio's back country, coffee planters spread inland and southwestward, into the Paulista West. This was the hinterland of the city of São Paulo, which until the mid-1800s had been a small colonial town above the coast southwest of Rio. In the last half of the century, coffee transformed São Paulo into Latin America's primary center of capital, technology, and political power. São Paulo city stands on the heights of a dramatic escarpment, roughly two thousand feet high, looking down to the coastal lowlands and its port, Santos. The state of São Paulo is a vast rolling plateau at the city's back, its hillsides less steep than the Paraiba watershed. The region falls off toward the west, drained by several rivers that flow into the Paraná River basin. Large areas of the plateau support a red soil that is rich with iron oxides but dangerously subject to laterization, a process that turns it into barren hardpan if its vegetation is stripped away.

For thousands of years nomadic hunters had roamed these hills. Roughly a thousand years ago they were succeeded by the semisedentary Tupi-Guarani farming culture. After 1530, Portuguese adventurers conquered, slaughtered, or enslaved the tribes. As historian Warren Dean writes, "Everywhere the Europeans acted rapaciously in their first contacts with the primitive inhabitants of the New World. In Brazil they were hunted for slaves to work on the coastal plantations. Raid after raid decimated them and shattered their culture. Most of the survivors withdrew far into the backlands," under pressure from these *bandeirantes*.[10] The Europeans managed to assimilate a few captured Indians into plantation life. "As servants and auxiliaries the Tupi taught [the Portuguese] how to dominate the wilderness; as concubines they bestowed upon them a mestizo population."[11]

At first, the São Paulo coffee frontier was settled by smallholder squatters, or *caboclos*, marginalized people in the social struggles of colonial coastal Brazil. As Dean describes the scene,

> In between the decamping aborigines and the nodes of town life on the edge of the plateau stretched a broad territory, still insecure and unclaimed, where only scattered army posts intruded. Into this were drawn people who sought a refuge from the oppressiveness of colonial rule. The landless could find land. The young and able were free of the draft, a terrible scourge because of intermittent war with Spain in the River Plate. Criminals were beyond the reach of the law. In fact the law often exiled them to the frontier. . . . The escaped slave headed for the frontier often—the hired slave hunter was called for good reason the "captain of the forest."[12]

The squatter settlers worked the land by the slash and burn techniques that they learned from the Indians' multicropping system. They planted crops with a digging stick in the fertile soil. Unlike the Indians, though, the settlers harvested little more than maize, which was a high portion of their diets.

In the early 1800s there were only a few tiny towns in the Paulista West, surrounded by forest and linked precariously to each other by trails and mule trains. Around Rio Claro town, for example, was a landscape of scrub pasture, second-growth woodlands on the hills, on red soils still fertile after even two hundred years of sporadic cultivation for corn, rice, beans, sugar, and citrus. Other areas were open fields with thin sandy soil, supporting only scattered brush, stunted trees, and a few cattle.

By the mid-1800s the landscape of the Paulista West had been transformed into estate holdings. Outsiders gradually gained title, evicted most smallholders, and subordinated many to tenancy. Cash surplus generated by the colonial economy was invested in new lands by coastal plantation owners, merchants, bureaucrats, and professionals. Buying virgin land was vital to them, since they, too, depended on fertile new soils. They continued the colonial system of crown grants, which were given only by the viceroy or governor. Grantees were required to begin cultivation or the title lapsed, which many titles did. By 1818, 98 percent of Rio Claro land was held in those grants. New grantees immediately began land speculation. Many never lived on their lands and sold portions of their grants to sugar speculators. Those who stayed practiced the most casual farming methods, which reflected the difficulty of establishing title to specific locations. Many modern commentators argue that the key to sustainable land husbandry is a stable population with secure rights to their property. The Paulista West of this period, typical in its moving frontiers of capitalist agriculture, had no such stability.

The first plantations in the Paulista West were sugar estates, founded by speculators from the older sugar belt along the coast. Large plantings of coffee trees began in the 1840s; within twenty years coffee entirely displaced sugar in the region. Coffee beans were more stable than semirefined sugar, and could be transported on mule back along the winding trails to the coast more successfully.

Soils varied widely in quality, and early planters did not understand the soils' relation to coffee production. Many coffee trees were planted in inappropriate locations and failed. The planters were convinced of only one thing: virgin forested land meant undepleted soil fertility. This speculative mining of Nature was based on a system of extreme human exploitation: the groves were worked by African slaves. In the rainy season, slaves hoed the soil several times to uproot weeds and keep the surface loose to absorb rain. Nearing picking time, they cleared the soil under the bushes, so that some pickers could strip the berries from the entire branch and others gather them from the ground. Planters did little fertilizing or mulching except for post-harvest raking of old stems and leaves back under the bushes.

Coffee remained the dominant crop in the Paulista West until the 1930s. Its international position received a great boost after 1870, when the British Empire's Asian sources of coffee for European markets were crippled. A blight that first appeared in the British colonies of southern India and Ceylon in the late 1860s had devastated coffee production there, forcing the colonial planters to replace coffee bushes with tea. That blight never spread to the Americas. Ironically, the resulting bonanza for Brazil's planters was the converse of the story of rubber a few years later. The rubber tree native to Brazil's Amazonian rainforest was devastated by parasites when it was planted densely in its native setting, but it could be grown in the dense, profitable plantations of tropical Asia. What Brazil gained in coffee it lost in rubber. In both cases, Nature dictated the path of commerce, and the United States provided the motivating power of the product's largest market.

By the 1860s the planters of the Paulista West reached the farthest limit of profitable coffee cultivation for the era before the railroads. Winding trails, rarely over six feet wide, were the only transport lines; mules had to ford streams or cross rivers on unsteady ferries. A major extension of the region available for coffee came in 1865 with the first British-financed railroad. Groups of plantation owners followed up by building branch lines with their profits. Planters thus controlled railroad profits as well; their companies gave their own stockholders contracts for wood for railroad ties, fuel, and construction materials. With greater mobility, most planters moved to São Paulo and turned their plantations over to hired administrators, who forwarded coffee to brokers in Santos, on the coast below, to sell to exporters.

Labor problems loomed large throughout the era. In 1850, Brazil abolished imports of slaves from Africa, so the planters began experiments with wage labor on the coffee plantations, using European workers who might stay on plantations for a few years because, at first, they knew nothing of local farming techniques. The Brazilian government paid their passage, using public funds from the entire country to underwrite the coffee planters' largest expense. By the 1870s there was a rising tide of farm workers from southern Italy, forced from their ancestral homes by long-term soil degradation resulting from their own agricultural system and brought to São Paulo by Brazilian recruiters.

In 1888 the Brazilian government declared total abolition of slavery. Most slaves were happy to leave the fazendas, but there were many European laborers to replace them, using this point of entry to a new and more hopeful life.

By 1914 more than one million immigrants from southern Europe arrived, drawn by the magnet of coffee and swelling both rural and urban populations of the region. Under severe pressure from the insecure and changing labor market, planters continued to minimize the care of the land. The old processes of mismanagement were encouraged more than ever by international demand in the last years of the century, driven especially by the American market. The consumer economy of the United States was becoming the key to the ecological transformation of southern Brazil, though almost no Americans understood anything of the consequences of their caffeine intake.

AMERICAN MARKETS FOR THE BLACK GOLD

Brazilians had both the capital and the political power to keep the Northerners largely confined to the trading houses of the coast. But, conversely, Brazilians had to work with the foreign buyers in the port cities through which the brown stream flowed. Rio de Janeiro was the only Brazilian coffee entrepôt until 1848. In the 1870s, at the zenith of Rio's trading, its exporters handled the production of over four thousand plantations, which sent over four million sacks—each weighing sixty kilograms (132 pounds)—through their warehouses yearly.[13] Each planter had an agent or factor in Rio, who received coffee and sold it to a sacker, who blended and sold it to exporters. Wealthy factors' homes were elegant, adorned in the European style. Factors had warehouses where they graded coffee in as many as nine grades, to meet their foreign buyers' increasingly precise demands. From the 1850s to 1880s there were anywhere from one hundred to two hundred coffee factorage and sacking firms in Rio. Foreign buyers developed long-term working relations with the local brokers.

But trouble was brewing for the Rio exporters, as their source region spiraled into ecological decline and lost ground to the hinterland of São Paulo. By 1900 Santos permanently replaced Rio as the world's largest coffee export city.[14] In Santos, factors and sackers were more often the same individuals than in Rio; the Santos system was a more narrowly controlled oligarchy whose members were well on their way to dominating national politics.[15]

None of this would have happened on anything like that scale had it not been for the bonanza of international markets, which turned the coffee berries into gold for those who controlled them. The expansion of European and American markets through the nineteenth century was the driving force. A few leading

importers, most of them based in London and New York, controlled international prices. In conjunction with widely variable coffee production from one
year to the next, they produced a series of booms and panics that made coffee as
wildly speculative as any commodity that ever crossed the equator.

London had dominated transatlantic coffee shipping ever since the late
eighteenth century, when it succeeded in monopolizing the West Indies' coffee exports. By the mid-1800s, London specialized in the premium mild Arabica coffees of Central America and the Caribbean. But British consumers had
cast their lot with tea as their primary source of caffeine. Their demand for
coffee never ranked with that of their stepchildren across the North Atlantic.

After mid-century, New York, Hamburg, and Le Havre dominated the
international market for mass consumption of the coarser Brazilian Robusta
coffee blends. New Yorkers had begun importing coffee early in the city's
expansion, in shops that also featured tea and spices. The heady aroma of commercial coffee roasters was familiar on Manhattan's streets from the 1790s
onward. In 1864 the New Yorker Jabez Burns perfected a more efficient coffee
roaster, boosting lower Manhattan's ability to process large amounts of berries.
Simultaneously, the pump of consumer demand was being primed by adven-
turous Yankee businessmen who were traveling around Latin America looking
for investment opportunities. Some of them headed inland from Santos on the
new railroads and brought back enthusiastic reports from the fazendas.

By 1880, two of the leading coffee exporters in Rio were New Yorkers: Hard,
Rand & Company, and Arbuckle Brothers. Their power to manipulate coffee
purchases reflected events in the commercial heart of New York City. From the
1870s onward, as Americans' demand for coffee expanded in line with a flour-
ishing industrial economy, a series of coffee booms and busts showed how
volatile the market could be, and how much it could be manipulated by insid-
ers. Stakes were high; through the 1870s as many speculators lost their shirts as
prospered. Coffee wholesaling was closely tied to the New York Stock
Exchange for speculation capital, and major traders like Arbuckle on Wall
Street attempted to corner international as well as domestic markets. High
international coffee prices in the 1870s stimulated coffee production in Brazil
and various other countries. Coffee from Java, produced by Dutch colonial
planters, was still important in American markets, while trade with Santos was
just starting up. In 1881 the notorious New York "Syndicate" or "Trinity" of
O. G. Kimball, B. G. Arnold, and Bowie Dash cancelled all imports of coffee

from Java, whose price collapsed on the New York Exchange. But the price of Brazilian coffee fell with it, from $.1625 to $.095 per pound in under a year. Several firms went bankrupt, with collective losses somewhere between $5 million and $7 million.

The New York Coffee Exchange was founded that year in an attempt to bring coherence to the trade. Its historian describes it as "a central location to standardize sales, collect data on market conditions, and further develop the futures contract."[16] It was so successful in rationalizing the trade that a year later it was replicated in Le Havre for the French import market; by 1890 Amsterdam, Hamburg, London, Antwerp, and Rotterdam had followed suit. Similar systems emerged more slowly in the ports of coffee producing countries: it was not until 1914 that a formal coffee exchange was set up in Santos.

As global coffee trade became more streamlined, it became even more volatile. Major competitors gained access to a communications breakthrough in the 1870s: the international telegraph, which further helped to destabilize the coffee economy. Rapid-fire manipulation of prices became possible, based on telegraphed news of crop conditions and supplies from countries like Brazil. In the Great Boom of 1886–87, predictions of a bad crop in Brazil led a cartel of buyers in New York, New Orleans, Chicago, Brazil, and Europe to drive the wholesale price upward toward $.25 per pound. Then they received revised news: a bumper crop was coming after all. The New York price immediately fell by one-third; in the spring of 1888 several major European firms collapsed.[17]

By the end of the 1880s Arbuckle Brothers emerged as the most powerful trader on the New York Coffee Exchange. They had dozens of competitors, but no one else imported even half of Arbuckle's volume. Together, by 1900, the New Yorkers imported 676 million pounds of coffee, 86 percent of the country's total. However, New York could not control the entire country's coffee imports. By 1900 the national retailing system was simply too big and diverse for any city to dominate. New Orleans increasingly controlled the coffee markets of the lower Mississippi region; its trade rose between 1900 and 1920 from 44 million to 380 million pounds, from 5 percent to 29 percent of national consumption. For western states' markets, the San Francisco Exchange expanded exponentially in the wake of its recovery from earthquake and fire; from 36 million pounds processed in 1913, it rose to 160 million in 1919.[18] All sections of the country and all sectors of society were participating in a caffeine binge that had no limits, and southern Brazil was its major supplier. In 1920 the New York Exchange imported an astounding 767 million pounds, but that was only 59 percent of a steadily expanding national total. Centralization was one way the international system attempted to manage a typical characteristic of tropical crop production: its boom and bust cycles of periodic overproduction.

By 1890, Brazil was growing only half of total U.S. imports, but São Paulo still had vast areas of native forest that could be brought into production. By 1900 the region was producing record crops nearly every year: in 1901–2 its fazendas produced 15 million bags; the next year the figure rose still further to 20 million, as additional areas of São Paulo's hinterland came into production, reflecting a new round of forest clearances five to seven years earlier. Trade in Santos was demoralized by the glut. Prices collapsed; from their high of $.19 per pound in 1890, they crashed to $.05 in 1903. Many estate mortgages were foreclosed, especially in the old area of Rio's hinterland, and some estates began passing into European hands.[19]

In response to these precarious economic swings, the state government of São Paulo, dominated by the coffee planters, made the decision to intervene massively in the market. In the harvesting season of 1903 it agreed to buy the next crop and hold it for sale later, when market conditions improved. It labeled this strategy "valorization," equalization of prices, so as to give each year's crop similar value. Both the fiscal and ecological consequences of the valorization policy would be far more vexing in subsequent years than anyone imagined at the time. Valorization committed the São Paulo government to occasional massive purchases in Santos; for that it needed large infusions of cash whenever overproduction drove international prices down. The valorization mechanism encouraged maximum expansion of coffee production by guaranteeing planters a profitable price, without fixing any limits to government purchases. But coffee production throughout the subtropical hill regions of three continents was also rapidly rising in response to the high prices of the 1890s. In 1901–2 the global crop was nineteen million bags; another bumper crop in 1906–7 produced 24.3 million bags, including Brazil's crop of 20.2 million.

In order to support the valorization strategy, in 1907 the São Paulo state government tried to borrow heavily from the Rothschilds in Paris, who had been Brazil's bankers for sixty years. The Rothschilds refused to enter that highly speculative game, so São Paulo approached the banker Herman Sielcken of Hamburg and New York, who raised enough cash for the São Paulo government to buy two million bags at $.07 if necessary. But then the state was deluged by the biggest crop in history; the government had to buy nine million bags, yet the price was still only just over $.06 by late 1907.

High stakes gamblers, Americans (including John Arbuckle) joined Sielcken, along with other Europeans. Now the Rothschilds decided to enter the bailout but laid out several conditions that would affect future coffee production and land use. They proposed that the Brazilian government prohibit estate owners from planting new coffee trees and levy fines on those who did, and it had to guarantee not to export over nine million bags from the next crop, or more than ten million in later years. So, in 1908, the São Paulo government borrowed $75 million from its New York and European creditors, who set up a committee of seven to sell the coffee in timing that would not upset profitable prices. The committee included representatives of São Paulo, Antwerp, New York (Sielcken), London, Le Havre, and Paris. This system promised to stabilize Brazilian production under foreign domination. In the following years, North Atlantic bankers and brokers controlled nearly 90 percent of Santos' exports. The foreign creditors even began expanding their loans to the fazendeiros themselves, foreclosing on some bankrupt plantations.[20]

It was not long before domestic American politics intervened, derailing the attempt to restrict the expansion of Brazilian coffee production. In 1912 Senator George Norris, the famed crusader against cartels and monopolies, charged the bankers with conspiracy to manipulate trade illegally. The resulting congressional debate produced a 1913 law empowering the U.S. government to seize coffee imported in restraint of trade. This effectively killed all American participation in future valorization systems and assured that violent price and production swings would continue.[21]

By 1913 there was still a severe international coffee glut. The bankers granted São Paulo two more loans, for a total of $60.5 million. They were forced to repeat the procedure again in both 1918 and 1922. All of the loans were gradually repaid and the coffee released on international markets. But little was done to control coffee production in southern Brazil, and the extent of degraded land continued to expand.[22] Ironically, though the international bankers' attempts to restrict coffee production had been made purely to support the long-term financial interests of producers and traders, the effect, if implemented, would have been to restrict the acreage under coffee, an environmentally beneficial result. Stabilizing demand, and thus planning for production, would have avoided wild speculation and frontier expansion.

Large areas of Rio's hinterland were already degraded and the São Paulo hills were well on their way. Severe erosion followed forest clearance.[23] The coffee frontier continued moving inland and southward, claiming additional forest regions as the international market drove it onward. Cheap land with virgin soils was still so readily available that planters could move entire estate operations to new locations and pay the costs of forest clear-cutting less expensively than to apply the intensive labor and revised land management techniques necessary to sustain production on old lands.

But a cataclysm was about to occur in Europe, the outbreak of global war. World War I produced a decisive shift in the international market for Brazil's coffee. In the early stages of the war, Germany's supplies from the Americas were cut off by its enemies' navies, giving the United States another opportunity to dislodge a major competitor from the lands to the south. By the end of the war, Brazilian coffee was exported largely to the United States. In 1919, American imports were 1,338 million pounds from all of Latin America, a figure that represented a remarkable 11.7 pounds for every American.

American coffee consumption continued to rise throughout the prosperous 1920s, the low-income 1930s, and the high-income 1940s.[24] During the 1920s, Brazilian landowners responded to that enticing market by continuing to clear forest for access to new coffee soils. Then, in 1929 and 1930, as the Great Depression descended on the global economy, exports to the industrial countries began to sag and prices fell similarly. In 1931 the Brazilian government established new price supports for coffee, and workers suffered wage cuts or were thrown out of work.

Among coffee producing countries, only the Brazilian government restricted new planting during the Depression. But its efforts were futile: an additional law requiring fazenderos to uproot a portion of their trees failed to reduce production, because the planters destroyed only their oldest trees, concentrating their subsequent work on their younger, more productive groves. Some planters used payments received for uprooting trees to establish new groves on the sandy soils of the western São Paulo tableland. Still using no shade trees, they would find that these poor soils supported coffee production for no more than twenty to thirty years. Other planters replaced their groves on the degraded soils with cattle, cotton, or sugar. New small-scale coffee growers attempted to work the less fertile soils in the interspaces among the old estates. But the clearing of additional forest on the coffee frontier was still the responsibility of the large fazendas. The scourge continued to spread across the land.[25]

In November 1937 the São Paulo government changed its policy to one of dumping coffee on international markets. This strategy pushed international prices to their lowest levels in the twentieth century, since all of Brazil's competitors (including the second largest producer, Colombia) refused to restrict production or exports. Supply and demand problems were proving virtually impossible to manage under existing arrangements. During the Depression, Brazil had been forced to destroy almost 80 million bags of coffee. The government attempted price supports in 1937, but this only aided foreign competitors.

By then war was brewing again in Europe. In the relatively prosperous year of 1936, Germany had imported 14,821,488 pounds of Brazilian coffee, and France had bought 20,850,865 pounds (in contrast, the United States bought slightly over 1 billion pounds). But after Hitler's armies invaded Poland in late 1939, European markets for Brazilian coffee were closed for six years. Under these difficult conditions, the major coffee consuming countries finally united their efforts in 1939, in the familiar strategy of creating a cartel, called the International Coffee Agreement, which adopted a new system of quotas. Europe's quota system could hardly function, though, without the cooperation of the world's largest coffee buyer, the United States. In November 1940, Washington joined the agreement by setting quotas for American coffee purchases from fourteen producing countries. In 1941 the United States went further, setting price ceilings, as it did for many commodities. A year later it presided over a new Inter-American Coffee Agreement, to guarantee a wartime supply of New World coffee to the United States. This system lasted through the war years, until 1946. It stabilized purchasing and marketing of Latin American coffee, buffering the rural economies of Brazil and its competitors against wartime disruptions and further consolidating the United States' dominant position in the market.[26]

AFTER 1945: INSTANT COFFEE AND THE FAST FOOD CULTURE
With the end of World War II a new era began in the American consumer economy. Less damaged than the European economies, the U.S. economy dominated world trade for the next twenty years. Peacetime promised a vision of limitless security and affluence for an ever-widening segment of a booming population.[27] The automotive industry, bloated in its capacity in the wake of

the intense wartime production effort, turned to mass marketing of family cars, which intensified the dream of speed and mobility.[28] The advertising industry blossomed, projecting visions of a new consumer utopia to a restlessly mobile industrial and suburban population. Supermarkets and shopping malls trumpeted a cornucopia of consumer abundance, instantly accessible. Exotic products, including bananas and other tropical fruits, became commonplace on the markets' shelves.

This was the postwar culture that also invented fast food. Technological breakthroughs in energy-intensive food processing made eating and drinking easier than ever for the mass of consumers. More highly processed foods, laced with sugar and preservatives, pervaded the American diet.[29] One of the most profitable inventions was instant coffee. Powdered coffee for mass consumption demanded the strong taste of Robusta beans that were a Brazilian specialty. So the world's biggest and fastest expanding coffee market focused its drawing power on Brazil.

In the 1950s, Americans' consumption of coffee spiraled upward, both total consumption and per person. By 1961 the United States imported 22,500,000 bags, or 3 billion pounds. Latin America supplied 85 percent of the total. A 1963 survey reported that the average American over age ten drank three cups daily, for a national total of 441 million cups daily. It concluded that "coffee and the coffee break are today an intimate part of the American way of life." The value of these beans was second only to petroleum products among U.S. imports.[30]

The end of the war in 1945 led to rapid depletion of international stocks; prices shot up, tripling between 1946 and 1952. By 1949 Brazil's massive coffee surplus was exhausted. Most coffee trees in São Paulo were old and badly damaged by then, as were the soils in which they grew.[31] Other parts of Brazil rapidly increased production, especially Paraná state, where coffee fast replaced the natural forest. The forest of Paraná was unique, dominated by Araucaria or Paraná pine. This tall conifer was not a true pine, but a genetic relic of ancient times in southern latitudes. The physical properties of its lumber were similar to pine, however, and the forests of Paraná were harvested intensively to meet Europe's urgent need for reconstruction after the war.[32]

Fortunately for the state's economy, coffee would grow well in the soils and climate of the Araucaria zone. By the late 1950s, though the natural forest was greatly reduced, it was successfully replaced by another tree crop. This transformation was a continuation of the old practice of opening new virgin soils to coffee but, unlike in Rio and São Paulo states, coffee was a stable crop on the less steep contours of Paraná. In 1959 Paraná passed São Paulo as the leading coffee producer state of Brazil.

Internationally, in response to endlessly expanding markets, 1958 world coffee production hit an unprecedented level at 45,780,000 bags. A year later even that figure was slightly exceeded; Brazil's contribution was 25,500,000 bags. Those exports contributed roughly half of Brazil's total foreign exchange earnings. For comparison, Colombia, the world's second largest producer, marketed 6,500,000 bags that year, only one-fourth of Brazil's production. Those were the years when the American market totally dominated trade; it imported nearly 20,170,000 bags of coffee in 1958, 81 percent of that from Latin America. That year American firms imported 37 percent of its total from Brazil. By comparison, its Colombian imports were 4,200,000 bags, 21 percent of its half-billion daily cups.[33]

Yet not all was well for the coffee producers. World coffee prices remained dangerously volatile. In 1957, coffee purchased unroasted at dockside in New York cost 51.85 cents per pound; by 1961 the price fell to 35.14 cents per pound. In 1958, groping for effective stabilization mechanisms as the price skidded, the principal importing and exporting countries founded the Coffee Study Group, which launched a global survey of coffee production and trade. A year later, international coffee politics suddenly intensified when Fidel Castro swept into power in Havana and threatened to export his revolution throughout Latin America. After John Kennedy became U.S. president in 1961, he launched the hemisphere-wide Alliance for Progress, partly as a Cold War strategy to thwart Castro's influence in other politically and socially unstable countries.[34] In August 1961, at the hemispheric conference at Punta del Este, Uruguay, which launched the alliance, Kennedy's representative announced that the United States would join a long-term intergovernmental program to stabilize coffee price levels. The new Democratic administration thus overturned the Eisenhower administration's opposition to governmental intervention in international commodity pricing.

Stabilizing the global market had the potential to stabilize production and reduce its environmental impacts. But did it, in fact? In 1962 the world's major coffee exporting and importing countries signed the International Coffee Agreement, which established comprehensive, centralized international control of coffee stocks. Under the agreement, no more coffee would be released onto global markets than would maintain prices at that year's levels. More significant for coffee production and the lands where the trees grew, the agreement also vowed to promote coffee consumption internationally and work to reduce tariffs and quota limitations.

Adjusting production to demand would prove to be very difficult. As the British expert, J. W. F. Rowe, noted in 1963, most overproduction was in Brazil, which would have to pay its planters to reduce production. Funds for that would have to come from the United States. Rowe predicted accurately that this would not happen; in the end much coffee, especially in Brazil, would still have to be destroyed. The familiar, absurd pattern would be perpetuated in which "many men and much [sic] natural resources will continue to be employed in producing coffee for destruction."[35] Political support for the existing system was simply too powerful among the planter politicians of southern Brazil and their friends in Washington, while American and European consumers were willing to approve any system that supported their drinking habits.

Kennedy's government saw the 1962 agreement from a different perspective than Rowe, carefully building political support for the new regulating system on the basis of the enormous thirst of American consumers. On the morning the agreement was signed, the President's press release noted that the U.S. market was responsible for 50 percent of the world's coffee trade—441 million cups daily! Stretching the analysis a bit, the press release presented statistics showing that this trade was responsible for 662,000 jobs in the United States, two-thirds of them related to producing goods for export to the thirty-seven countries that produced coffee for the American market (more than 16 percent of all U.S. exports in 1961), and one-third directly related to processing imported coffee. The White House calculated that 1,146 U.S. communities, in all fifty states, were linked to that economic activity.[36] In sum, Cold War politics helped to drive Latin American coffee production upward; this in turn ate away at the hill forests.

Across the social spectrum, Americans were addicted to a beverage that continued to devour the forest ecosystems of southern Brazil. Was there any hope that coffee production processes could be made more sustainable, more environmentally benign? Then the supply of new and inexpensive land in regions appropriate for growing coffee was no longer limitless, and land values were rising steadily. The financial equation was beginning to lead Brazilian coffee growers to intensify production practices on their lands by increasing agrochemical inputs.

A United Nations survey in 1962 encouraged the estate owners to adopt input-intensive methods. It reported that modern techniques had begun in the 1930s, including closer planting of trees, introducing more productive stock, and contour planting for soil retention. More fertilizers were beginning to appear, including both manure and chemicals. But soil enrichment of any sort was still used on only a small percentage of the new plantations: by 1958 only 13 percent of Brazil's coffee area used chemical fertilizers and 29 percent used organic manures. Most chemical fertilizer was used on older plantations, to prolong their productivity. Three-fourths of the soils under coffee by then, especially in Paraná, were sandy. These soils were especially deficient in nitrogen, but the U.N. agronomists estimated that the planters used only 14 percent of the nitrogen fertilizers that should be used under those conditions.[37]

In a complementary strategy, the Brazilian government in 1953 had begun encouraging crop diversification over coffee in São Paulo. By the late 1950s the state was in the midst of an agricultural revolution, as production of cotton, oranges, sugar, and soya escalated, mostly for export. As agricultural land became more profitable under the new capital and chemical intensive methods, it also became more expensive. Land ownership in São Paulo state became even more concentrated. Mechanization and export cropping proceeded at the expense of food production, as coffee was being phased out. Landowners either reduced workers' wages or laid them off. Unemployment increased and food shortages developed, leading to growing labor tensions and even food riots.[38] The Paulista planter aristocracy dominated national policies concerning cattle and Amazonian development. This, in turn, led to Brazil's Amazon development strategy, as an escape valve for rising social tensions. By the 1970s, large numbers of landless laborers, whose forbears had migrated into the region in search of work on the coffee estates, began to join the exodus to western Amazonia. An even greater ecological disaster on the rainforest frontier was beginning, in part the legacy of the coffee travesties of the prior century.

Warren Dean's ironic conclusion about the coffee era in São Paulo is fitting:

Coffee enlarged the fortunes of [the big planters] and secured the plantation system. Plantations, on the other hand, were not essential to the development of an export trade in coffee. Unlike sugar, coffee does not have an unrelieved history of large-scale cultivation. The plant responds to extra labor inputs and skillfulness of tending with greater output and higher quality berries. Thus in nineteenth-century Jamaica, Puerto Rico, and Colombia coffee was the salvation of a smallholding peasantry. The exporters of Santos, therefore, necessarily directed their coffee to a mass market unable to pay for better quality and inured to an undistinguished product. A great paradox: the freeholding peasants of the Caribbean raised their superior coffee for an affluent European middle class, while their factory- and farm-working counterparts in the United States drank the product of slave-driving latifundists.[39]

The counterpoint between social and ecological change was stark in southern Brazil; it was less easy to define in Colombia.

COLOMBIA: FRONTIER FARMERS, MOUNTAIN FORESTS AND EXPORT MARKETS

The American and European coffee thirst became so great that even Brazil's massive production was often insufficient to quench it. New York and the other major import centers also turned for supplies to northern South America, on the other side of Amazonia from Brazil to the Andean hill lands of Venezuela and Colombia, former Spanish colonies that had been independent from the early 1820s onward. After 1900 Colombia became permanently the second largest producer of coffee for the U.S. market. There, just as in Brazil, the American impact on the land was indirect. Just as in Santos, foreigners remained in coastal ports as coffee buyers and rarely bought or managed coffee producing lands.

But that was where the resemblance ended. The society on the land that coffee purchasers helped to shape contrasted sharply with southern Brazil. When coffee first arrived in Colombia in the 1830s, there was no slave system like on the Brazilian fazendas. Instead, the Colombian hill zone was settled by a complex, shifting patchwork of landlords and squatters; both organized coffee production successfully. But on the northern tier both the social and ecological outcomes of the global coffee economy were very different. International coffee markets, especially in North America, made possible, even irresistible, the domestication of yet another natural ecosystem, with resulting loss of soil and biotic diversity. As in Brazil, the ecological results of massive coffee planting in Colombia were damaging.

In Colombia, small growers on the agricultural frontier played a major role in replacing ancient forest because coffee was an ideal cash crop for frontier squatters. But the more profitable it was, the more an alliance of landlords and urban traders was determined to control its flow. As the country's major cash crop, coffee became the focus of social conflict between landlords and peasants, which chronically disrupted production and frustrated the English-speaking buyers on the north coast. In each case—extensive or tiny groves—one ecological consequence was the same: the elimination of natural forest cover on the mountainsides of the northern Andes. Another fundamental ecological difference between large plantations and small coffee holdings was that the large monocrop groves eliminated many of the other species of flora and fauna that were natural to the forest, while the small holdings tended to preserve many of them in the remaining patches of woodlands or the multilayered tree and annual crops that the peasants intermixed with their coffee groves (see map on page 66).

The northern Andes of Colombia and Venezuela stretch northeastward in a great arc from the Ecuadoran border nearly to Caracas on the Caribbean coast.[40] The cordillera lies just north of the equator, so elevation rather than latitude produces a temperate climate. At these latitudes coffee grows at elevations of 3,000 to 6,500 feet. At the same time as the early expansion of coffee production in southern Brazil, the first experiments at commercial production in the northern Andes began in northwestern Venezuela in the 1830s, shortly after its independence from Spain. Coffee production tripled in the 1830s, mostly from virgin forest clearances in higher elevations than cacao (which had been the primary export crop in Colombia before 1810), with prices rising until the late 1840s. Coffee was exported to Europe along with cacao, sugar, cattle hides, and indigo; coffee provided one-third to one-half of Venezuela's total export value in those years.[41]

From the start, the northern Andes specialized in the mild café suave for European speculators, who provided loan capital but charged high interest rates. Rising competition from Ceylon and Brazil drove prices slowly down after the late 1830s, but the links between the coffee market and domestic affairs were tightening. When coffee prices crashed after 1842, the damaged Venezuelan planters rose in rebellion against their government in 1846–47. The northern Andes's cycle of civil violence tied to the coffee cycle had begun. Continuing agricultural depression through the 1850s triggered the Federal

War of 1858, which disrupted the rural economy. Production returned to its pre-1858 levels only after 1870, when a new golden age for coffee began in the Andean region.[42] But by then Colombia was on the way to passing its neighbor's production levels. Coffee groves gradually spread from the narrow Andean belt of Venezuela southwestward into the more extensive mountain ranges of Colombia, which became the world's second largest producer of coffee by 1900.

Colombia is the only country in South America that lies on both the Atlantic and Pacific coasts. It is divided into four distinct biogeographical zones. The northernmost is the wide savanna of the Caribbean lowlands. Behind the coastal plain rises the Andean region, which dominates the western third of the country in three parallel chains of ridges towering 10,000 feet to 18,000 feet high, carved by the Magdalena and Cauca rivers. Just west of those ranges lie the Pacific lowlands, one of the planet's wettest and most biologically diverse rainforests. Finally, the entire southeastern half of Colombia, beyond the Andean chain, is a remote, vast segment of Amazonia. Even now this region supports primarily a sparse Indian population, and its borders with Brazil and Peru are only vaguely demarcated.

In the colonial era, agricultural estates clustered in the Caribbean lowlands, the hinterland of Cartagena, Barranquilla, and Santa Marta, which were the most important ports on that stretch of the Spanish Main. In this seasonally flooded savanna, which extends east into Venezuela, cattle ranching dominated the landscape.[43] From there, settlement spread slowly inland, southward toward the mountains, concentrating first in the department of Norte de Santander, just west of the Venezuelan border.

The northern Andes, the modern coffee zone, has no pronounced seasons. Climate varies by elevation, in three human settlement zones: the coastal lowlands (1,000–3,000 feet), the middle hills (3,000–6,500 feet), and the zone of high-mountain settlement (6,500–10,000 feet).[44] The forested mountainsides of the temperate middle hills provided the coffee frontier—and the worst environmental damage—from the mid-1800s onward. Three north-south cordilleras constituted formidable barriers, hindering inter-regional travel and trade until the 1870s. In other words, the Colombian Andes presented many local frontiers, settled one by one. Unpopulated areas, or *baldios*, were abundant until nearly the end of the century. The Colombian government saw them as a challenge to development and a welcome outlet for social tensions in older settled areas. The environmental history of the Colombian Andes thus became inseparable from the country's socioeconomic and political history. In turn, its economy also became inseparable from the global coffee market and in particular the consumer economy of the eastern United States.

Before the Spanish conquest, Indian communities had concentrated in the hill zone, cultivating mixed-food crops on small plots of land. The conquerors in the late 1600s and 1700s established haciendas in the rich bottomland soils of the river valleys. Much of the new coffee before 1850 was grown on private estates dating back to the seventeenth century. Marco Palacios, Colombia's leading coffee historian, concludes that "[t]he establishment of the coffee hacienda did not take place at the expense of communal lands and the minifundia holdings [in the interior], as had been the case in other parts of Latin America, where commercial agriculture had come into sharp conflict with peasants and local communities. Colombian coffee-growers were able to claim, perhaps justifiably, that the consequences of their activities had been to further the advance of civilization in a wild and hostile environment."[45]

From 1850 onward, coffee spread southward into the hills of Cundinamarca around Bogota, the new capital. The heavy bags of coffee cherries were shipped down the Magdalena River and sold to eager buyers from the Northern world in the Caribbean ports of Santa Marta and Cartagena. In the 1870s, merchants from Bogota entered coffee speculation; investors in Medellin began competing with them in the 1880s. Owners of large estates entered coffee production in the same years, using knowledge learned in the tobacco trade. Together they became a class of absentee owners and exporters. In the hills above Bogota, quinine plantations were established in the 1870s; when quinine failed, they were transformed into coffee groves on the higher slopes or cattle ranches below. Newly consolidated cattle haciendas drove peasants off their lowland farms, creating a floating labor market; the coffee gentry badly needed their labor, at the lowest possible cost. The dispossessed peasants became either sharecroppers on the estates or small colono farmers on the hill frontiers.

The Colombian government, eager to turn the land into marketable commodities, encouraged frontier settlement by giving unsettled baldio land to any settler who would cultivate it. Dispossessing the indigenous populace of the mountains, the government sold wide areas of Indian communal lands in the highlands above the export-crop zone to coffee speculators large and small. The increasing immigrant population grew various crops, including subsistence foods, tobacco, cacao, and coffee. They cultivated marginal hillsides, gradually exhausting cultivable land through soil nutrient depletion and erosion.

The national legislature generally supported small settlers, praising the peasants as hardy frontiersmen. But when export booms occurred, such as in the 1870s and 1880s, the resulting wealth was captured by merchants, financiers, commercial farmers, and land speculators. When land prices rose, the government happily sold baldios to the highest bidders. That strategy reinforced the wealth of urban speculators in Bogota and Medellin.

The international marketing system for Colombian coffee brought competitive buyers from Europe and the United States into the picture. American purchasers helped determine the investments and markets that fueled Colombian coffee production and settlement in the middle Andean hills. Foreign buyers set up their offices in the north coast ports as the nineteenth century wore on. Exports grew rapidly from 1870 to 1897 then stagnated until 1909. By the turn of the century, U.S. purchases exceeded the European market and totally dominated Colombia's exports for the following six decades. From a market share of 16 percent of coffee exports in the mid-1860s, the Americans' rose to 72 percent in the 1903–7 period.[46] The role of New York investors became steadily more important, as green coffee importers adopted a policy of pre-paying for annual crops. In contrast with Santos, Colombian exporters attempted to open their own offices in Manhattan but the New Yorkers successfully prevented them. In turn, the Colombians prevented the New Yorkers and their European competitors from dominating the shipping houses in the Colombian ports, at least until 1920.

Under such powerful economic incentives, the hinterland began to be opened up by new transport technology, just as it was everywhere around Latin America. In the 1870s, steamboats began plying the Magdalena and Cauca Rivers.[47] Gradually railroads replaced them, funded to a large extent by and for the coffee industry. By 1920, Colombia built 1,300 kilometers of rail lines. A dramatic breakthrough came in 1915 with the completion of the Pacific Railroad from Cali in the far southwestern hills to the Pacific port of Buenaventura. The newly opened Panama Canal, pride of American engineers and politicians, had decisively reduced transport costs from the west coast of tropical America to North Atlantic ports, and Colombia's luxuriant Pacific coastal rainforest belt was laid under siege.

Reflecting those infrastructural changes, the great coffee boom in the central cordillera appeared after 1910, spreading into the Antioquia region from Medellin southward. Antioquia, known nationally for its people's entrepreneurial spirit, was primarily responsible for a 450 percent increase in Colombia's export earnings between 1870 and 1918. By 1920, coffee produced 70 percent of the country's export revenues.[48] Thanks largely to Antioquia, national exports rose from one million sixty-kilo bags in 1913 to 3 million in 1930.[49] When Brazil's valorization strategists held coffee off the market, Colombia happily filled the gap; its increased production kept international prices from rising, which frustrated Santos. By the 1920s, as Palacios writes, "the more difficult stages of the settlement of the western part of the country were over. The area contained the most fertile and ecologically most propitious conditions for the cultivation of coffee, perhaps of anywhere in Latin America." [50]

On the middle slopes between the Cauca River and the high mountain ranges, peasant settlements with their varied crops produced a patchwork landscape of farm and forest; coffee was the cash crop that made them barely viable. Squatter colonos seldom had secure titles to their land, so they were vulnerable to takeover by the wealthy. In some areas, colonization was dominated by the landed elite, though Antioquia was a rather more open, egalitarian frontier society than the older centers. On the small colono coffee holdings there, farming techniques were land and labor extensive; the peasants used little manure or fertilizer. They planted and replanted coffee trees in random relation to soil and contour. They planted trees in low density, interplanting other crops, which, Palacios suggests, gradually exhausted the soil.[51] But they maintained shade trees over their coffee groves, in contrast with the Brazilian slave plantation owners. Their roots must have maintained greater soil stabilization and their crowns a wider range of microspecies diversity than groves grown without shade. And their intercropping with subsistence crops provided an element of greater stability than the large estates.

During World War I transatlantic shipping was disrupted and European purchases of Latin America's coffee were almost totally curtailed. At the end of the war, when European buyers returned, coffee prices leaped upward. Then, in mid-1920, in a brief but sharp depression, prices collapsed. American importers took control of the trade when all Colombian exporters went bankrupt. This was strikingly similar to Cuban sugar's Dance of the Millions at the same moment, when New York banks went even further, foreclosing on many of the great Cuban sugar estates. Colombia's banks suspended operations and had to borrow heavily from New York and European banks. The Bank of New York and Battery Park National Bank seized all coffee stocks of two major Colombian traders. All Colombian firms in New York went bankrupt that year. Importers like the Great Atlantic and Pacific Tea Company's subsidiary, the American Coffee Company, began to buy green coffee directly from producers on the land, cutting out Colombian traders. E. A. Kahl, the German immigrant coffee trader in San Francisco, who knew Colombia well, was also deeply involved in these maneuvers as West Coast manager of W. R. Grace and Company. From then onward into the 1950s American importers were dominant in the Colombian coffee trade. Between 60 percent and 80 percent of Colombian exports were coffee, and 80 percent to 90 percent of that went to the United States.[52]

Colombia's export economy grew rapidly after 1921 with the help of an accelerated inflow of North American capital. Investments in oil, plus loans to national and state governments and banks totaling $200 million in the decade between 1920 and 1929, developed industry, communications, energy, public services, and transport.[53] This trend was reinforced by expanding world coffee demand. Colombian coffee exports tripled between 1915 and 1929, and their value increased over 400 percent. Total government revenues from coffee quadrupled between 1919 and 1929. Major credit for the new dynamism went to FEDECAFE, the National Coffee Federation, founded in 1927 as a trade association that

> has worked with commendable efficiency to regulate internal prices, assure supplies of credit, control the quality of the Colombian product, and much else besides; and all those involved in growing and selling coffee were invited to belong. In practice, the federation was dominated by the larger growers and the coffee merchants, who naturally derived the principal benefit from its services. At the same time, though, the mere fact that the small grower was himself an independent operator did give him a sense of having a stake, even if a modest one, in the existing system.[54]

Vast tracts of hitherto "worthless" public lands attracted large-scale entrepreneurs, especially in the newer western coffee zone. Elite speculators increased pressure on colonos already there. But the boom and bust cycle of the global economy continued to plague such suppliers of primary commodities as Colombia. When the Depression hit in late 1929, it reverberated immediately into the mountains of Colombia. By January 1930 the international price of coffee fell by 50 percent, destroying the financial base of many marginal coffee farmers. European colonial preference schemes, which turned to Europe's colonies in Africa and Asia for as much of their supplies as possible, further cut down markets for Latin American coffee, leaving Colombia even more at the mercy of the North American coffee market.

Colombia's coffee zone was a perennial breeding ground for social violence. Under the pressures of the Depression, many dispossessed colonos attacked and occupied the larger estates. The Colombian government attempted to mediate between landlords and peasants, purchasing 240 estates in the heart of the coffee zone to subdivide for peasants. In those locations, small coffee fincas replaced large estates. But an agrarian reform law in 1936, which seemed to favor settlers, was used by landlords to dispossess marginal or unruly workers. Endemic social upheaval prevented any effort at careful, sustained management of the land.

World War II and its aftermath did little to alleviate either the social tension or the consequent stress on the land. In 1945, peace returned to the international arena but not to Colombia. Three years later one of Latin America's longest civil wars began; Colombians bluntly call it La Violencia. Endemic violence lasted for seventeen years, until 1965. By the time it sputtered to a halt, some 200,000 people had died and 800,000 were left homeless.[55] This epic but confused civil war was many faceted. It was not just a peasant war but also interregional, urban versus rural, Liberal versus Conservative, and more. In the mountains where coffee grew, class violence intensified beyond the levels of the 1930s and became more severe than on the lowland haciendas. Many peasants left particularly bloody areas for still more remote mountain frontiers, squatting without formal title on public lands on newly opened frontiers. Guerrilla organizations flourished in hill frontier regions.

Few observers of the bloodshed in those years were concerned about the impact of this social and political maelstrom on the agricultural and forest ecosystems where it played out. Conclusions must be tentative but some insights are possible, shedding light on the indirect impact of American coffee buyers on a society and landscape from which they drew their supplies. In 1948, the American T. Lynn Smith reported at the Inter-American Conference on Natural Resources and Conservation that soil erosion was acute in the temperate zones north of Bogota, as well as in large parts of the Andean zone of Antioquia. The result was a major drain of population off the land or else "hopeless resignation to abject poverty and misery." Smith laid the blame on the landlords, arguing that in colonial times the Spaniards had forced Indians off valley lands in favor of cattle ranches. The Indians had retreated into the hills, where they grew wheat and potatoes. The steep slopes, gradually stripped of vegetation and soil, were "converted into badlands absolutely beyond reclamation, and the destruction is continuing at what is probably an accelerating rate."[56] Those hill areas, of course, were the zone of mixed cropping and coffee estates.

In the postwar years, Colombia's coffee production and exports continued to expand. In 1958–59, a global boom production year, Colombia produced 6,500,000 bags. The United States imported 4,255,000 bags, 21 percent of its total imports. Another 1,077,000 bags went from Colombia to Europe, primarily West Germany.[57] By 1970, of the 4.5 million hectares of land in Colombia's coffee zones, approximately one-fourth was in coffee. FEDECAFE, searching for new efficiencies in handling coffee, turned to a program of modernizing warehousing and credit, the commercial aspects of the coffee industry. This expressed the trend of the national economy as a whole. The postwar years saw industrial diversification and renewed foreign investment in industry, while large-scale mechanized farming gradually replaced traditional low-yield cattle ranching in the country's lowlands. By the 1950s the national elite emphasized industrialization and efficiencies of large-scale operations, which meant consolidation of land ownership into fewer, larger properties.

Foreign coffee experts, whose advice was funneled largely through the International Coffee Organization, were virtually unanimous in their belief in the virtue of large-scale coffee farmers as agents of modernizing production methods. In the conventional wisdom of the time, they perceived the peasant smallholders as inefficient and backward, stolidly resistant to change. In contrast with them, major Colombian growers began making a transition toward intensive production methods. By 1960, technological changes were visible on the coffee plantations; they became common on the large estates after 1970.[58] Farmers began to increase the density of trees per hectare by three to five times; they used more productive tree varieties; and at last they began to employ contour planting and soil stabilization. But they also increased applications of chemical fertilizers and pesticides. In the long run this reduced species diversity on and around the modernized estates, in contrast with the peasant holdings that could not afford the greater capital expense.

The ongoing struggle between landlords and colono peasants expressed the larger picture of national politics in those years. Between 1931 and 1971 the Colombian government distributed eleven million hectares of baldio land to individuals and land companies. In certain instances landlords also sold some land to peasants but generally this was the least fertile, most marginal land. Other landlords turned tilled land into cattle pasture to eliminate the presence of unruly workers. Landless peasants moved to the cities or became seasonal labor on coffee, banana, and cotton estates, or else continued the migration to upland frontiers. The trend toward land consolidation, with more systematic management of larger groves, including soil stabilization, in turn stabilized land use on larger coffee fincas somewhat, though at the increasing cost of agrochemical pollution. But marginal peasants continued putting pressure on forest frontiers. As long as the social problem was not resolved, forest loss and soil degradation continued to spread there too.

The international pipeline of coffee production and consumption thus connected the steaming mug on an American breakfast table with the machete and hoe on a remote north Andean mountainside. Yankee housewives and factory workers depended on Hills Brothers and Maxwell House, whose agents bargained with Colombian exporters who overlapped with the large coffee growers of the core zone and the squatters on farther, marginal land. Americans provided the largest market, until the end of the 1960s, when rising European purchases roughly equaled American totals. Internal sociopolitical and biogeographical circumstances did the rest. Northern marketers and consumers had no direct responsibility for the consequences on the land. Yet they were linked to those changes in a complex causal web, helping to perpetuate the violent movement of the social and ecological frontier.[59]

CONCLUSION: TOWARD A SUSTAINABLE TREE CROP?

American coffee consumption always had a more indirect environmental impact than sugar or bananas. In the coffee cycle, from production to consumption, Americans played two roles: as purveyors to the world's largest market and as consumers of the black brew. They played little or no role in actual management of the land. Nonetheless, the American market was the engine that drove coffee-centered agroecosystems in Brazil and Colombia, just as the European market drove coffee to replace forests in the hill regions of other tropical and subtropical lands.

Coffee production had transformed hill lands throughout tropical and subtropical Latin America since the 1830s.[60] As a dominant cash crop for international markets, coffee strengthened the hold of landed oligarchies in some countries, and was the key to successful peasant pioneer farming on the forest frontier in others. The United States was central to this transformation, since Americans became the world's greatest coffee consumers by the late 1800s. Their virtually exclusive source of supply was Latin America until the 1950s, when American purchasers began further diversification by moving into African production areas as well. They turned primarily to the French colony of Ivory Coast, though Ivorien coffee exports continued to flow primarily to France.[61] In contrast to sugar and bananas, but much like rubber, coffee did not have to be quickly processed and transported to market. Coffee could be produced by small farmers as competitively as by landlords or corporate plantations. Peasant households could be financially viable if they grew coffee as their cash crop, in conjunction with a variety of subsistence crops in their multispecies agroecological systems. Their more complex strategy supported the continuing presence of a wider spectrum of flora and fauna than the one-crop large estates.

When intensified production (based on new varieties and denser planting of coffee bushes) emerged in the 1950s, along with more sustainable management of hill soils, the larger producers were in a better position than the marginal farmers to adopt the innovative methods. But their coffee trees excluded virtually all other plant and animal species. Brazilian growers at last began to nurture shade trees in the coffee groves in the 1950s. Then thirty years later, new varieties of coffee trees whose products did not require shade from the intense sun, began to displace the older shaded groves throughout the Americas. Throughout recent decades, intensified production has been sustained by increasing applications of commercial fertilizers and pesticides, a strategy that eliminates adjunct species and places chemical residues in the soil and downstream waters.

Finally, as large-scale coffee production advanced, it displaced subsistence farmers, who were forced either to squat on new forest lands or migrate to the burgeoning cities. In Brazil, by the 1960s and 1970s, the production area stabilized somewhat and land management improved but farm workers were displaced into cities or onto the Amazonian frontier, where an even greater ecological disaster was growing. In Colombia, conditions on the land remained notoriously unstable, as the struggle between landed and landless roiled onward.

None of this mattered to coffee advertisers in the United States, who convinced their public that Juan Valdez, the resourceful and contented independent coffee farmer, would tend his small groves in perpetuity to satisfy his Yankee consumer's need for caffeine and sociability. Northern coffee traders and consumers fueled both social conflict and environmental stress by their purchases. Even if American traders spent long years in the coastal marketing offices of Latin American producers, they had no concern for what happened to the landscapes of the supplying countries, as long as they could continue to buy the coffee beans at competitively low prices and in assured supplies. American consumers knew virtually nothing of the ecological or social conditions in the source areas that provided their rituals of first morning cup at home, mid-morning coffee break at the workplace, and a final cup with dessert in the evening.

4

The Tropical Cost of the Automotive Age: Corporate Rubber Empires and the Rainforest

THE ERA OF INDUSTRIAL RUBBER

Sugarcane and bananas replaced lowland forests of the Caribbean basin, northern South America, and the Philippines. Coffee eroded the mid-elevation hill regions of tropical and subtropical America, Africa, and southern Asia. Still another industrial crop, rubber, further domesticated tropical forest ecosystems. From the start of the automotive era, vast groves of rubber trees extended the domestication of tropical Nature into new regions. Among them were the American rubber industry's plantations in Indonesia and Malaya in Southeast Asia and Liberia in West Africa. The rubber hunters experimented with several latex-producing species, but the *Hevea brasiliensis* tree dominated them all. Yet, when grown in concentrated plantations in the natural forest of Amazonia where it had evolved genetically, Hevea was subject to a disease as deadly as the banana diseases. Only when planted far from its natural setting, in the rainforests of southern Asia, and then equatorial Africa, could the Hevea trees thrive. On those two continents it displaced natural forest in wide tracts.

Somewhat similar to coffee, rubber could be commercially grown either on vast one-crop plantations or as the primary cash-earning commodity on multicrop smallholder farms. The rubber industry, and the global consumer demand that it created and satisfied, thus had a wide impact on moist tropical societies and ecosystems. Moreover, more than in the case of coffee, it turned out to be possible to create varieties of Hevea that raised the trees' productivity ten times over that of natural trees. Intensification of production, particularly on the corporate estates, became a hallmark of the industry and one of the most dramatic triumphs of tropical agronomy.

However vast the clearings of natural forest for rubber, the acreage would have been far greater in the long run than it ultimately reached had not the industry developed a second source to complement it: synthetic rubber refined from petroleum, which came on the market during the crisis of supplies in World War II. The technological breakthrough catalyzed by that military emergency transformed the global rubber economy. Since 1960 roughly two-thirds of global rubber production has been derived from synthetics, and the other third from trees on lands that had once sustained rainforests. In this segment of tropical forest clearance, to a greater degree than any other tropical monocrop except bananas, the United States led the way via innovations in automotive engineering and marketing.

The story of rubber began in the early 1800s. Rubbery substances derived from the latex of various tropical trees and bushes had long been in use. But in hot weather they tended to melt and in cold settings became brittle. In 1837 the American Charles Goodyear invented the vulcanization process, which stabilized latex products over a wide temperature range, opened up a vast new range of possibilities for the industrial era, and gave Goodyear's company an early lead in developing product lines and markets. At first the new product was used primarily by the clothing industry of New England's mill towns to produce wet weather boots and clothes. Toward the end of the century, this market was superceded by tires for bicycles, and then automobiles and a burgeoning range of other commercial and industrial uses.

Unsure of where their sources of latex might be found, commercial adventurers from Europe and the United States searched the world's tropical lowlands. *Hevea brasiliensis,* a tree endemic to the Amazonian rainforest, proved to be the best source of latex. After 1890, as world demand for rubber burgeoned, Hevea latex rapidly eliminated all others from international trade, and the tree was taken to Africa and Asia, where single-species plantations replaced rainforest over large areas.

AMERICAN SPECULATORS IN AMAZONIA

Beginning in the 1820s, British and American explorers and speculators engaged in a strategic race in the Amazon basin, mapping the vast unknown territory and searching for any product that they could commandeer, including rubber. In 1849, two U.S. Navy officers, Lewis Herndon and Lardner Gibbon, conducted a navigability survey of the main river. Herndon was the brother-in-law of Matthew Maury, head of the National Observatory in Washington and chief booster of U.S. trade with Amazonia. In hyperbolic prose typical of the age, Maury reported that Brazil "has arrayed herself against the improvement and the progress of the age, and she has attempted by intrigue so to shape the course of events that she might lock up and seal with the seal of ignorance and superstition and savage barbarity the finest portions of the earth."[1] Global progress would result from increased international trade and Americans of imperial ambition would lead that historic trend, Maury trumpeted, foreshadowing today's globalization boosters.

By the 1850s Maury and other explorers probed all major tributaries of the Amazon, searching for the occasional fairly dense stand of Hevea. The finest of all Hevea forests were along the vaguely defined border between Brazil and Bolivia, on the Madeira branch of the river. George Church, an American adventurer, worked with the Bolivian government to build a railroad into its portion of the Amazonian lowlands. Backed by British capital, he began constructing the notorious Madeira-Mamore Railway Company in 1872, but his workers collapsed in large numbers from jungle diseases. Though Church went bankrupt, he was not finished. He went next to Philadelphia, in the hopes that the large pool of unemployed laborers might be willing to go to civilization's farthest frontier for a pittance. In 1878 he again left for South America, this time with Irish, German, and Italian workers. In the brutal working conditions of the jungle, their ethnic rivalries turned into brawls, and those who did not die scattered to other towns, racing away from what had become a green hell for them.

Next, Church hired landless peasants from drought-haunted Ceará state in northeast Brazil, when in 1877 the northeast suffered one of its most severe droughts of the century. Desperate for any form of survival, 100,000 dispossessed Cearense workers flooded up the Amazon, many of them into Acre, the remote border region where Indian tribes had never before seen more than a handful of Brazilians. But by 1881, 500 out of Church's 1,400 men had died from yellow fever, and his operation collapsed, marking the end of the first ignominious Yankee effort to tame the Amazon.

But the Bolivian powerbrokers were obsessed to find a link to the Atlantic. They were determined to gain free passage down the Amazon, which the

Brazilian government opposed. In 1866 the two governments agreed on the Treaty of Ayacucho, which drew an arbitrary line across terra incognito, giving the remote jungle region of Acre to Bolivia. The rootless peasants and their backers in the business houses of Manaus and Belem provided a new opportunity for American speculators to dabble in rainforest politics. The "Bolivian Syndicate," whose investors included J. P. Morgan, the Vanderbilt family, and a cousin of the future president Teddy Roosevelt, attempted to raise capital to back the Bolivian side.[2] The international imbroglio precipitated a brief war between Brazil and Bolivia, which Brazil won, annexing a wide, remote region.

Over many millennia in the Amazonian rainforest, several closely related species of Hevea had evolved. The most productive was *Hevea brasiliensis,* which grows naturally in several regions of the Amazonian basin, always scattered as one species among hundreds. Only a few Hevea trees grew, widely dispersed, in each acre of forest. This prevented the parasites that had co-evolved with it from concentrating their attacks, as they could when humans planted the trees in dense groves.

Extracting the precious white liquid and shipping it out of the jungle was another matter entirely, requiring the skills and tenacity of people who could survive the extremely difficult living conditions of the basin. Outside speculators were failing in their efforts to gain direct control of forest tracts; they had no hope of participating directly in the latex extraction. Hevea latex was tapped by hardy men *(seringueiros)* who knew the obscure trails through the forest from one stem to the next.

Foreign markets' demand for the seringueiros' work began to accelerate after Goodyear's invention of vulcanization. By the 1860s the Amazonian forest began to feel the industrial world's capacity to penetrate even the most remote ecosystems and social systems, as the flow of immigrant workers from poverty-stricken Ceará began to increase. They were controlled by powerful men who grasped ownership of forest tracts, by legal or illegal means, from the indigenous tribes, whom they displaced, destroyed, or occasionally forced to collect rubber. The owners supplied the tappers with food, tools, and loans and bought the tappers' crude rubber at riverside trading posts. It was a brutal life; the tappers were locked by debts and the threat of violence into servitude to the owners. No outside government could reach far enough into the interior to restrain the exploitation. In turn, these men sold the collected crude rubber to investors or their agents in Belem, the largest city at the mouth of the Amazon and capital of the vast state of Pará. By 1880, foreign buyers, both British and American, set up offices in Belem to purchase large orders of what they dubbed Pará rubber from the merchant houses there.

International markets for Pará rubber expanded rapidly after the late 1880s, led by the newly booming tire industry. In 1900 the Amazon basin produced 25,000 metric tons of rubber; by 1909 that figure rose to 40,000 tons. Demand rose even faster, so prices doubled in that decade to almost $3 per pound. Market prospects like these were enough to give the jungle itself market value, for whoever owned the land might hope to control the profits. The remote interior of Amazonia underwent a boom in speculative land sales in the 1890s, as soon as the Brazilian government adopted simplified land registration procedures.

Some of the companies in Belem came to be controlled by foreigners who had larger capital reserves than local people. But foreign speculations never succeeded in controlling the upriver networks, which were dominated by the new Portuguese-speaking land barons. The foreigners' failure was not for any lack of grandiose ambitions. In the dawn of the new century, a group of American rubber manufacturers organized the United States Rubber Company, dreaming that they could monopolize Amazonian production. Assuming that a big enough barrel of cash could enable them to dominate the trade, they planned to raise $50 million in capital and buy out Amazon Steam, the only steamboat company that was plying the river as yet. They hoped the Pará state government would pay them navigation subsidies in rubber lands, not cash. But their Brazilian competitors, much better placed politically, prevented that from happening. This was yet another grandiose failure of ambitious Yankee investors who did not understand that they knew nothing about the jungle or its people, or that this mattered.[3]

In the face of inefficiency, corruption, and ethnic antagonisms in the business of collecting wild rubber, British strategists attempted to grow Hevea in dense plantations. In Brazil they could not conquer the tree's fatal disease, the South American Leaf Blight, a fungus that had co-evolved with Hevea in the forest. Hevea trees had survived over the millennia by growing widely dispersed among other species; capitalist concentration of production demanded the opposite. Leaf Blight was as impossible to control on plantations as was Panama Disease in concentrated banana groves.

When foreign business interests learned how to cultivate Hevea, they succeeded not in its Amazonian home but in Europe's colonies in tropical Asia,
where climate conditions were favorable for intensive plantation of rubber
trees and its worst disease did not follow it. Moreover, in Southeast Asia colonial investors could dominate political conditions and the workforce was
much easier to control. In the early 1870s the British succeeded in taking
Hevea seedlings out of Brazil, first to Kew Botanical Garden in London and
from there to their colonies of Ceylon and Malaya. They established their first
full-scale plantations in 1900, and the young trees began to produce latex in
commercial amounts in 1910. The resulting transformation of world rubber
markets was sudden and decisive. By 1912 Brazilian rubber sales on the world
market collapsed, however, and the entire network of Brazilian penetration
into the interior of Amazonia fell to pieces. The great forest remained largely
intact, though the population of Pará state stabilized thereafter at double or
triple what it had been in 1870. And the global extraction system had forced
many Indians into the money economy. Like the great rainforest that supported them, their rhythms of life had begun to be undermined.

AMERICAN RUBBER CORPORATIONS IN INDONESIA

As soon as it seemed clear that the British experiment with plantation rubber
in Southeast Asia was viable, American companies joined them, happy to be
out of the Brazilian quagmire. They were following in the wake of four centuries of European adventures in the colonial extraction of Southeast Asia's
natural wealth. Rubber embodied the American discovery that tropical agricultural products in Southeast Asia had value independent of trade with
China. At the end of the eighteenth century, American voyages into the
Pacific and to the China coast had not stopped at the latitude of their future
Philippine colony. They reached still farther south into the East Indies. Thus
the American navigators and their sponsors on the New England coast were
drawn into the current of several centuries of Europe's romantic fascination
and avaricious eagerness, the two-pronged imperial impetus that transformed
the ecology of tropical Southeast Asia.

The American role in changing the face of those lands was subordinate to
the colonial grip of the Dutch and British. But shortly after 1900 the clearing
of Southeast Asian moist forests became one of the major tropical regions that
American industrial wealth helped to transform. American rubber purchasers

began to fear that the British might establish a monopoly of global supplies through their new colonial plantations in Ceylon and Malaya, possibly in conjunction with Dutch interests in the East Indies. American rubber companies therefore began searching for their own production sites in Southeast Asia in 1907. The political umbrella of the U.S. colony in the Philippines might have saved them the trouble of negotiating a secondary position in European colonies. But the 1902 law restricting purchase of more than 1,024 hectares of public lands discouraged them from exploration there. Instead, they looked to new frontiers of capitalist agriculture in Dutch and British colonies.

Sumatra became the center of U.S. operations, on the agricultural and demographic frontier. Sumatra is a massive island, 1,085 miles long and an average of 185 miles wide, lying across the narrow Straits of Malacca from peninsular Malaysia. The island hangs from the Barisan mountain range, which falls sharply southwestward into the open depths of the Indian Ocean. To the northeast the mountains fall more gradually into wide coastal mangrove marshes before subsiding into the sea. Several short rivers drain the hill forests into the Java Sea.[4] Until the onset of plantation agriculture in the late nineteenth century, the lowlands supported a thin population of Muslim Malay rice farmers. In the higher reaches, Batak hill tribes practiced multicrop swidden agroforestry. Local sultans, their capital towns located near the mouths of the short rivers, skimmed tax revenues from the export of forest products, but they had little effective control over the land and its people.

Dutch pioneers did the initial work of taming tropical Nature and its human inhabitants on Sumatra before American investors appeared. The Dutch experimented with various crops—tobacco, tea, rubber, coffee, sisal, agave, and palm oil. In 1863 Jacobus Nienhuys planted the first export tobacco on the Deli River. This became the famous Deli leaf, the world's most desired cigar wrapper. The first shipment arrived in New York by the early 1870s, to great American interest, as an alternative to wrapper leaf from the hills of western Cuba. American imports were shipped under Dutch control through Amsterdam and Rotterdam. The highest figure for U.S. imports was in 1920, when Americans bought 9,823,000 pounds of tobacco, for $17,616,066. Amounts and values declined thereafter, until in 1959 the amount was only 19,756 pounds, costing $131,466.[5]

Land clearing in Sumatra was made possible in part because of these American purchases. Sumatran tobacco plantations replaced largely natural forests.

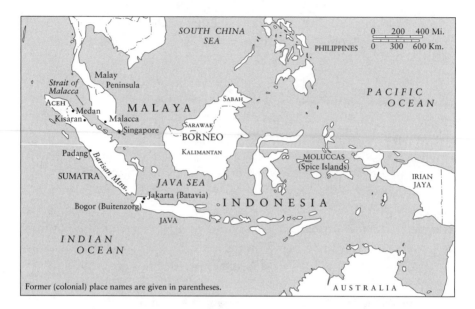

Southeast Asia

The sultans saw the European interest as an opportunity to extend their authority. With Dutch support they mounted pacification expeditions against the Batak hill tribes, a process complete by the 1890s. The Dutch planters, at least nominally members of the Reformed Church, set about to impart European values of social production into what they saw as degenerate, slothful cultures. Tys Volker wrote for the planters' association, "The conditions prevailing in these overwhelmingly Batak districts were, to put it frankly, bad. The natives were degenerated and enslaved to gambling and opium, even women and children being gambled for."[6] Through its tobacco planters the expansionist Dutch regime brought what it projected to the world as peace, human dignity, and prosperity. The planters conquered the wilderness, established orderly agriculture, and civilized the towns.

> The visitor to the modern "greater Deli," witnessing the intense activity of this region and the present day run for the extreme South, can hardly imagine that this region, where in every respect welfare and prosperity are prevalent, where the native population is very well-off, where no pauperism exists, was 65 years

ago nothing but untrodden primeval forest, with here and there settlements of native Bataks and Malays [who have] come as colonists.[7]

By 1900 tobacco cultivation had expanded so far that it spread beyond good tobacco soils; the new plantations were proving unprofitable. Planters began looking for alternatives; first they interplanted coffee with tobacco. But when Indonesian coffee was undercut by Brazilian competition, the planters desperately needed to find a new crop with promising markets in Europe and North. In an ironic trade with Brazil, that product would be rubber.

The British had begun the first Hevea plantations in Malaya in 1876. The success of those dense groves convinced the Dutch to begin their first large plantation of Hevea, in 1906, on Sumatra. But successful rubber production would need massive capital, large acreage, secure land tenure, and a seven-year wait for the first latex. Local lords could negotiate leases for agricultural land directly with Western firms. The standard lease was for seventy-five years, with high payments to the sultans, reinforcing their power and wealth over the peasantry.[8] Virtually all land that foreign investors thought was worth cultivating was leased to them; very little was left to the peasant population for meeting its own subsistence needs. This disregard for the rural population's needs would work against both the planters and the sultans by the 1930s, when organized protests by food-deprived peasants began the disruption of the estates that crippled them in the 1940s and 1950s.

The environmental consequences of the new plantation system would prove to be equally broad. The clearing of natural forest was only the core of the transformation. The web of transport and settlement infrastructure that supported the plantations, and the work force of imported Javanese and Chinese coolies, produced far more wide-ranging impacts across the Deli region. The population of the East Coast region rose from 568,400 in 1905 to 1,693,200 in 1930.

Massive forest clearances commenced immediately after 1900. From 435 acres under rubber in 1902, the figure grew exponentially, to over 320,000 acres planted in rubber groves by 1914. For operations on this scale, the Dutch planters required additional capital. Fortunately for them, the United States Rubber Company was pulling out of Brazil. U.S. Rubber was about to transform itself from a commercial rubber buyer to an estate manager. It first attempted to centralize purchasing, with agencies in Belem and Manaus, London, Singapore, and Colombo, but this was insufficient.[9] Searching to develop its own supplies in tropical Asia, in 1907 it sent Stuart Hotchkiss, scion of a family of Massachusetts rubber processors, to survey the potential of the Deli region. Acting on his recommendation in 1910, the company purchased a fifty-two-year lease of a 14,511-acre Dutch estate, the New Asahan Tobacco Company, which had repeatedly tried and failed to cultivate Deli wrapper on soils unsuitable for tobacco.[10] By 1913 U.S. Rubber added several other estates for a total of 75,947 acres, suddenly the largest single holding in the world designated for rubber cultivation. At its greatest extent, just over 100,000 acres or 150 square miles of property were held by its new subsidiary, the Dutch American Plantation Company. "Hoppum," as the company was referred to throughout the rubber world, was incorporated in Amsterdam for administrative convenience. Dutch investors bought shares in Hoppum, though U.S. Rubber maintained American financial control; supervisors in Medan were a mixture of Dutch and Americans. This made it possible for the United States to free itself of its increasingly noncompetitive Brazilian sources.

By 1913 Hoppum cleared and planted 32,500 acres. A year later, as war broke out in Europe, Hoppum built the world's largest rubber processing plant on the coast southeast of Medan. Responding to escalating wartime prices, Hoppum converted 14,200 acres more from forest to plantation in 1915. By that time fourteen thousand imported Chinese and Javanese indentured workers toiled under ninety European and American supervisory staff.

The first Sumatran rubber shipments to the United States were made in 1915, via the new Panama Canal. Now U.S. Rubber could ship its product directly to the United States from Deli, rather than through the older European entrepôts of Batavia and Singapore. Three other U.S. companies soon joined the Sumatran adventure, led by Goodyear, the United States' largest tire producer, which began purchasing crude rubber at Medan in 1916. In 1917 Goodyear followed U.S. Rubber into estate management, leasing a 16,700-acre concession covered almost entirely by primary forest. In three years it was cleared and planted in long straight rows of Hevea.

As one American commentator bluntly stated, "Capital development . . . turned the East Coast from a jungle into a vast commercial garden."[11] The U.S. Rubber Company controlled 88,000 acres of that land, as well as 22,000 more across the strait in Malaya. The major corporations brought with them an entirely new scale of technology. As Stuart Hotchkiss observed, "Preparatory to establishing a rubber plantation, it is of course necessary to make an exhaustive study of the country from the technical standpoint of soil conditions, rainfall, freedom from wind, transportation and labor supply."[12] As head of U.S. Rubber's operations there, Hotchkiss brought in plant geneticists and soil specialists, who organized careful surveys of soils, built bunds to inhibit erosion, and manured intensively to maintain soil fertility. However, not all of their imported techniques fit Sumatra's circumstances. They removed all stumps from cleared fields and insisted on clean weeding of the rubber groves. This thoroughness in the early years guaranteed a degree of soil depletion that had never occurred in pre-European land tilling systems. By the 1920s the plantations were obliged to supplement the soil's natural nutrients with chemical fertilizers.

The entire system rested on an elaborate strategy of labor control. The Dutch first relied on indentured Chinese coolies for their tobacco plantations in the 1870s; this system expanded directly into the first generation of rubber plantations. After 1920 most indentured laborers on the estates were Javanese landless peasants, imported on contract in large numbers. Batak tribals of the North Sumatra hills were prohibited from settling in the plantation region, though they had begun expanding beyond their easily tilled valley lands several decades before, and had begun migrating toward the new international economy. They knew the land, and thus could not be reliably controlled, in contrast to imported coolies on contract.

Labor conditions in the pioneer decades were notorious, as they were on many forest frontiers of the new global economy. The conquest of the tropical forest entailed a heavy toll of life and health from the coolie laborers. The colonial planters organized an essentially industrial labor discipline. In the early years they imported only men, whom they housed in barracks. The laborers were called out every day at dawn and worked as long as the sun shone, cutting and burning the forest, planting seedlings in the fires' ashes, weeding the young plantations as long as sunshine reached the understory, and tapping the mature trees. Controlling all aspects of their workers' lives, the planters also provided markets, mosques for the Javanese laborers, and even athletic fields and prostitutes for any men who had energy left after the grueling day's work.[13]

The Chinese were alien to that landscape and few could hope to escape these rigors until their contracts were completed. Those who attempted to leave were pursued by Karo Batak tribals whom the planters rewarded for their capture. They were then lashed severely and returned to their barracks. After the 1920s, when the Dutch plantations began to bring Javanese women as well as men to Sumatra, the managers reluctantly allocated small plots to the worker families to use for kitchen gardens. How much this extended the area of forest clearance is unclear, one of the shadowy peripheral impacts of the plantation system.[14]

A congressional investigation of tropical plantation labor in the mid-1920s resulted in a warning to the American companies not to emulate their European colonial compatriots' systematic brutality. Like their counterparts in the banana business, Hoppum and Goodyear provided better housing than on the Dutch plantations and subsidized food. Perhaps most important for their own interest, the companies set up basic medical care (especially to control labor-depleting diseases such as malaria). Jungle clearing produced widespread malaria, where little had previously existed; the sun could now penetrate to the ground, and stagnant pools of water proliferated. The worst incidence of malaria was in newly planted groves; the older, cleaner estates reduced malaria from over 4 percent to under 1.2 percent.

In the immediate postwar depression, crude rubber prices in Singapore, Amsterdam, and London collapsed, falling from a wartime high of over $1 per pound to $.115 in the summer of 1921. The British rubber corporations in Malaya and Ceylon, which had built up large stocks from their first generation of trees, were faced with fiscal disaster. So Winston Churchill, then British Colonial Secretary, appointed Sir James Stevenson, president of Johnnie Walker Distillery, to head a review commission. The Stevenson Plan of 1922 restricted production on Malayan rubber estates and prohibited planting of new higher yielding trees.

But the Dutch refused to join the system of production controls. In the United States, Henry Ford's new assembly lines were producing an automobile production boom. Moreover, Goodyear's newly introduced balloon tires, which gave a more comfortable ride to the mobile middle class, required 30 percent more rubber than the old high pressure tires. In combination, these factors resulted in a rising international rubber price of $.35 per pound by early 1923. By then, American plantations on Sumatra were coming into full production, but American demand was expanding so rapidly in the era of the Model T that U.S. companies had to buy most of their supplies from others, through their purchasing offices in Batavia and Singapore. By mid-1925 the international price spiraled upward to $1.23. The Stevenson Plan restrictions were still enforced in Malaya, however, especially the ban on new plantings.

American importers were determined to free themselves of European-controlled sources. In addition, American attitudes were generally hostile to any regulation of free markets. Herbert Hoover, then secretary of commerce, denounced the Stevenson Plan's restrictions, as severe violations of free trade. Hotchkiss, on the spot in Sumatra, was guardedly favorable to the Stevenson strategy, for in 1923 U.S. Rubber reported $128 million losses from the collapse of unregulated prices. But rubber company executives shared Hoover's view. Their resistance to the British strategy paid off, for American imports of crude rubber rose from 692 million pounds in 1923 to 888 million pounds two years later.[15]

In 1927 Goodyear leased another huge estate southeast of Medan: 28,600 acres, all virgin jungle except for a small area that had been developed by a former Japanese lessee. Goodyear mobilized sixteen thousand workers to clear that forest and create Wingfoot Plantation, which ultimately boasted 40,028 acres. By 1927 the total impact on the lowlands of Sumatra was over 536,000 acres cleared of forest and planted to Hevea, producing 63,510 tons for export. In 1933, at the height of their operations, American holdings in Sumatra totaled 218,393 acres, including 131,000 acres actually planted.

In a botanical breakthrough of major importance, Hoppum pioneered a new technique of bud-grafting high yielding varieties on older, hardy rootstock. Planting with high-yielding clones began on a large scale in 1925. In order to approach the full genetic potential of the new trees, Hoppum also imported large amounts of American fertilizers. By 1925 the United States supplied 75 percent of all sulfate of ammonia imported into Sumatra. The new trees more than doubled latex yield. This was a decisive step toward the extraordinary increase in productivity that the growers ultimately achieved — more than ten times what the first trees yielded. Intensification, rather than clearing more forest, had become the corporations' major strategy.

Genetic and chemical innovations alone, though, could not solve all the problems on the estates. The loss of forest cover was not the only environmental cost of the new agroindustry. Deforested watersheds were running dry after the monsoon rains ended. So the companies had to build an elaborate irrigation system for the dry season. This turned the planters' attention to the

condition of forested watersheds in the mountains above their estates. In the
early 1920s the planters' association began to demand that the colonial government restrict tribal swidden systems in the forest, though they themselves
had slashed and burned vastly greater acreage of forest than the indigenous
farmers above. Ironically, the rubber planters were emerging as the first forest
conservationists in Indonesia. But as with many Western foresters and conservationists they blamed marginal peasants and tribals for their problems.

The boom years of the 1920s also saw a great expansion of small-holder
rubber production on the periphery of the Sumatran estates. Malay farmers
learned that they could grow Hevea trees as their major cash crop just as competitively as the estate planters, integrating at most a few hectares of rubber
into the varied subsistence production of their annual and tree crops. A cen-
sus in the late 1930s indicated that over one million hectares had been cleared
by small holders, who tapped their own trees and processed the latex into
sheets of semirefined rubber, which they sold to Chinese middlemen.[16]

During the Depression, rubber was as much at the mercy of collapsing
demand and prices as any tropical crop. Prices on the New York market hit
their lowest point, $.027 per pound, in June 1932, as supplies piled up in ware-
houses. Faced with precipitous price drops, the corporations chose to increase
production because the new bud-grafted product was just reaching the market.
In order to meet this crisis, the major producers formed the International Rubber Regulation Commission (IRRC) in 1934. By then there was a much higher
degree of common interest between the Europeans and Americans and common policies could be enforced more effectively. The commission imposed
cutbacks in production even on American acreage in Sumatra. The IRRC
allowed no new planting of any sort, and limited replanting to 20 percent of
existing acreage, for bud-grafted clones.

By the mid-1930s, as the Depression's worst effects weakened and consumer markets began to expand again, U.S. imports slowly responded, rising
from 427,000 tons in 1932 to 496,000 in 1936. By 1940–41 American firms
produced 20 percent of all Sumatra rubber, which accounted for 14 percent of
U.S. imports from the Netherlands East Indies. These were the highest yielding years of all. The companies continued to ship until March 1942, when
Japanese armies destroyed Wingfoot Plantation's headquarters.

In addition to the economic roller coaster, the Depression years produced
wrenching social and environmental disruptions in the Deli region. The Euro-

pean planters laid off many workers in the early 1930s, forcing them off the plantations and onto adjacent lands. On or off the plantations they became squatters, struggling to keep from starving. They cleared small patches of forest or cut down rubber trees in their search for cropland. Conflict between estate managers and squatters meant that land use on the periphery of the estates was uncoordinated and changeable. Long-term settled tilling of the soil was out of the question.

By the time of the Japanese invasion, Sumatra was running an annual deficit of at least 120,000 tons of rice. In the naval and commercial uproar of the following months, rice imports ended and large-scale starvation threatened. Japanese policy encouraged peasants to occupy the tobacco and rubber estates, cut down the older rubber trees, and grow their own food. Many plantations were taken over by local warlords and labor unions. Three years of war and Japanese occupation, followed by four years of struggle for Indonesian independence, left the plantations badly battered and their former workers in turmoil. A very different era in Indonesian and global rubber production would emerge in the 1950s.

FIRESTONE IN LIBERIA: LAND EXPLOITATION IN WEST AFRICA

Unlike any of the other primary products from tropical trees and plants, rubber came to be considered a strategic material in the minds of American military and foreign policy planners. The term "strategic materials" arose during World War I, denoting those raw materials that were considered critical for military preparedness, and the sources of which any powerful country had to control if it was to survive international conflict. In contrast to nonstrategic commodities, the United States and other major industrialized countries willingly put their full military and diplomatic machine behind the corporations that mined, pumped, or produced the strategic resources. The list was primarily metals but it included petroleum and rubber. From World War I onward, therefore, rubber imports assumed a strategic priority beyond any other tropical crop.

American planners saw that since rubber was a strategic raw material it was urgent to break out of British domination of international supplies and prices. By the early 1920s Americans were purchasing 85 percent of the world's cars and three-fourths of global rubber production, of which 80 percent was for automobile tires.[17]

Herbert Hoover, then secretary of commerce, encouraged rubber conservation at home and development of non-Southeast Asian sources, and he personally urged the Dutch not to cooperate with their British competitors.[18] Harvey Firestone was already working to break British domination of the world rubber market. During the war he had presided over the Rubber Association of America, which allotted the rubber that the British had allowed the United States to import.[19] Later he observed bluntly, "When the war broke out, the United States was building two great industries. When the war was over, we had built them. . . . I mean the automobile industry and the tire making industry. An automobile without a tire is useless; and so is a tire without an automobile. And yet these two great industries depend absolutely upon the will of foreign countries for their lives. They depend on rubber, and no rubber is grown in the United States." Firestone was unwilling to tolerate such a situation. In 1923 he appealed to Congress for support in identifying tropical locations outside Europe's colonies in Southeast Asia. Firestone argued that strategic priorities and corporate interest were identical: "If our business were to perform a public service, it was our duty to keep open the way to the sources of raw material."[20] Congress agreed, funding a global Rubber Survey, to identify locations around the tropical world where rubber might be grown beyond the reach of the British Empire.

Firestone ordered his manager in Singapore to organize teams of specialists to study possibilities in the Philippines. He personally lobbied Congress to force the Philippine Congress to set aside the 1,024-hectare limit on foreign land purchases. Firestone insisted that rubber was a different matter from sugar. "If America is to attain any degree of independence in its source of supply of rubber as well as other materials, which are now in the hands of foreign monopoly, our government must assure the industries interested that it will lend its utmost assistance in protecting our investments."[21] But the Philippine Congress refused, so Firestone turned his attention to tropical America and Africa, coordinating closely with Hoover.[22]

Firestone then set his intentions on Liberia, where an early American experiment in growing Hevea rubber had paralleled the European efforts in Southeast Asia. In 1910 an American entrepreneur had established a plantation called Mount Barclay. He abandoned the operation in 1914 but, even a decade later, though overgrown with secondary vegetation, those acres still had healthy trees, which could be tapped. Liberia was an improbable country.

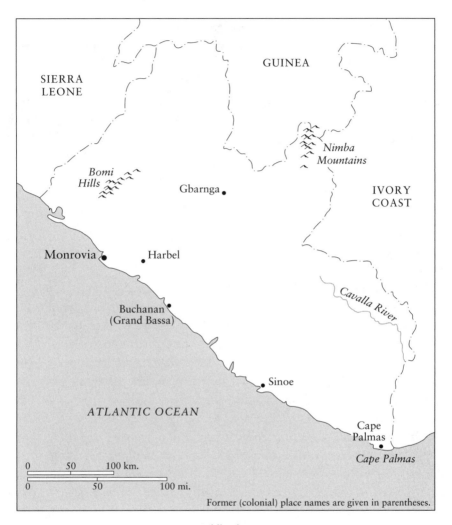

Liberia

In 1816 the American Colonization Society was incorporated by an alliance of Northern white American clergymen and businessmen and southern slave owners to return freed slaves to their "ancestral homeland." Their aims were mixed: to Christianize the region, begin American trade with West Africa, and eliminate free black people from the United States.

On the west coast of Africa the American Colonization Society purchased 43,000 square miles of land from local ethnic groups and established a base, calling it Monrovia. What was to become Liberia lay on 350 miles of Atlantic coastline. The shoreline had no deep-water ports, was heavily forested and marked by lagoons and the tidal flats of a series of small rivers. Sandy soils supported dense mangrove forests. Inland, primary forest was dotted with many patches of "low bush," scrub secondary vegetation resulting from local villagers' shifting cultivation of crops.[23] The rivers that flowed down from rolling hills in the interior were navigable for only a few miles inland before shallows and rapids made it impossible even for small craft to float. Even the immediate inland reaches were navigable only during the rainy season, from June to October. Inland, the Nimba hills rise to over five thousand feet, supporting a forest where many species of flora and fauna thrived, stretching as much as 150 miles.

Numerous ethnic groups had emigrated from the savannas of the continent's interior over the previous several centuries.[24] They grew upland rice interplanted with cassava, and a variety of vegetable and fruit crops, moving gradually from one location to another. Those who controlled the hills discouraged outsiders from traveling along the forest trails. Even by the 1920s there was no railroad to the interior and few good roads were built.

Facing this prospect, the immigrants from the United States settled only along the coast, despite the constant threat of malaria there. In 1848 they declared the Republic of Liberia; the newly invented country was dominated thereafter by the Americo-Liberians, whose ancestors were from various African countries but not this coast. They were townsmen and traders, not field hands; none knew African crops or farming methods or wanted to eat African foods. Their American background held them together and apart from those they confronted; they assumed their cultural superiority to the people they confronted. The Americo-Liberians' national motto was "The love of liberty brought us here." But that liberty was for themselves as a group, not for the varied Africans whose homelands they partially controlled. Their domination of the entire country, especially the hinterland away from the coast, would ultimately depend on international capitalist investors.

Coastal and hinterland tribes had a long history of rivalry. The coastal tribes had been involved in slave raids inland for European buyers and they maintained a monopoly of trade with inland areas, keeping foreigners from leaving the coastal littoral. In contrast, the tribes of the interior were shifting agriculturalists. Aside from some connections to inland trade routes they did not live in a money economy and they had no conception of private property. The land was used collectively by household and village groups for sustenance, not owned by individuals. No land surveys were ever carried out.

After 1830 when settlers tried to buy land from them, their chiefs sold or leased land several times over, not understanding what the outsiders meant by purchase. The newcomers faced uncertain descriptions of land, rival tribal claims dating from long before the new immigrants' arrival, and vague language on sale deeds that did not distinguish between individual rights and sovereignty. The hinterland became a zone of intensified interethnic conflict. The American Colonization Society tried to prohibit the settlers from directly purchasing land from the hill people, but speculators often evaded the prohibition, in hopes of growing coffee or other crops for export.[25]

A nation-state was in gestation, and its infancy was turbulent. Politics were largely the business of the American immigrants. In 1869 the True Whig Party won the Liberian presidential election and stayed in power for most of the following one hundred years. The government dealt with the hill region through indirect rule, maneuvering with local chiefs. It taxed inland Africans for development funds and forced chiefs to sign away title to numerous tracts of land. In response the tribes of the hinterland launched a series of ethnically based riots and rebellions from the 1880s onward. These were fueled by a long international depression in which many Americo-Liberian crop plantations collapsed and coastal merchants were ruined.

Then the race for rubber reached West Africa. In 1906 the Liberian Rubber Corporation, a subsidiary of the British firm Dunlop, opened the first interior rubber plantations. Fearing that Europeans might entirely displace American interests in Monrovia, Booker T. Washington, Liberia's most prominent booster in the United States, convinced President Theodore Roosevelt to guarantee Liberian independence. In early 1909 Secretary of State Elihu Root pronounced, "Liberia is an American colony. . . . Our nation rests under the highest obligation to assist them toward the maintenance of free, orderly, and prosperous civil society."[26] The Liberian government had already requested U.S. support to maintain its independence from the European empires.

In 1912 American bankers took over a British loan when the Liberian government defaulted. After that the United States effectively controlled the Liberian economy. Americans were not interested in a formal empire anywhere in Africa, but control of one region of Africa's wet tropical zone might

well suit American commercial and industrial interests. Liberia remained a
backwater into the 1920s. But gradually the Liberian government established
control over inland areas,[27] supported by Harvey Firestone. Once again the
foreign corporate magnate and the local elite would work hand in hand in the
conquest of the land and its ethnically varied inhabitants. In 1924 Firestone's
team studied Liberia, focusing on the neglected rubber plantation. They found
promising conditions, and reported:

> The land for the most part is well drained, much of it consisting of gently slop-
> ing hills with intervening wide, winding depressions. Forests cover almost the
> entire area, but there is comparatively a small amount of "big bush" or virgin
> jungle. This is due, for the most part, to the rotating system of cultivation prac-
> tised by the natives for centuries. . . . This system has not robbed the soil of its
> fertility, and at the same time has made the work of clearing for rubber planta-
> tions less expensive because secondary-growth timber is much easier to remove
> than virgin jungle.[28]

Firestone immediately hired five hundred workers on the old 2,000-acre
Mount Barclay plantation, fifteen miles inland from the coast. They cleared
the brush from between the lines of rubber trees and began tapping. But an
operation that small was only a pilot project; Firestone envisioned supplying a
major portion of the booming American rubber economy from Liberia. This
entailed elaborate negotiations with the Liberian government. The U.S. government stepped in on Firestone's behalf. The American consul managed the
discussions and Washington hinted that major financial support might be
available to strengthen the Monrovia regime.[29]

In 1926 the Liberian government granted Firestone an enormous concession: 1 million acres of land for ninety-nine years. In return, Firestone would
build port and harbor facilities, roads, hospitals, sanitation, and hydropower.
Firestone would also provide medical staff, a sanitary engineer, a mechanical
engineer, an architect and builder, a soil expert, and a forester. This was an
arrangement clearly in the tradition of private chartered companies in the
European colonies of Africa, which were appointed by the regime to provide
the accoutrements of organizational and technological modernity. In return,
the companies were guaranteed wide-ranging power and profit.

In order to exploit an estate of such a vast scale Firestone projected $100
million capital costs. In 1934 the first trees were tapped. Rubber soon pro-

duced over 50 percent of Liberia's exports in value. By the mid-1930s Firestone was the country's principal employer, with over ten thousand workers, a figure that grew to twenty-five thousand by 1946. This single foreign concession transformed labor patterns and rural society over an entire geographical region. Previously, the hill cultures had been subsistence farmers, uninterested in wage labor. As one observer noted, "Work was largely seasonal and intensely social; work was performed collectively for family or village ends. In general, a non-individualistic ethic resulted from the traditional kinship system."[30] The rubber baron was transforming them into the capitalist mode of existence.

From the beginning, Firestone used the Liberian government to solve his labor recruitment problems. Laws administered by the Department of Interior enhanced the powers of local chiefs, assigning them recruitment quotas and paying them for sending workers to the plantations. A Firestone agent walked into the forested interior with a government representative, from one village to the next, to negotiate quotas, pay the chiefs, and transport the workers to the plantations. The chiefs selected the men who would go for a minimum two-month work period, which was often extended to several periods.

Firestone's officers deliberately recruited among all the interior tribes, pursuing a policy of social homogenization. They paid each chief a "dash," or gift, in the traditional manner, for allowing men to work for the outsiders; the men would return a portion of wages to their village or clan. The negotiations covered all aspects of wages, living conditions, food, and medical care. The arrangements were more flexible and noncoercive than labor recruitment in the French and Belgian colonies of central Africa at the same time; workers could leave at any time, and the chiefs might require them to return home for farm work or other responsibilities.[31] Firestone himself described the recruitment process rather complacently:

> When an agent has assembled a group of natives—let us say about 200—they start for the plantations accompanied by a 'messenger' who represents their chief by supervising the welfare of his people. This trip along a forest trail, in some instances several hundred miles long, is a great adventure. Many of the men never traveled that far from home before.[32]

But the new system, which merged the power of the corporation and the authority of the government, was open to abuse. In later years, an American investigation came to a rather different conclusion but rationalized the system as the unfortunate cost of social and economic modernization.

> The recruitment practices for concessions are not nearly as extreme as those exposed during the forced-labor scandal of the late 1920s, or, indeed, as some present-day abuses. However, there is no denying the coercive features of recruitment. The chiefs . . . levy fines (and, we are told, more drastic penalties) on their recalcitrant subjects. Despite the feudal cast of the system with its abuses and defects, it probably gave initial impetus to the creation of a wage-earning labor force. The dislocations have undoubtedly been unpleasant and painful for many, but the disruption of tribal patterns in one way or another is an inevitable consequence of development.[33]

The main plantation was headquartered at Harbel near Monrovia. Workers there were not allowed to maintain the village way of life. Only the men were brought to the vast plantation, where they lived in dormitories and ate food supplied by the company. Consequently, there was a high turnover in the labor force. A secondary plantation, on the southeastern side of the country at Cavalla, was organized along different lines. It employed three thousand workers, mostly long term, with their wives, who grew their own rice on small plots; they maintained village patterns of social life. Either way, labor troubles were frequent. Among the coastal Kru there had already been periodic resistance over payment of the government's hut tax. Inland, there was a traditional pawning system, in which an impoverished man could indenture himself or a relative to a chief until a debt was paid. Often this dragged on for years. In places, there was even a continuation of some semislavery, just as there was elsewhere in nearby European colonies.

In 1930 the League of Nations appointed the Christy Commission, which substantiated many allegations. President Charles King broke off diplomatic relations with the United States in anger at the challenge to his authority, but he was forced to resign in late 1930. King's successor, Edwin Barclay, continued to repress unrest, both among his own America-Liberian critics and the ethnic minorities. The United States reestablished diplomatic relations in 1935, and Firestone continued to prosper through that alliance. As an environmental consequence, vast acreage was transformed from second-growth forest and cropped fields into massive groves of rubber trees, which tolerated few other species of plants or animals.

WORLD WAR II: STRATEGIC CRISIS AND THE RISE OF SYNTHETIC RUBBER

In the late 1930s, as war loomed again in Europe and the Pacific, diversification of rubber sources became an urgent strategic concern of the U.S. government. Direct confrontation with Japan over Southeast Asia's strategic materials began to accelerate. Japanese leaders feared an American and British embargo, especially of aviation fuel, unless Japan left China; Japan wanted the Netherlands East Indies as a petroleum and rubber source. The American Consul General in Batavia cabled Washington, asserting that 92 percent of the U.S. supply of natural rubber was at stake.

The U.S. government had been attempting to stockpile rubber from Southeast Asia for some time before that, but Great Britain had been only partially cooperative with the American goals. At the end of 1939 the United States had less than a three months' supply of rubber on hand and attempted to expand purchases from the International Rubber Regulation Committee. When Nazi Germany's invasions of adjacent countries began in late 1939, the British-controlled Committee began to loosen its restrictions. Nonetheless, by May 1940 the United States still had only five months' supply of tin and three months' supply of rubber in stockpile.

In June 1940 the Reconstruction Finance Corporation was empowered to create satellite purchasing corporations for strategic materials. It created four of them, including the Rubber Reserve Company. By early 1941 stockpiling accelerated. In July 1941, President Franklin Roosevelt created the Economic Defense Board under Vice President Henry Wallace. But in mid-December, even after the Japanese attack on Pearl Harbor, it still had only 30 percent of its rubber target, and less than that of various minerals.[34]

Firestone's production in Liberia was steadily accelerating, but it never accounted for more than 7 percent of the enormous American market. Only a qualitative breakthrough in rubber production could solve the dilemma. Fortunately for the war effort—and in the longer run for the remaining rainforest reserves of the tropical world—a new source of rubber, synthetic rubber derived from petroleum, became available as the war continued, transforming the entire industry.

From the 1860s onward, European chemists had been attempting to synthesize rubber from a wide variety of source materials.[35] The essential rubber compound, which was called isoprene, could be distilled from turpentine, at least into an elastic mass. Collaboration developed between the British and German petrochemical industries, until it broke down during World War I. The Allies blockaded German imports of tropical natural rubber during the war. In desperation Germany managed to produce 150 tons per month of methyl rubber, but in that form it lacked stability. The vehicles' tires were made of solid methyl rubber, which lost its shape when the vehicles were parked for any length of time. So the Weimar regime dropped the effort to synthesize rubber from petroleum.

Meanwhile, in the United States, DuPont succeeded in polymerizing a form of rubber that it called Neoprene. Competitive German efforts revived by the late 1920s, as the country attempted to become strategically independent of imported natural rubber. In a parallel effort, I. G. Farben (IG) and Standard Oil of New Jersey negotiated a contract to develop synthetic petrol. IG was already making synthetic rubber from acetylene. In 1930 IG produced acetylene from natural gas; in a stroke of great good fortune for Standard Oil and American strategic interests, this new product was covered in the basic information-sharing contract. Standard's ambition was to "supply the United States with a synthetic rubber which would completely replace the imported natural prod-uct."[36] So it was interested in IG's new Buna-S rubber, which was related to the acetylene process, though by 1933 trials were still not encouraging.

After the Nazi regime took power, it imported natural rubber from Brazil and elsewhere but wanted independence from tropical products. It pushed improvements of Buna, but tire treads stripped from their casings when Buna was used heavily. By 1939, at the beginning of the war, Germany had improved Buna enough to meet military requirements, and was able to use it for many wartime purposes.

As international military tensions rose during the 1930s, Roosevelt's strate-gic planners watched German and Japanese developments, realizing that the United States was just as vulnerable to disruption of natural rubber supplies as its potential enemies. As early as 1934 both State Department planners and the Army and Navy Munitions Board argued that the United States must maintain a large strategic stockpile of rubber.[37] But Congress, under severe budgetary constraints during the Depression, was not interested in paying for large purchases. It was only in June 1939, with the Japanese army already occupying large areas of China and Hitler's military machine in full operation, that Congress allocated $100 million for all strategic stockpiles, including metals and other materials as well as rubber. By the end of that year, the American stock was only 125,800 tons, hardly a three-month supply. Germany already occupied Poland and Japan was threatening Southeast Asia.

In June 1940 Jesse Jones, the powerful chairman of the Reconstruction Finance Corporation, established the Rubber Reserve Company, to coordinate accelerated rubber purchases. Jones urged Congress and the oil and rubber corporations to launch a crash program to perfect synthetic rubber. This would entail an unprecedented degree of cooperation among them.

As early as 1933–34, Firestone had attempted to use DuPont's Neoprene to supply the Army with airplane tires. But these tires, like their German counterparts, wore out quickly, so the company looked elsewhere. Once again it turned to what Germany was beginning to produce. In 1938 German Buna-S had arrived in the United States, and Firestone made experimental tires that summer. In May 1939, Firestone produced Buna from its own somewhat different formula. But IG Farben held the patent to Buna-S. Fortunately, Standard Oil Company of New Jersey held a portion of the rights and was able to buy the sole rights from the Germans, which it then shared with Firestone.

In the summer of 1940 Firestone unveiled synthetic tires at the New York World's Fair. In July, Harvey Firestone Jr. conferred in Washington with the Council of National Defense. In a radio broadcast that month he asserted, in an eloquent mix of patriotism and self-promotion,

> Events abroad have swept into the discard many previous conceptions of military strategy and tactics. Speed is the very essence of modern warfare. And the realization of this significant fact emphasizes again the vital importance of rubber, the material that makes such speed possible. . . . The army tank, once a cumbersome, unwieldy vehicle which waddled along no faster than a man could walk, now races along its rubber track blocks at forty miles an hour. No longer does the infantry, footsore and weary, plod twenty-five miles a day. It covers twice that distance in a single hour in its rubber-tired cars and trucks.[38]

Simultaneously, Standard Oil continued improving Buna, now with help from Congress. In 1942 Congress passed a bill encouraging corporations to make synthetic rubber from grain alcohol. But President Roosevelt vetoed it, favoring rubber from a combination of petroleum and coal, and set up the Baruch

Committee, to oversee the accelerated research program and the use of federal funds. At a cost of $700 million, in two years the companies reached full-scale production of synthetic rubber based on petroleum and coal, making 1 million tons of rubber per year.

This was paralleled by the British rearmament program in the late 1930s. Britain struggled with severe shortages after the 1940–41 German air raids. In tropical Asia, it was then caught by surprise in early 1942 by the sudden Japanese conquest of Malaya. The only natural rubber supplies left for Churchill's compatriots were from Ceylon and India. In desperation, Britain linked with the United States for wartime supplies of synthetic rubber. The British received their first American synthetics in late 1943; by 1944 they were using 75 percent synthetics. Many products, including clothing, could not use the synthetic, but until May 1945 there were heavy pressures to broaden uses of the synthetic and reduce the percentage of natural rubber in many uses.

At end of the war, Britain rapidly reconverted to natural rubber, a process that was complete by December 1945.[39] Until 1947 the British government purchased rubber from its Southeast Asian colonies to deliver to the United States, to pay its wartime debts and accumulate dollars for reconstruction. That flow helped stabilize rubber production there and prepare the plantations for the boom era of the 1950s.

After 1945 the global rubber economy rose steadily, with the reindustrialization of Europe and Japan, and the continuing expansion of the industrial economies of the United States and elsewhere. But because of the rise of synthetic rubber, this did not result in a continuing massive removal of tropical forest. There was a rising percentage of synthetic rubber in the international economy, and particularly in the American industry, which was by far its largest component. Between 1948 and 1973 world demand for rubber rose 6 percent per year. Natural rubber production grew by 3.3 percent per year, but synthetic rubber increased nearly three times as fast, by 9.3 percent per year.[40] Synthetic rubber production passed natural rubber first in 1962; by the time of the OPEC oil price rise in 1973 it had reached a stable two-thirds of total global rubber production. This meant that the impact of a steadily rising global demand for rubber had much less cumulative effect on tropical land use than it would have, had synthetic rubber not assumed its major role because of the war. Ironically, in this case warfare had the long-term impact of limiting a single crop's destruction of a major tropical ecosystem.

The rubber industry in the United States, with its limited supply base of natural rubber, pushed for further rapid development of synthetic rubber. Until the mid-1950s most production of petroleum-based rubber was in the United States. By 1973, when global production reached 7,295,000 tons, still 40 percent was produced in the United States and Canada. The American rubber industry pursued backward integration: by the 1960s five tire companies controlled more than 55 percent of American production of the synthetic, and only one-fourth of synthetic rubber was produced by the petrochemical industry. Western Europe and Japan began large-scale production only after 1960, pursued mostly by petrochemical companies.

Supplies were influenced by the U.S. government's policy of continuing rubber stockpiling, under conditions of the Cold War and especially the Korean War, and into the years of the Vietnam War. The American stockpile rapidly increased in 1951–54 during the Korean War, reaching its highest level in 1954, at 1,250,000 tons. Then it was gradually phased out between 1959 and the mid-1970s. During the Korean War, the American government feared renewed shortages and decided to maintain a large domestic synthetic rubber industry under private ownership. In other words, rubber production continued to be influenced by the strategic materials debate. This revealed a distinctive segment of American attitudes toward tropical resources in relation to U.S. hegemony.

The primary market was for the booming civilian automotive tire industry, the core of the American Dream. Two-thirds of all rubber is used by the auto industry, and no economy or consumer culture has been so gripped by that industry as the United States. In 1950 there were 265 cars for one thousand people in the United States, 139 in Canada, 21 in West Europe, and 1 in Japan. By 1973 there were 481 in the United States, 355 in Canada, 216 in West Europe, and 134 in Japan.[41]

NATURAL RUBBER PLANTATIONS AFTER 1945

Natural rubber, not its petroleum-based competitor, is what determines land use in the tropical lowlands. Global production, after its immediate postwar low of 851,000 tons in 1946, quickly revived to 1,890,000 tons in 1950. By 1973, just at the onset of the OPEC petroleum era, the figure rose to 3,493,000 tons.[42] Much of this was produced on acreage that had already been growing rubber trees, as production became more efficient, but additional acreage was also achieved by further cutting of primary forest. Throughout the postwar years the geographical pattern of natural rubber production has remained stable; over 90 percent has been produced in tropical Asia, about 6 percent in equatorial Africa, and only 1 percent in Latin America.

The significance of these figures must be understood in terms of natural rubber's markets. The United States remained a major consumer, but not permanently the largest. In 1973 North America (including Canada), purchased 757,000 tons of natural rubber from the tropical world. By then Western Europe had surpassed it, with its far greater direct sources of post-colonial production, buying 921,000 tons. And Japan's purchases from Southeast Asia had risen to 335,000 tons, as Japan's consumer economy became a major source of pressure on tropical resource systems. The automotive industry was far and away the largest consumer of natural rubber, especially in the United States. In 1970, 400,000 tons of natural rubber went into auto, truck, and bus tires, in contrast with 168,000 tons for other uses. In contrast, the European Economic Community consumed 384,000 tons of natural rubber in tires and nearly as much, 317,000 tons, for other purposes, while Japan's pattern was similar to Europe's. The auto industry, still led by Americans, was the most insatiable consumer of all.

The difficulty American firms faced in renewing production in postwar Southeast Asia was illustrated in Indonesia, which became independent in 1949. Goodyear gradually returned to its plantations on Sumatra in the midst of both Indonesians' struggle to transform the economy from a colonial to a "national" base and peasant unions' struggle to overthrow the sultans who had collaborated with the Dutch. In persistent, bloody fighting between 1946 and 1948, most of the sultans and their immediate supporters were either killed or dispossessed and their palaces ransacked.

Several new peasant organizations led massive squatter campaigns after 1945. By the early 1950s there were approximately a half-million squatters on the Sumatran estates, many of whom claimed the right to stay based on occupancy rights in traditional *adat* law. Many had settled on the estates during the Japanese occupation; others had arrived in the turbulent patriotic struggles of the late 1940s. By 1957 they occupied at least 115,000 hectares in East Sumatra.[43] They flooded some lands for wet-rice production, thus damaging hydrological systems. Rubber production continued to be crippled.

American companies were reluctant to reopen under Dutch rule, which was tenuous at best in the fighting against Indonesian nationalists. In addition, they would have to return to over-aged stands of trees, since there had been little planting of new stock for several decades, just as everywhere else in Southeast Asia. Production figures for 1951 were half of prewar totals. But there was a price boom during the Korean War between 1950 and 1954. The war caused international prices to triple in 1951, before settling back to prewar levels three years later. American firms, seeing a major opportunity to supply their military's wartime demands, reopened their plantations on Sumatra, led by Wingfoot, in 1950–51. During the early 1950s all U.S. companies were reincorporated in Indonesia, for the Indonesian government was not hostile to them as it was to the former Dutch colonial managers. The Americans immediately began the major job of replanting the old groves with higher-yielding clones.

Sukarno's government between 1949 and 1958 was ambivalent toward foreign investors. Sukarno wanted the continuing income but he also wanted greater long-term control over the plantations. Many of the original leases were running out and the Jakarta government proposed to renew them for only thirty years. The planters resisted the proposed new dispensation, so in 1957 Jakarta confiscated all Dutch estates.

In 1958 political turmoil once again determined the flow of rubber production, when Indonesia plunged into civil war. Most estates on Sumatra were seriously damaged, as rebels tried to cut off the government's income. By then the major American rubber companies had reliable alternatives: specifically, to buy their rubber directly from middlemen in the world's great sales emporium, Singapore, which handled production from Indonesia and Malaysia. They were no longer interested in struggling with the political conditions on the estates and in Jakarta. By the early 1960s, U.S. Rubber was gone from Indonesia and Goodyear's operations were being liquidated.

The period of optimism was very brief, for in 1965 revolutionary upheaval exploded again. Several months of nationwide social chaos left some 500,000 dead. Sukarno was packed away, replaced by a military command trained in the United States, which was headed by General Suharto. The Suharto era, in sharp contrast to Sukarno's militant nationalism, welcomed foreign investment.[44] But no American rubber producers were interested. They had opted

out of the financial risks and management headaches of running the plantations. It was economically rational to wash their hands of responsibility for
any further incursions into the rainforests of Southeast Asia.

The environmental changes, which had initially been caused predominantly by lowland forest clearance for plantations, were now increasingly
entangled with the broader trend of population and land use in post-1945 East
Sumatra. The senior American specialist on Sumatra in those years, Karl
Pelzer, wrote in 1957, "There is, at this time, no shortage of land in North
Sumatra, but there is a scarcity of land which is easily accessible, well drained
and protected against destructive floods or the encroachment of tidal salt
water."[45] Over the years, the corporations had commandeered most of the
best agricultural land in lowland Sumatra. The rapidly rising population,
much of it a consequence of the rubber magnates' recruitment from Java and
beyond in earlier years, had little land available for cropping. So rubber trees,
many peasants' cash crop, spread inexorably into the forest in thousands of
tiny patches, in a way that was somewhat similar to coffee planting in Colombia. In recent years, in the higher hill areas of southeastern Sumatra, smallholder coffee has continued to play that role, as the ancient forest cover has
been replaced bit by bit.

In spite of, or perhaps because of, the political difficulties of the 1950s on Java
and Sumatra, Indonesia's rubber industry had gone through a period of expansion.[46] Over 700,000 tons of rubber were exported every year through 1958. A
new production zone was emerging on Indonesia's rainforest frontier in Kalimantan, the vast Indonesian segment of Borneo, where social conflict between
landlords and peasants had not yet developed. This was the work of small holders, as the government was sending large numbers of surplus farm laborers there
from Java, diverting the flow from its former channel to Sumatra.

After 1965, General Suharto's authoritarian regime ushered in a new era of
political stability and economic growth favorable to the export sector. The
rubber economy saw rapid expansion, almost entirely at the expense of primary forest on the formerly undeveloped outer islands, especially Kalimantan.[47] By 1973 the country's total exports were 886,000 tons. The acreage
utilized included 465,000 hectares on large estates, and over four times as
much, 1,841,000 hectares, on smallholdings. In this system productivity was
low: 382 kilograms per hectare in Indonesia in 1973, in comparison with 879
in peninsular Malaysia. This was more wasteful of land cleared from forest;

more forest had to be felled and burned in order to achieve similar production. But the profits thus gained benefited a broader spectrum of the population, instead of only the plantation elite.

Indonesian rubber relied on Singapore as its main market, as well as Malayasia's port of Penang. In a system similar to the peninsular Malaysian operations, Indonesian Chinese traders purchased semiprocessed sheets of rubber from the growers and exported them to Singapore and Penang for further processing and sale to purchasers from Europe and North America. So American and European rubber buyers were ultimately partners in the global economic web that was responsible for the accelerating transformation of Borneo's rainforest away from a natural ecosystem teeming with diverse plant and animal life.

One other important tropical source of natural rubber was still important for American markets: Liberia in West Africa. Though Liberia's production in the 1960s was only about 2 percent of the world's natural rubber supply, it provided closer to 7 percent of the United States' imports of natural rubber. Americans believed it was a showpiece of the contribution of Yankee enterprise to the development of tropical economies and societies, reassuring anyone who cared to notice that their global impact was a boon to humanity. Firestone Rubber in Liberia loomed symbolically even larger than its actual dominant impact on that small country.

LIBERIA: FIRESTONE'S HEYDAY AND DEMISE
During World War II Harvey Firestone fared well in his Liberian venture. The North African struggle between Allies and Axis gave Firestone an important role in strategic American operations. He formed a subsidiary, the Liberian Construction Corporation (LCC), and built Robertsfield Airport down the coast from Monrovia, Liberia's first major airfield. After the war LCC continued its monopoly of civil engineering works for the Liberian government, completing the first all-weather highway to the interior border. This was the first major project financed by U.S. government development aid, and it extended Firestone's reach through many aspects of Liberia's economy and society.[48]

By 1960 Harbel plantation, the largest in existence, spread over 74,000 acres, and the smaller Cavalla plantation added 13,000 more. Together they produced 80 million tons of crude rubber per year. Their production averaged

12,000 pounds per acre, equal to the highest in the world. By the early 1960s, Firestone's research division was producing new tree varieties that gave close to 30,000 pounds per acre per year, which it processed in the largest latex concentrating plant in the world.[49] In the 1950s this single corporation paid 26 percent of the Liberian government's total tax income.

Production (and ultimately resource management) depended on political stability. As in many other cases in the developing world, there was a natural convergence of interests between the foreign agroindustrial corporation and the host regime. In Liberia's postwar years much depended on William Tubman, who was president from 1943 to 1971. According to Tubman, rapid economic growth was an essential underpinning for the work of modernizing Liberian society. Furthermore, development would extend the government's control throughout the country. In the early 1950s he launched an Open Door economic policy, encouraging foreign companies beyond just Firestone. By the mid-1960s Tubman gave forty major concessions and many smaller ones to foreign corporations, for exploiting the country's land and mineral resources. Several of the earliest and most massive contracts went to members of the inner circle of rubber and other strategic interests in the United States.

Major new concessions to American firms began in 1947, when Tubman granted a lease of up to 150,000 acres meant for growing Robusta coffee, cocoa, and oil palm, plus other possible mining rights, to the Liberia Company, a corporation organized for the occasion by Edward Stettinius, who had visited Liberia during the war and had seen the country's natural resource potential. After Stettinius's death, Juan Tripp became president of the company; Tripp was also president of Pan Am World Airways. The Liberia Company created the 25,000-acre Cocopa Plantation in the interior and began planting rubber in 1956. By the mid-1960s it was producing coffee and cocoa, as well as 5,500 acres of rubber there. Like Firestone, it also incorporated lumber operations with its land clearing operations: by 1960 it was milling an impressive 200,000 board feet of lumber annually, for use on the plantation and sale to markets around the country.

In 1954 the major tire manufacturer B. F. Goodrich gained an even more massive 600,000-acre concession for agriculture, mining and logging. Goodrich established a 58,000-acre development between Monrovia and the iron mines of the Bomi Hills; by 1968 that plantation had 11,000 acres in rubber. Like Firestone's operations, a plantation of this size entailed building a massive new infrastructure, a major element of the Liberian government's interest. By 1961 Goodrich paved forty-three miles of new roads, and constructed warehouses, shops, a power plant, housing, schools, and a twenty-four-bed hospital.

During these years independent Liberian producers also rapidly expanded their rubber holdings; they rose from 150 to 2,300 farms from 1941 to 1960. Most of these owners were members of the Americo-Liberian elite, government officials and their friends. High international rubber prices during World War II and the Korean War helped them gain economic eminence. By 1960 their annual output increased from 600,000 to over 14 million pounds. Firestone played a critically important role in this trend. It distributed over 10 million trees, similar to its own number; it gave surveys and advice to new plantations, including technical specialists and management plans; and it extended credit for start-ups. They, in turn, marketed all production through Firestone. However, this system disconnected the transnational corporation from responsibility from the social and political ramifications of labor management. As one commentator asserted,

> Many of Liberia's most important politicians and government officials (and their relatives) are independent rubber farmers who are reluctant to have their own wage bills increased. Moreover, Liberian farms are generally much less efficient than Firestone and realize much lower rates of profit. Accordingly, it has been the government's unofficial policy to keep wage rates below the level set in a free labor market. The technique that keeps wage rated down without producing a severe labor shortage is involuntary labor recruitment under government auspices.[50]

By the terms of all concessions, foreign companies were granted extensive "reserve areas," within which were intensive "development areas." Reserve areas were required to be developed within several years. But the land rent of six cents per acre on development land was a steal; that rate had been unchanged since the first concessions just after 1900. Firestone paid royalty on the amount of rubber produced; others were expected to pay income tax after initial tax-free periods, usually of fifteen years. Each concession could legally import duty-free all equipment and supplies.

As for its infrastructure, rail lines were entirely within the concessions and used only for company business. New paved roads were open to the public, benefiting national development more generally. Perhaps most important for its impact on Liberian society, the contracts stipulated that tribal lands were to be appropriated by the government for development, with compensation to tribes. In a social setting of long-standing ethnic rivalries, this system, funded by the international rubber economy, was an invitation to abuse by the Liberian-American elite. Integrating the country into the global corporate web thus drove the economy inland away from the coast, penetrating regions that previously only Firestone had entered. The oligarchy was widening its base, but the gap between it and the majority poor was also widening.[51]

In a strategy reminiscent of the way older rubber corporations had incorporated ethnic divisions into their labor hierarchies in Southeast Asia, Firestone divided the tasks on its plantations by ethnic identities. One of Firestone's managers wrote, "Tribe loyalties and distinguishing talents endure. Belles, for example, excel as builders; Krus as boatmen and fishermen; Mendes as policemen, Buzzis as technicians, Bassas and Gios as farmers, Mandingos as traders. Rubber growing requires all these skills and many more."[52] By structuring old tribal distinctions into its corporate labor management, the company accentuated the ethnic divisions of Liberian society. This paralleled the Americo-Liberian government's continuing distrust of the other ethnic groups. Its dominance depended in part on the loyalty of tribal leaders interested in the profits from labor recruitment. Labor troubles continued to simmer. A series of strikes in the 1960s hit Firestone and Goodrich, as well as some Liberian-owned estates. Government troops cracked down and arrested the organizers.[53]

Tubman's long era as Liberia's president ended with his death in 1971. In the following years the increasing split between the Americo-Liberian elite and the vast majority of the indigenous population took Liberia into a period of instability. The international rubber economy, and Firestone in particular, was tangled in the process of socioeconomic change that ultimately led to a socially and ecologically debilitating civil war. In 1980 armed factions began battling for control of Monrovia and its hinterland, and a military coup led by Samuel Doe overthrew the government; the Reagan administration in Washington supported him. In power, Doe favored his own ethnic group, the Krahn, and unleashed a reign of terror against other segments of Liberian society. In response, American-educated Charles Taylor invaded the country from neighboring Ivory Coast with an insurgent force in 1989, launching a six-year civil war. Five other armed factions, also based on ethnic groupings, emerged in the course of the war.

Until 1994 all factions tacitly agreed not to destroy Firestone or the smaller plantations, for any rubber which each faction could export would help finance its military operations. Taylor established his fortress inland from Monrovia, up the road from the Firestone center at Kakata. When he finally attacked Monrovia, fighting quickly engulfed the Firestone plantations. Groves and facilities were largely destroyed, part of the chaos that had descended on an artificial nation maintained by the industrial world's hunger for a tropical crop. By the time a tenuous peace was negotiated in 1995, 150,000 people, mostly civilians, had died in six years, out of the total national population of 2.6 million; 800,000 refugees had fled the country, and 1 million more were forced from their homes. Only in 2005 was the chaos brought under control enough that orderly elections chose Ellen Johnson Surleaf as Liberia's first woman president.

By then Liberian society was shredded, the land lay in ruins, and the plantations were paralyzed. The rubber industry, dominated by the American rubber manufacturers, had left a complex and ambiguous legacy. It had made decisive contributions to raising incomes and health and literacy rates among its plantation workers, and it was one of the most biologically stable monocropping systems in the tropics. Yet it had also contributed to the ethnic and class tensions that ultimately tore Liberian society apart. It has still not been possible to assess the ecological fallout of the civil war and its antecedents in detail.

CONCLUSION: THE MOTOR CAR IN THE JUNGLE

By the early 1970s, less than a third of world rubber production came from natural rubber. Petroleum-based synthetics seemed destined to dominate the industry. At that juncture, what might be concluded about the ecological consequences of American capital and consumption of natural rubber? Certainly, corporate plantation rubber was as powerful a weapon as bananas for the conquest of the rainforest. Large-scale corporate investment was driven in turn by an equally fundamental aspect of industrial society, its markets. Rubber came to have thousands of uses, but its engine was the automotive industry and its cultural counterpart, the dream of personal mobility. Yet strategic motives had also been central to the evolution of the American rubber firms. In the race for control of sources and profits, American firms had become entangled in an elaborate rivalry with European empires, especially Great Britain in Southeast Asia. The strategic aspect of rubber use marked it off from economic rivalries over sugar, fruit, or coffee.

Rubber-induced ecological change in the tropical forest took two contrasting forms, reflecting the contrast between corporate and smallholder production, just as coffee and bananas ultimately did. European and American corporations carved out separate spheres of influence. The Southeast Asian estates in particular, both those established by foreign corporations and later those controlled by local elites, mobilized massive labor forces, reconstructing ethnic relations of entire societies and concentrating alien populations in rainforest zones.

Foreign corporations determined land use, choosing a monocrop; foreign management controlled cultivation systems. In order to create the plantations, they clear-cut the forest, burning the biomass or in some cases organizing salvage logging of valuable hardwood trees. At first the newly cleared land was prone to erosion during the beating rains of equatorial monsoon climates. But estate management improved rapidly. Soil erosion came under much better control as management experience increased. In the more competitive era after 1945, agronomists produced new varieties of rubber trees that dramatically increased yields. Hence, existing acreage in the groves could meet rising market demand, thus reducing the pressure to expand onto other acreage. But in order to sustain higher productivity, estate managers resorted to increased applications of commercial fertilizer and pest controls. In the longer run these agrochemicals threatened to pollute subsurface and downstream water supplies.

The contrasting pattern of natural rubber production in Southeast Asia, and later in Liberia as well, was smallholdings. In a pattern resembling production of coffee and bananas, small-scale producers integrated rubber trees with the varied food and fiber crops which they already grew. American firms like U.S. Rubber and Goodyear did not become directly involved with smallholder production in Southeast Asia, but Firestone took a leading advisory role in Liberia, in a strategy similar to the British firms in Malaya and Ceylon. The American connection to smallholder production was more indirect, but momentous nonetheless. American buyers purchased much smallholder rubber from middlemen in Singapore (and later Monrovia on a smaller scale). On behalf of American consumers they thus provided a large portion of the global market that sustained massive small producer rubber expansion. In a real sense, that demand created even the smallholder groves.

Small rubber groves were more dispersed and had less monolithic impacts on ecosystems, and they did not displace food cropping to any critical extent. Those groves had more stable inter-relations with the peasant agroecosystems. But—again like coffee and bananas—they were considerably less productive per land unit, and the farmers were slower to adopt intensive methods. For any given amount produced, they required greater acreage. Thus they may have had a greater tendency to expand into new land taken from forest or previously cleared for crops. But at the same time they were much slower to induce accumulation of agrochemicals in soil and water.

By the early 1970s some proponents of synthetic rubber expected the entire natural rubber industry to be on its way to oblivion. But a major shock jolted the global rubber economy in 1973, when the OPEC countries imposed sudden steep price rises for petroleum. As a United Nations survey phrased it,

> In 1973 the world rubber economy suffered its first severe exogenous shock: the oil crisis and subsequent sharp rise in crude oil prices. For an industry whose major component—synthetic rubber—depends so heavily on petrochemical feedstocks, the sudden drastic increase in crude oil prices in 1973–74 represented a major change in cost structures and production economics. The other component of the industry—natural rubber—was less affected directly, but was still subject to all the indirect effects of the oil crisis: acceleration of world inflation, changes in consumer expectations, and rising doubts about the long-term future of world elastomer demand in the energy-intensive automotive sector.[54]

The immediate price rise of natural rubber was less than half of synthetic rubber's price rise. OPEC had unwittingly introduced a new unpredictability into the rubber economy, and a new level of demand for Hevea rubber. In addition, its superior properties became decisive in tire markets in the 1980s, when radial tires, first created by Michelin's technicians, came to dominate the market. By placing cords at 90 degrees to the spin of the tire, then adding a steel belt beneath the tread, they produced longer life, better fuel consumption and more effective handling.

By the early 1990s natural rubber had risen again to well over one third of global production. As Wade Davis succinctly notes,

There is today no product that can match natural rubber's resilience and tensile strength, resistance to abrasion and impact, and capacity to absorb impact without generating heat. Today the tires of every commercial and military aircraft . . . are 100 percent natural rubber. . . . The enormous tires of industrial machinery are 90 percent natural. Nearly half of the rubber in every automobile tire originates on plantations located thirteen thousand miles away.[55]

Those thousands of miles represented the global ecological links of the automotive age and established a horizon beyond which consumers did not care to look.

5

The Crop on Hooves: American Cattle Ranching in Latin America

YANKEE CATTLEMEN AND THE RANGELANDS OF NORTHERN MEXICO

The European introduction of domestic livestock into the Americas was probably an even more radical shock to New World ecosystems than the introduction of European crops. When cattle, horses, sheep, and goats spread across the land, they were mobile and fecund, running wild and multiplying staggeringly fast. Livestock voraciously consumed native vegetation. Where they grazed, indigenous plant species were replaced by hardier European grasses that had hitchhiked across the Atlantic with the animals. The effect was similar to that of introduced crops: native plant and animal communities were reduced or eliminated. But unlike most plant crops, the mobile cattle and the Old World grass seeds on their hides, ranged across the land, ignoring all human boundaries.[1]

Throughout the past five centuries European cattle were a powerful adjunct to frontier extraction systems, making indigenous cultures, as well as native ecosystems, subservient to capital investors and beef eaters. Cattle were associated with all scales of crop production, from squatter subsistence to plantation capitalism. They were ubiquitous on all agricultural frontiers.

When Yankee ranchers entered the livestock industry of the subtropical New World, a stream of American international interests, different from crops, was inaugurated. Traditionally, ranching was tightly linked to agriculture for both subsistence and the market. Beginning in the 1820s, in what was then northern Mexico, an intricate fusion of Anglo and Hispanic cultures and economies emerged to exploit the land and its living systems. This produced closer links between the United States and Latin lands than any of the cultivated crops.

The roots of Yankee cattle interests in the tropics penetrate into the hacienda culture of Spanish colonial Mexico, which Anglo settlers met in south Texas when they began drifting beyond Louisiana after 1820. Those settlers were the forerunners of the beef suppliers for the meat-packing industry of Chicago after 1860. As the era of industrial ranching began in the late 1800s, a counterpoint evolved, both within the United States and internationally, between the lean range-fed beef of traditional Hispanic cattle, and corn-fed, lot-fed, modern cattle breeds. The result was permanent degradation of wide arid regions, where the vegetation was reduced to a low-level stasis, with varying amounts of soil erosion.[2] Not all was lost; in later years, natural savanna began to be transformed into managed grasslands when a few ranchers began working their pastures more intensively, seeding them with exotic grasses introduced from Africa. But the cattle industry's new scientific management was as double-edged environmentally as the new agronomy. From the mid-1800s onward, new breeds of cattle raised for international markets invaded the wet tropical lowlands in commercial concentrations, turning moist forest ecosystems into degraded pasture that could be grazed only for short periods.

The beginnings of this transformation trace back across the Atlantic to the Iberian peninsula of late medieval times. Spain's cattle culture centered in the rolling highlands of Castile and Extremadura, evolving on grasslands that were parched each long summer when the moist winter winds from the Atlantic had died away. Both the grasses and the Criollo cattle breed that developed there had to be drought resistant. So did the ranchers whose lifestyle became one of the most prestigious and powerful in Spain.[3]

In the Americas after 1492, this transplanted phenomenon overwhelmed grasslands and probed into woodlands. Cattle were introduced onto Caribbean islands by Columbus's men.[4] Ranching became a tradition in Cuba, on the central lowlands outside Havana, where they supplied the export trade in hides and tallow. By the shipload these products were sent back to Europe to supplement its increasingly inadequate supplies of cattle and pasture.[5]

The great ranching saga evolved in Mexico, where cattle spread in every direction from the early colonial base in conquered Tenochtitlan. Faced with few natural enemies, the cattle multiplied massively, running half-wild. They roamed with the conquistadores into southern Mexico and Central America's Pacific lowlands and settled there permanently even after their masters left again.[6] The indigenous people, under siege from European epidemic diseases already, had no way of protecting their croplands from the ravages of the feral cattle. Many Indians deserted their lands and faced death by hunger, as well as disease, thereby making it easier for a new Creole landlord class to consolidate the haciendas of the later colonial period.

By the late 1600s permanent haciendas were founded in the Central American lowlands, providing cattle products for both local use and regional trade. In the rolling lowlands around Lake Nicaragua and Lake Managua, where large areas of pasture had been gradually cleared, British traveler John Bailey wrote in 1850,

> One of the principal sources of wealth consists of cattle, [especially] on the eastern side of the lakes, . . . a space containing many hundred square miles, but without towns, and with little more population than is required for attending the herds. This tract affords admirable pasturage . . . besides furnishing what is required for the consumption of the inhabitants of the more populous districts, many thousands are annually driven off to the fairs of San Miguel in Salvador . . . and also Guatemala.[7]

From Mexico City the Spanish colonial interests turned northward into the Mesa del Norte, the mountain slopes and intermontane valleys and tablelands between the Sierra Madre Occidental and Oriental. There the volcanic soils supported pine, oak, and mesquite forests on the steeper slopes. In the bottomlands, agricultural Indians had grown the classic Mesoamerican triad of crops—maize, beans, and squash—for centuries. In the wide regions that received less than twenty inches of rain, the natural grasslands faded away into drought-resistant shrubs, especially mesquite, which was nutritious for browsing cattle, and finally into the northern desert of Sonora and Chihuahua. Even there livestock could find moist grasslands on the higher mountains, as well as by springs, perennial streams, and marshes toward the bottomlands.[8]

As the Spaniards and their cattle moved northward in the mid-1500s, they overwhelmed the descendants of the Aztecs and Toltecs, whose numbers were decimated by up to 90 percent, leaving wide areas of deserted fallow fields.[9] Cattle were linked to the European economy by silver mines in the mountains

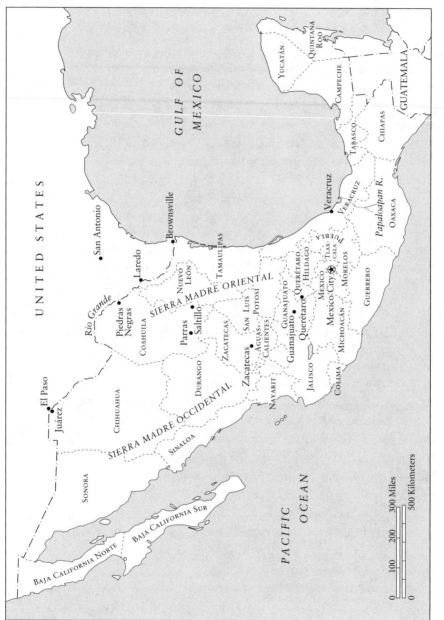

Mexico

of Zacatecas and Guanajuato. They were used for draught power and for their hides and tallow, which were exported to Europe for its industry and warfare.[10] The grasses of the high plateau fed exploding numbers of cattle, which overgrazed the land within a few decades. Tens of thousands of steers were slaughtered each year for the men of the mines and for export. The carrying capacity of the pasture declined rapidly. When easily accessible lodes of silver were played out, the region saw a leveling of cattle numbers to a far lower number that was sustained on the tired land for centuries more.[11]

Spaniards and their livestock spread more slowly into the lower semi-deserts and ranges of the north, confronting hotter temperatures and scantier rainfall. Ultimately, colonial Mexico reached northward through the deserts of Sonora and Chihuahua into the present-day U.S. states of California, Arizona, New Mexico, and Texas. Miners introduced cattle on their northern claims, establishing ranches that survived when the silver mines played out.[12] Where population was sparse, cattle required little labor, unlike agricultural crops.[13]

In the northern borderlands, most outposts that survived were Catholic missions, run by Jesuit priests, then Franciscan friars, who had a far more powerful organization to support them than any individual hacendero could summon. In 1785 one visitor to a mission ranch in Texas wrote, "The only wealth that this mission has enjoyed since its erection has been that derived from the herds of cattle. . . . All the missions had considerable property of this kind."[14]

In colonial Texas, the Spanish founded the new Presidio of San Antonio de Bexar (the modern city of San Antonio) in 1718, which organized the cattle industry along the San Antonio River, teaching local Indians Christianity and horsemanship. By 1780 smaller outposts were created as far east as Nacogdoches, on the fringe of the Mississippi lowlands' pine forests. Along the more humid coastal lowlands inside Padre Island, on bluestem prairies and salt marshes, a secular society of private ranches gradually extended northward.[15]

The Spanish land grants resulted in continual conflict between ranchers and the Indian communal system over the use of grazing lands and untilled fields.[16] Many cattle escaped from the undermanned haciendas and multiplied, to await later settlers. In 1780 the total number of cattle in Texas was estimated at somewhere between fifty and one hundred thousand. Thousands of cattle and horses settled in Texas almost before Mexican human settlers.

Cattle became late colonial Texas's primary export: the hacenderos sent herds west to California, northeast into Louisiana, and south into Coahuila. In the early nineteenth century, after the United States took Louisiana, the Texas breeding zone sent longhorn cattle to stock farms in Tennessee, Kentucky, and even Illinois and Ohio. The integration of Hispanic and Anglo rangeland economies had begun.

In the long depression of the late eighteenth and early nineteenth centuries, Texas and Coahuila became a virtually autonomous, self-sufficient backwater region. Toward the west and north the numbers of Hispanics were effectively limited by counterattacks from Apaches and Plains Indians.[17] But by then the region's semiarid grasslands had suffered serious long-term consequences. Cattle and sheep had overgrazed and trampled the grasses, compacting and eroding the soils in a process of devegetation and desiccation. Native grasses were replaced by tough woody plants, such as chaparral. Cattle carried Old World grasses with them, especially the variety which came to be known as Kentucky Blue Grass. As historian David Weber tells it, "Old World grasses had adapted for centuries to close cropping and bare or compacted soil, and evolution had equipped them with seeds hardy enough to survive a journey through the digestive system of ambulatory quadrupeds, or with barbs or hooks that enabled them to hitch a ride."[18] So the land was shaped in unknowing preparation for a new invasion from the Northeast, as Anglo-American farmers and cattlemen spread into east Texas after Louisiana became part of the American empire. Jefferson's dream of an American imperium in midcontinent was to be established by bovine as much as human conquerors.

The cowboy culture and ranching economy of the Great Plains was a fusion of Hispanic cattle ranching with a north European livestock economy that had matured in the eastern U.S. woodlands and pastures. There, Anglo farmers and cattlemen managed north European cattle breeds in conjunction with mixed crop agriculture. These cattle were not well adapted to arid grasslands; they had little experience with drought or xerophytic (drought-resistant) species of grass. In the 1820s, Yankees began moving westward from the southeastern states and New Orleans into east Texas, against the protests of the Mexican government. In the following quarter-century, Texas became a region of cultural fusion, with Anglo political and commercial systems ultimately in control. In the frontier region, Anglos mixed with Hispanics and Indians, especially the agricultural Choctaws of the lower Mississippi.[19] They swept all the others into the culture of commercialization and fundamentally changed life on the land.

Politics increasingly shaped the use of Texas grasslands. By 1824 the Mexican government, newly independent from Spain, granted 272 land titles to Americans in Texas. In 1836, the gringos launched an open rebellion when Sam Houston declared the region independent. Texas entered the United States officially in 1845, precipitating war with Mexico three years later. When the United States won, it took possession of a vast region, roughly the northern half of Mexico. Big Yankee ranches began to settle the west Texas rangelands in the 1850s. Texas was moving toward the brief but spectacular longhorn era, when, for a few years, its ranchers exploited their grazing lands as never before, in response to a great new hunger radiating out from Chicago and the eastern states.

In sum, even in the colonial era the arid rangelands of northern Mexico were linked into a wide market economy, but only weakly. This was a pre-industrial economy, with none of the long-distance efficiencies that emerged in the 1860s. That second transformation of American cattle lands was to prove far more powerful and far-reaching than the first.

INDUSTRIAL CAPITALISM ON THE GRASSLANDS OF THE AMERICAS

From the early nineteenth century onward, Great Britain and the United States integrated the grasslands of western North America, including Mexico, the temperate zone of southern South America, and Australia and New Zealand, into the global economy as the primary source of beef and mutton for their dinner tables. In the late 1800s, Americans began moving beyond Texas into the cheaper grazing lands of northern Mexico. In 1900, American interests aggressively entered Argentina, processing and shipping its beef to England with a system developed in the midwestern United States. Significantly, they did not attempt to market South American beef in the United States, since the Great Plains proved capable of satisfying the American market and generating major exports as well, until far into the twentieth century. But the east coast's bankers and Chicago's meat packers took major roles in domesticating the planet's grasslands far beyond U.S. borders. In this work they joined with an international network of breeders of hybrid beef cattle.

Tropical crop plantations were systems largely fabricated on the spot. The modern beef industry was not; it was devised in London and Chicago and the ranches of the western United States and then exported southward. The mechanization of the meat trade began in Cincinnati in the 1830s, dressing and shipping hogs, in order to transform abundant corn harvests into pork. By the early 1860s Chicago passed Cincinnati to become the continent's great center of beef processing. The first key was railroads. Chicago's railroads to the east coast began running in 1856.[20] In 1862 the young city on Lake Michigan slaughtered a million cattle for the first time. Processing such vast numbers was the key technical and organizational challenge. In 1865 the world's largest meat-packing operation, the Union Stock Yards, opened. Then the early 1870s saw the first refrigerated storage rooms and mechanizing slaughtering process. One commentator called these innovations "the brutal and inventive vitality of the nineteenth century."[21]

Cattlemen whose names later spread into Latin America now appeared. Their early struggles shaped the entrepreneurial style of their aggressive push into southern nations. One was Gustavus F. Swift, who began life in 1839 in New England, working first as a local butcher and then as a cattle buyer. Swift went to Chicago in 1875, to confront the center of operations. He soon began using refrigerated cars; in 1882, he shipped his first beef to New York. Swift and his competitors, determined to dominate the national industry, decided to reduce local butchers in the East to the role of salesmen of chilled meat, eliminating their local independence.

Swift's major competitor was Philip D. Armour, a meat packer and grain trader from Milwaukee. Armour, the most aggressive speculator of them all, had tried out the Gold Rush in California in 1851, but later returned to the Midwest. Like Swift, Armour too moved to Chicago in 1875. Chicago was no less lively than San Francisco, as "turbulence and confusion pervaded the Chicago grain market, where the price of the world's bread was decided. [The beef trade was a] vortex of cracks and crashes."[22] By 1890 Armour owned grain elevators with nine million tons capacity, 30 percent of Chicago's total. He also made a heavy investment in California citrus to exploit the possibilities of refrigerated shipping to the east coast.[23]

These entrepreneurs were creating a national grid of speculative investment. Facing westward, they saw a massive rangeland supply base. In the aftermath of the Civil War, railroads were laid across bison country, over mountain ranges, to the Pacific; by 1870 one train left Chicago every fifteen minutes. Men and cattle walked hundreds of dusty miles to meet them. In 1867 Chicagoan Joseph G. McCoy laid out a safe trail from Texas to an almost abandoned settlement, Abilene, Kansas, on the new Kansas Pacific Railroad. This linked the longhorns with the national processing and marketing system. That fall he shipped thirty-five thousand steers from Abilene to Chicago. As William Cronon writes, "Called into being by the same urban markets that had sent the hunters scurrying across the plains in the first place, the new herds would be tied to the cities by the same iron rails that had turned the plains into a slaughterhouse."[24] As cattle replaced bison, a single economic cycle replaced varied ecological cycles.

This led directly to a new chapter in the international competition between England and the United States for the fruits of the southern continents' lands. England's investment in the beef industry of the western United States was its last great effort to exploit North America as a frontier for its consumption. From 1800 onward, the British passion for beef, especially when it was richly marbled, began to be satisfied from the newly perfected Shorthorn crossbreed. But pasture acreage in England, Scotland, and Ireland was too limited and expensive to supply the burgeoning urban population's hunger. Only imports from distant lands would suffice when that became technologically feasible.

London's Smithfield Market became the focal point of both import and domestic trade. In the 1860s live cattle and salted beef began to be shipped to England from the United States, but the supply was still inadequate and expensive. In 1875 New Yorker John Bates shipped the first chilled beef to England in ice-cooled rooms. This market boomed instantly; by the end of 1876 three million pounds of fresh beef were crossing the Atlantic each month.[25] British financiers responded aggressively: the 1870s were the era of major British investment in railroad construction in the western United States.[26] It was no coincidence that this was immediately after the conclusion of the Indian wars and bison slaughter on the Great Plains. On the over-stocked range, the blizzards of 1886–87 destroyed tens of thousands of cattle, and many British investments collapsed.[27]

As early as 1860 there were already 4.5 million cattle in Texas.[28] As soon as the War between the States was over in 1865, the eastern and British beef markets—and the new means of getting beef to those consumers—caused an explosive acceleration of beef production in the U.S.-Mexican border region.

When the railroad reached Abilene, herds of cattle moved northward from Texas on the Chisholm Trail to the connection with the Chicago stockyards. They had already been driven from Texas to Louisiana and even to Cincinnati since the 1840s, and to California in the 1850s. But the scale of the drives expanded massively when the railroads were hammered into the land. In 1867 the first steers were driven to Abilene and then shipped by rail to the Chicago. In an 1869 count, 350,000 cattle walked the Chisholm Trail from San Antonio to Abilene; by 1871, 700,000 head traveled the same route to market. Between that year and 1885 the herds multiplied and spread explosively. Five and a half million beasts moved to market and to stock more northerly ranges that had been cleared of bison herds and their Native American co-inhabitants. In those fifteen years twelve states were filled with cattle.[29]

The era of the long drives and the vast longhorn herds was relatively brief but it permanently disrupted a great grassland ecosystem. By the mid-1880s cattle ranching was grossly over-exploiting the region's resources. A sudden economic crash ended the era in the winter of 1886–87, when the worst blizzards of the century destroyed millions of cattle.

A new kind of competition arose in the form of corn-fed, stall-fed hybrid cattle, farther northeast where modern livestock and pasture management were intensifying production. New techniques were developed on the short-grass prairie from Indiana to Iowa, some of which could be transplanted to less expensive lands in Mexico and beyond. Simultaneously, another competitor for the prairie was moving in: settled farming. Cropping required more water than ranching did and was more labor intensive, displacing cattle onto poorer pasture. This groundswell of change raised the cost of land steadily, until it was no longer financially viable to graze cattle. By the last years of the century, the ranchers had to find cheaper rangeland for raising young beef (feeder cattle), then fatten them in intensively managed pastures and feedlots close to packing houses and transport to markets.

Texas ranches gradually consolidated into fewer, larger spreads and began a long process of modernization, technical change, and capital intensification. The largest of them was the King Ranch. In 1853, shortly after the United States annexed Texas, Richard King bought an old hacienda on Santa Gertrudis Creek south of Corpus Christi. Sprawling across the arid mesquite brush, this was the first portion of what ultimately became a 1,200,000-acre family ranch and a symbol of modern scientific cattle and pasture management.[30] In the early 1900s, the King Ranch developed the only new breed of the century in the United States, the Santa Gertrudis, a complex cross between Brahman and Hereford, designed to thrive in hot lowland settings, resist their diseases, and produce maximum beef. The King Ranch was to play a major innovative role in bringing a widening variety of Latin American habitats under the hoof.

By the turn of the century, U.S. government lands had been sold to private speculators and dirt farmers. Settled farming and barbed wire fences were rapidly encroaching on the open prairie, the ranchers' former domain, and land values were inexorably rising. The beef industry began to look southward to the wide savannas of Latin America. A new supply of cattle would come from the arid and still inexpensive grasslands of northern Mexico. Profits would come equally from the southern hemisphere's extraordinary grasslands, the pampas of Argentina and Uruguay.

Cronon's insight into Chicago's imperial relation to the grasslands of the Great Plains could be extended globally, and nowhere more than Argentina. The conquest of Nature and the indigenous people of Argentina's wide lands was primarily the work of a British-Argentine alliance. The meat packers of Chicago invested only in beef processing; they did not purchase or manage ranch lands in Argentina. From 1900 onward the Chicago meat packers played a vital role in the process that linked Argentina's soil to Britain's dinner tables.

The pampas, one-fifth of Argentina's land surface, is the country's social and economic heartland, a flat plain covering ancient granite with hundreds of feet of sediment, fine clay, sand, and dust. No major rivers run through the pampas, but in the seasonal rains huge shallow lakes cover the lush grasses of the prairie. For centuries the only human inhabitants of the pampas were the Araucanians, nomadic hunting tribes who mastered European horses and weapons by the 1560s. The transformation of that land had begun in the sixteenth century, when cattle introduced by the first Spanish explorers escaped and multiplied at astounding rates, faced with no natural predators or diseases, except for packs of wild dogs, another European introduction.[31]

The colonial population expanded very slowly around the Rio de la Plata on the Atlantic coast, for the early Spanish found little that interested them there. Only in 1776 did Madrid found the Viceroyalty of Rio de la Plata, with Buenos Aires as its capital. For the slowly expanding urban market there, gaucho horsemen began capturing the wild herds of the pampas. In the colonial period, just as in Mexico, the cattle were slaughtered mostly for leather and tallow; 60 percent of the meat was said to be left at the site. Around 1800 the first solution to that waste was the saladero, a meat-salting plant for whole carcasses.

Euro-American expansion across Argentina was still blocked by the Araucanian defense, for the indigenes could move faster and strike their enemies more decisively on the wide savannas. Conquest of the Araucanians became a national obsession in Buenos Aires and its hinterland. Finally, in 1879–80, President Julio Roca led the "Conquest of the Desert," a war of obliteration against yet another indigenous culture.[32]

In the immediate aftermath of Roca's Conquest, industrial technology and capital completed the domestication of the land. The first British railway had been built from Buenos Aires on the coast to Cordoba far inland in the 1860s; more lines were completed across the pampas by the late 1880s. Just as in North American ranching, the new transport system helped to create a great concentration of landholdings. Speculators and previously rich landlords soon took control of the pampas; by 1910 millions of acres were transferred into private hands. The new ranchers built elegant homes on their estancias and Buenos Aires became the Paris of South America, its population rapidly swelling beyond its 300,000 of the 1880s.[33]

This transformation depended almost exclusively on the insatiable consumer market for beef among the prospering urban middle classes of Western Europe. Europeans now demanded tender, fat-marbled meat. Their own cattle breeders had learned how to provide that quality and encourage a taste for it. By 1900 Argentine ranchers adopted new breeds from Europe, especially the Shorthorn, which demanded richer pasture.[34] Achieving a revolution in pasture management, they planted natural grasslands with alfalfa and wheat. They began fencing the pampas and established intensive feed pastures near the point of export, Buenos Aires, where the men who controlled the beef industry could now control the country's politics and cultural life as well.

The settlement and domestication of the pampas required a large new labor force. In the decades around 1900 a wave of immigrants arrived from Europe, which swept in marginal and tenant farmers from poor northern Italy and Spain. These tenant farmers were the real conquerors of the native pampas. Many became a permanent part of the rising Argentine population; others were seasonal Italian and Spanish laborers, called *golondrinas,* or swallows, who crossed the Atlantic annually for the wheat and corn harvests.

The domestication of the grasslands was remarkably rapid. Between 1872 and 1895 the cultivated area of the pampas increased fifteen times, to ten million acres; wheat exports to Europe were regularly above one million tons in 1890s. The export of beef increased similarly. On-hoof shipments dominated until 1900, when England banned live animals because of a massive hoof and mouth disease outbreak in South America. But frozen beef was considered not to carry the dreaded epidemic, so packing houses came to dominate the trade, providing frozen beef that could bypass Smithfield and other European slaughterhouses. From 0.2 percent of Argentina's beef exports in 1897, frozen shipments rose to 51 percent in 1907. In 1908 the transport of chilled beef (shipped at the freezing point) was perfected, providing better quality than frozen beef on arriving at Smithfield.[35]

Americans were highly competitive in this business. In the late 1880s Swift had chased cattle southwestward from Chicago, building processing plants in Texas and elsewhere on the range.[36] Moving into Argentine business was only one more step. Chicago firms entered the industry in Buenos Aires immediately when Britain banned the import of live beef in 1900. The Yankees had no need to develop markets for Argentine beef in the United States, but American capital reinforced the scale of European consumption.[37] By 1929, at the onset of the Great Depression, of the total American investment in manufacturing in Latin America as a whole, more than one-third, $82 million, was in Argentina, mostly in meat processing.[38]

The pampas was transformed ecologically. By 1960 Argentina's pastureland (for both cattle and sheep) amounted to 124,353,000 hectares, or 45 percent of the national land. However, only 11 percent of that was sown to alfalfa and carefully managed. The rest was degraded pastures where natural grassland communities had been replaced by thistles and other hardy European weed species, in tandem with soil erosion and exhaustion. As Alfred Crosby summarizes the change, "Today only a quarter of the plants growing wild in the pampas are native, and in the well-watered eastern portions, the 'natural' ground cover consists almost entirely of Old World grasses and clovers."[39] But American investors and consumers remained at a great distance from the ecological changes that the meat packers were fostering.[40]

SCIENTIFIC RANGELANDS

In the early 1800s a new era of cattle breeding emerged in Europe, producing hybrid cattle adapted either for meat or for milk, though not both in the same animal. These animals demanded more nutritious fodder; their commercial development was dependent on the new science developed from the eighteenth-century European revolution in pasture management.[41] A branch of this movement flourished in the United States as the 1800s advanced, moving gradually westward from the intensive cattle management of the eastern ex-woodlands to the great prairie west of Chicago.[42] It flourished in stockmen's associations and was propagated in their periodicals and at county fairs.

The new stock breeding was transferred into Latin America beginning in the mid-1800s, when British sugar planters in Jamaica experimented with powerful, disease-resistant Zebu stock from India in an effort to improve the Criollo cattle's performance as draft animals in moist tropical lowlands where they were poorly adapted.[43] Far more important in the long run was the effort to increase beef production. The potential of the natural grasslands stretched to the horizon of any stockman's imagination, if only a meatier animal could be bred. Elsewhere around the continent, by 1900 a series of crosses of the lean Criollo with Hereford, Shorthorn, and Angus of northern European ancestry were achieved in South America.[44]

Equally important for the long-term transformation of Latin American grasslands was the work of pasture specialists in importing hardy African grass species. Argentina and Uruguay led the way in replacing the natural pampas with alfalfa pasture. By the early 1900s little remained of the indigenous savanna ecology of the pampas, but the new pastures were the world's most productive for beef.[45] That was a unique situation; outside the pampas there was little incentive or capital available for change in range management until after 1945. The arid lands of northern Mexico were a very different, much drier ecosystem that promised more modest rewards to intensified investment and management.

The lowland rainforest was still another system. The wet forest climate and soils, if they were to be sustainably grazed on a commercial scale, required an infusion of intercontinental science. The species of grass that made the invasion of that forest possible were introduced from Africa, into several specific niches. All the six primary species of *Gramineaceae* grasses that have become widespread in wet tropical America (Guinea, Pará, molasses, jaragua, Kikuyu

and Pangola) co-evolved with ungulate mammals in woodland margin habitats of Angola, Rhodesia, and the Transvaal. Easily propagated in tropical
America, "these grasses have proven to be explosively aggressive, invading
and holding vast areas wherever they have received minimal support by
man."[46] All are more palatable and nutritious to livestock than the native
grasses which they displace.

As James Parsons concludes, "The African grasses stand up better to grazing and have higher nutritive values than native American species. In this
respect the invasions can be considered advantageous, although botanists may
mourn the disappearance of native members of the flora that it may cause."[47]
In contrast with the earlier European impact on the grasslands, the new system had major advantages. Unsystematically grazed and burned grassland
that was not turned into managed pasture continued a process of gradual
degradation. At least the new system of intensive pasture management had far
higher and more sustainable productivity than its predecessor. Its introduction into Mexico and other areas of Latin America was a long process, shaped
by local politics as much as anything.

YANKEES IN NORTHERN MEXICO

Americans' penetration of Latin American ranching, and their slowly expanding role in its modernization, began in the wide arid rangelands of Chihuahua
and Coahuila in northern Mexico. This was a harsh and fragile environment,
with uncompromising yet unpredictable limits to its carrying capacity. The
occasional rains fall between June and October; the land is desiccated for the
rest of the year. In the remaining months, up to 30 percent of the livestock can
be lost in any dry year. The high, dry pastures sustain drought-resistant native
grama grasses and chaparral shrubbery, especially mesquite, which can help
reduce cattle losses in times of severe drought. In extreme drought nopal and
other edible cacti still survive.[48]

Texan ranching investment in northern Mexico emerged in the early
1800s. As soon as Texas broke away from Mexico, Yankees and Englishmen,
brandishing far more investment capital than Mexicans could muster, began
buying out the old hacenderos.[49] These ranches remained highly risky investments until the last decades of the century, when presidents Benito Juarez and
Porfirio Diaz began aggressively attracting foreign capital.[50] From 1885
onward Yankee investors entered Mexican mines, railroads, logging, ranch,

and telecommunications systems.[51] The Mexican government expropriated Church lands and many traditional *ejido* common lands, turning some of them, especially in the north, into vast new latifundia. Their new owners included American and European land speculation companies creating an interlocking Mexican-foreign hacendero elite.

The most massive Yankee ranch in northern Mexico was owned by George Hearst, the founder of the publishing empire in California. When the San Francisco grandee met President Diaz in 1884, he decided to buy a thousand square miles of land in Vera Cruz, Campeche, and Yucatan, plus a million-acre ranch, named Babicora, in Chihuahua. He bought the spread from rancheros worn out by fighting Geronimo and paid twenty cents per acre for it.[52] Babicora sprawled across four high plateaus separated by ranges. "The land was high and arid, watered in places by artesian wells, and divided almost in two by a rugged spur of the Sierra Madre. Some of it was covered with marketable timber."[53]

Hearst and his son William Randolph appointed Jack Follansbee supervisor of Babicora. Follansbee became both a grandee in Mexican aristocratic circles and popular on the New York circuit.[54] In 1903 the young Hearst drove with his bride to Mexico City, where the aged President Diaz, a good friend of Follansbee, received them with honors. The Hearsts then visited Babicora, where forty-eight thousand cattle roamed on its million acres. Some of the land was rented to Mexican tenants growing beans and corn, but most of the plains were pasture for tens of thousands of Shorthorns and Herefords, managed by hundreds of vaqueros. Hearst sold cattle in El Paso each year. By 1910 Hearst's Mexican properties were valued officially at $4 million, and were probably worth much more.[55]

The Yankee stake in Mexican ranching, like all Yankee investments in Mexico, was badly damaged by the Revolution. In Coahuila by 1910, the majority of ranches had been owned by Yankees, partly as a drought reserve for Texan herds, because most of the Texas range was degraded and Mexican acreage was much cheaper. Gringos had also begun investing heavily in breeding stock for the Mexican haciendas.[56] In Chihuahua, as well, many haciendas, large and small, were owned by Englishmen and Americans. Hearst owned a $2 million ranch and the Cudahy meat-packing firm owned another. In addition, Yankee smallholdings were worth over $3.8 million, including $2.9 million owned by Mormon immigrants from Utah.[57] Many small holdings were destroyed or temporarily crippled by Pancho Villa or his opponents. Little was left except the knowledge of how to rebuild and expand on pre-Revolution experience, and that was enough.

Hearst's Babicora hacienda was equally in peril during the chaotic years, in part because of Hearst's participation in the expropriation of Indian communal lands under the Porfiriato. Local peasants' organizations emerged around 1900 in self-defense against both the new landlords and Apache raids from the north. In May 1908, fifty campesinos rode to Babicora, protesting what they insisted was the grabbing of nine thousand hectares of communal land and water rights. Hearst's men relented, and realigned their fences.[58] Several years later, Villa attacked the ranch, took sixty thousand cattle and killed one of the ranch's vaqueros. Hearst's newspapers denounced the Mexican revolutionaries. In the *San Francisco Examiner* on July 8, 1916, Hearst demanded that "the United States Government exercise the fundamental functions of all governments and protect its citizens; that it prevent the Mexicans from murdering any more of our citizens and that it punish Mexico for the murders and outrages already committed upon our citizens and our soldiers."[59] For the time his belligerent invocation of the American imperium was not entirely necessary, for most Yankee properties survived in their hands through the stabler 1920s. That was a favorable decade for Yankee ranchers, and Hearst continued to enjoy the international high life.

In 1921 Hearst and his equally flamboyant mistress Marion Davies went to Mexico City to meet the new President Obregon, who agreed to protect the Hearst estates, including his lands in lowland Campeche. The arrogance and high visibility of the Yankee capitalists left them vulnerable to rising Mexican political wrath against Yankee domination of the economy. Obregon's successor Calles confiscated several parts of Babicora, distributing them to peasants. Hearst also began to have reason to worry about his Guanacevi and San Luis mines and timber and chicle lands.

In 1935, under the reformist President Cardenas, a new law limited individual holdings to 100,000 acres, so the government expropriated 175,000 acres of Hearst's arable land; in 1940 it took 117,000 more. The rest remained under the management of Hearst's team, who maintained it as the most productive ranch in northern Mexico. Babicora Ranch was fully nationalized after Hearst died in 1951. In 1954 the Mexican government paid Hearst's estate a bargain price of about $2 million for the final 50,000 hectares, and turned it into 20-hectare plots for agricultural colonies. Breaking up an estate that was run in sophisticated ways—evidently including efficient water use and pasture management—and turning some of the best lands over to subsistence farming, may well have caused environmental deterioration, though that is difficult to measure against the rights and needs of campesino families.

Other states in Mexico's arid north saw a similar picture. In Coahuila, east of Babicora, by the late 1920s many ganaderias were U.S.-held, such as $2 million in ranches at Piedras Negras. When Frank Tannenbaum of the Brookings Institution in Washington surveyed the economy of rural Mexico in the aftermath of the Revolution in the late 1920s, he found that foreigners owned one-fifth of all Mexico's private lands, primarily in the northern and coastal states, where population was sparse and land cheap. Americans owned just over half of the acreage, followed by Spaniards, British, Germans, and French.[60]

The 1920s saw the beginnings of modernization of the Mexican cattle industry. The key element was Mexican imports of breeding stock and exports of beef cattle, which were almost entirely an exchange with the United States. Mexico's exports, which went almost entirely to the United States, faltered during the early Depression years, but then rose strongly, from a low of 60,000 cattle in 1934 to almost 550,000 in 1941.[61]

How important were American beef markets for the changing uses of northern Mexico's arid lands? From 1921 to 1949, U.S. imports varied from under 1 percent of U.S. beef consumption to a high of 5 percent in 1939.[62] Because that demand was concentrated in the fragile northern drylands of Mexico, it had significant long-range ecological consequences. Over the years the ranching system suffered a gradual elimination of vegetation, on both flatlands and hillsides. Erosion, especially sheet erosion caused by wind, removed thin topsoil, making it difficult to reconstitute and improve pastures when more funds and modern pasture management became available.[63]

American law prohibited the import of South American beef because of the danger of aftosa, or hoof and mouth disease, so American suppliers had long centered their interest on Mexico. In the immediate aftermath of World War II, Mexico suddenly faced a major crisis in its cattle industry, when aftosa began to ravage Mexican herds. The United States banned live cattle imports in 1947 as a result. In 1939, 754,000 head had been imported; by 1949 that was reduced to only 21,000 head. But by then, Mexican beef canneries sold canned beef to the U.S. Department of Agriculture, which shipped it largely to British markets. In 1949, 149 million pounds of processed beef passed through Yankee hands on that route.[64]

Eradication of aftosa necessitated improvement of stock management. Thousands of breeding bulls were shipped to northern Mexico from the United States from the late 1940s onward.[65] From that stock, Mexican breeders extended their work southward into Central America. Mexican cattlemen were dependent on range conditions in the western United States. In periodic droughts north of the border, Yankee cattlemen could now buy Mexican feeder cattle for fattening. A severe drought in the southwestern United States in 1956 led Mexico to begin large exports to the United States again four years later.

By the late 1950s little additional pastureland was available in northern Mexico. So, with rising profits and costs after 1945, ranchers increasingly turned to stock improvement. Northern Mexico's feeder calves were hardier, healthier, and hungrier than stock north of the Rio Grande. Consequently, there was a rising demand for them by the 1950s in the southwestern United States. In 1960, 318,000 feeder cattle were shipped across the border to the United States; two years later that figure jumped to 740,000. Chihuahua and Sonora increasingly aimed production for U.S. markets, using improved breeding, range and water management, and agricultural technology. By the late 1960s Chihuahua's cattle were 65 percent Hereford crosses.

Pasture management was another matter. In the early 1950s still only 3 percent of Mexico's pasture was improved with hardier grasses. More ranches began sowing their pastures to the drought-resistant black grama grass, which by 1970 covered large portions of the plateau from Mexico City to Juarez. Ranchers, moreover, had better access to a U.S.-financed research program, under the Rockefeller Foundation and the U.S. Department of Agriculture, which focused on improving both breeds and pasture. A Rockefeller Foundation Survey Commission first traveled around rural Mexico in 1941. It found that about one-third of Mexico was still native grasslands that could only be productively used through grazing. On the northern ranges, many fine herds of Hereford and Angus were maintained for markets to the north. In contrast, most of Mexico City's beef was lean and tough, still raised in the traditional manner.[66]

In conclusion, the larger operations had the technical and financial capacity to reconstitute severely damaged grasslands, and in some places the political power to control water resources. On the intensive commercial ranches many pastures were improved, though at the long-term cost of depleting both surface and underground water resources. Yankee capital and Yankee markets were a major driving force behind that trend. Beyond the reach of intensive management of the large commercial ranches was a mixed picture of Indian communities where the reforms of the 1930s had given them title to the land in an approximation of their old commons, but few other resources, technical support, or water. Most of the ejidos were badly degraded and poverty-stricken.[67]

PENETRATING THE LATIN AMERICAN RAINFOREST

After 1945, following more than four centuries of preparation on grasslands beyond the Old World, the cattle industry was primed to establish export-scale commercial operations in the lowland wet forests of tropical America. The rainforests had already been encroached upon by both subsistence settlers and large-scale commercial crop exporters. The transport and communications systems that had developed for northern markets were driving more and more wedges into the depths of the jungle. But ranching carried a unique complex of political power, control of extensive tracts of land, and cultural prestige. The ranchers' crop moved on its own locomotion; it could eat its way into the forest. Once again, trends in the economy and culture of material consumption in the United States were to have a profound effect on the ecological fortunes of its southern hinterland.

Postwar America witnessed a baby boom and an unprecedented rush for affluence and all its attributes. Like instant coffee, beef became one of the most prominent symbols of the life that affluence could buy: beef of all cuts on the dining table, and hamburgers in the new chains of fast food restaurants, like White Castle and McDonald's. By then the United States, with one-twentieth of the world's population, was responsible for nearly half of the entire global consumption of beef. In 1960 an average American consumed just under 100 pounds of beef per year, but that figure rose by 1976 to well over 150 pounds— nearly a half-pound of beef every day for every American—before starting to recede in the early 1980s.[68]

As pasture costs rose in the western states, the trend toward rising consumption of beef and rising prices of domestic production coincided with declining supplies of home-grown beef. This led American meat packers to begin looking outside their borders for low-priced beef. In the late 1960s the United States, long an exporter, became the world's largest importer of beef.

At the beginning of the import era in the late 1940s its imports averaged 35,000 tons annually, in contrast with Western Europe's imports of 480,000 tons from southern South America, Australia, and New Zealand. By 1970 American imports skyrocketed to 527,000 tons, while west European imports only doubled to 945,000 tons.[69] The trend continued until about 1980, which had important consequences for the economies of several Latin American countries, and for their lands as well, both savannas and forests, as those regions became economically dependent on the new market.

In response to the rapidly rising demand for beef, American suppliers could draw from the temperate savanna lands of southern South America. Argentina and Uruguay continued to ship processed meats to American markets. U.S. Department of Agriculture experts forged an agreement with the two southern countries on standards of sanitary conditions in approved plants. But an American law passed in 1964, on the insistence of the domestic beef lobby, set import ceilings for beef, veal, and mutton above which a quota system went into effect. The impact on Argentina and Uruguay was immediate. The two countries provided one-half of total U.S. beef imports in the 1950s, but by 1970 that figure fell to only one-quarter. Argentina's share dropped from one-third to under one-tenth.[70]

American meat processors and hamburger chains intensified their searches for new sources of disease-free beef. Expanding affluence throughout the Americas, as expressed in rising demand for beef within Latin America and by export to the United States, produced a major expansion of Latin American rangelands from the 1950s onward. By the 1960s livestock became Latin America's third most valuable export commodity, behind only petroleum (largely from Mexico and Venezuela) and grain (largely from Argentina).[71]

Beginning in the late 1950s Central America became a beef supplier for American markets. Its cattle were raised on grass rather than grain, making the beef very lean, suitable for only one sector of the U.S. beef market, the fast-food trade. Central American beef began to make its way into hamburgers, frankfurters, chili, TV dinners, baby foods, luncheon meat, salami, and other processed meats for humans, to say nothing of dog and cat food. Of these items, hamburgers became the leading category, accounting for more than one-third of the fast-food industry in the 1970s.

Development of the industry in moist forest zones posed a series of problems that were not present in the grasslands. The biotic complexities of rainforest ecosystems were an effective barrier against commercial ranching until the 1950s. Lowland pasture diseases such as blackleg, anthrax, and splenetic fever had been a hindrance to livestock, much as malaria and yellow fever had been to humans. In addition, roads remained poor except where corporate export operations like bananas had taken hold.

One source of innovations for the Caribbean lowlands of Central America came from Mexican ranchers farther up the coast. Beginning in the 1920s, the Mexican lowlands led the way in adopting new techniques of cattle ranching in the moist lowland forest. In colonial times and through the 1800s Mexican cattlemen had maintained small herds of Criollo cattle on the coastal savannahs and riverine marshes, to provide leather and tallow to Mexican markets. The Revolution of 1910–25 decimated most of the herds, but thereafter the numbers rose steadily again. This time they had a stronger market for beef in Mexico City, as roads improved and new railroads were built.

In Mexico's Caribbean coastal lowlands American rubber, banana, and sugar plantations had introduced commercial cattle operations as early as 1910.[72] There was reason now to improve the size and beef productivity of the herds. In the 1930s and early 1940s there was a considerable increase in cattle numbers in the wet lowlands of the Gulf zone. Ranchers introduced new Brahman bulls in 1932. As for pasture improvement, by the 1920s Pará and Guinea grasses were displacing large areas of native species.[73] Both traditional and improved pastures had ecological disadvantages. Where pasture was managed intensively in the Africanization of the grass complex, economic productivity rose at the expense of species diversity. Where cattle were run in neocolonial ways, grasslands were degraded, suffering invasions of woody shrubs as well as the exotic grasses.

The American banana corporations in Central America were also an important source of innovative cattle and pasture management. When Sam Zemurray began organizing large-scale banana production on Honduras's north coast around 1910, he paid attention to pastures as well as plantations, primarily to provide beef for his workers. His employees worked with local ranchers to introduce other aspects of modern pasture and cattle management. Corporate ranching had access to international innovations in cattle breeding and veterinary medicine. By 1929, when United Fruit bought out Zemurray, it inherited over $2 million in livestock, herded on 117,272 acres of managed pasture that was seeded with nutritious exotic grasses such as Guinea grass.[74]

None of this had widespread impact on the rainforests of the Central American Caribbean lowlands until the 1950s, when market demand was transformed by the rise of the American hamburger industry. Cattle ranchers still had little knowledge of the new techniques of cattle management. Anyone who wished to expand commercial operations faced formidable obstacles. On the wet Caribbean lowlands cattle were tormented by sunburn, ticks, and disease, defenders of the natural forest just as much as human and crop diseases were. Only local markets existed, and cattle walked to market, losing weight and quality along the way. Slaughterhouses or *abattoirs* were local monopolies, heavily taxed. One American expert who toured El Salvador at the end of the 1950s described the slaughterhouses as "small, poorly illuminated, unscreened structures of some antiquity. Tools, facilities, and techniques are rudimentary; and disposal of waste usually involves a rear wall, buzzards, and dogs."[75] Typically, there was no refrigeration in open markets and no packaging.

As one commentator succinctly put it, "Before the export boom of the 1960s, cattle managed Central America's pastures."[76] Criollo cattle survived with little care even on rough pasture, but they were poorly adapted to modern markets' demands. They gained weight slowly, their meat was tough and stringy, and they had low reproduction rates. They overgrazed the unmanaged pastures, lowering the pastures' long-range carrying capacity into scrub vegetation. Native grasses survived with little care, but like the Criollo cattle they showed low productivity.

In the 1950s cattle began replacing trees in massive numbers, as new developments in livestock management and meat processing methods brought a revolution in animal husbandry, pasture management, transport, and slaughtering and marketing to Central America. The new technologies and investments led to consolidation of larger properties, which in turn led the way toward more intensive pasture management. The social cost was high, for increasingly powerful ranchers forced many small holders off their ancestral lands.[77] The American role in that trend was selective, but in most of Central America it was an important force. In the new era of widening U.S. investments, Americans strengthened close links to local landed oligarchies, supporting them in their ways of working the land, so long as Yankee standards of beef quality were achieved.

In the two decades after the mid-1950s, beef exports from Central America soared from 20,000 tons a year to almost 150,000 tons, nine-tenths being dispatched to the United States. Nicaragua increased sales to the United States by five times between 1957 and 1967; Honduras increased its sales by twenty-four times. By the end of the 1970s, when American beef imports were at their zenith, the United States imported roughly 10 percent of its total beef consumption each year; most of that was raised in Central America.[78]

By the 1970s beef became Central America's fourth largest earner of foreign exchange, behind coffee, cotton, and bananas. Revenues from beef exports rose from $9 million, when the Alliance for Progress was launched in 1961, to over $100 million in the early 1970s.[79] The area of human-established pasturelands, together with the number of beef cattle, more than doubled in the thirty years after 1950. The expansion occurred primarily at the expense of natural forests.

All Central American beef destined for Yankee markets had to be slaughtered in the home countries, and according to U.S. standards. Beginning in 1957, the U.S. Department of Agriculture worked in tandem with local officials and slaughterhouse operators to set up modern packing plants. The first was opened that year in Nicaragua; by 1978 the five republics boasted a total of twenty-eight plants. The sixteen major ones had a capacity of nearly 900,000 carcasses per year. The hamburger connection was soldered in place.[80]

Investors in new plants included several American corporations, both meat packers and fruit companies. The first plant in Costa Rica and the first two in Honduras were foreign-owned. United Brands intensified management of its pastures in Costa Rica. In Honduras it managed 14,000 acres of improved pasture plus 34,000 acres of extensive rangeland, adding financial value to the high percentage of the concession land that had never been planted in bananas. Remarkably, by the late 1970s United's Honduran beef had bigger sales than its bananas. Not to be outdone, the other food distribution giant, International Foods, also bought two plants in Honduras. Other multinational fruit corporations followed United in their diversification campaigns, turning more marginal land into cattle production. By the 1960s Del Monte ran cattle on 99,000 acres of concessions in Guatemala and Costa Rica; Standard Brands had extensive ranching concessions in both countries. Even Goodyear Tire turned an old rubber plantation in Costa Rica into a cattle ranch.

Individual American entrepreneurs, as well as corporations, profited from the new possibilities. When Santa Gertrudis cattle were introduced into Central America in the 1950s, Leroy Denman of the King Ranch spent fifteen years in Guatemala on that work. Rudolph Peterson, ex-president of the Bank of America and head of the United Nations Development Program, bred cattle in Panama. Another Yankee speculator was Toby Orr from Montana, head of the Peace Corps in Costa Rica in the late 1960s. By 1972 Orr and twenty other Americans were operating ranches there.[81]

These men were vital channels for the modern inputs that were industrializing Central American agriculture and reducing the rainforest. Yankee multinationals marketed virtually the whole spectrum of new inputs for cattle operations, including animal feeds with veterinary supplements, introducing grasses, pasture fertilizers, barbed wire, and more. "The companies that sold tubes of refrigerated semen also dispensed worm medicines, fly sprays, tick dips, vaccines, vitamin/mineral supplements, and other imported ingredients for improved animal health and sanitation."[82] Fort Dodge Laboratories in Kansas set up processing and packaging of veterinary products in Costa Rica, Honduras, and El Salvador. Cargill Foods took enriched animal feeds into Guatemala. W. R. Grace introduced frozen bull semen, fertilizer, and improved grass seeds into Nicaragua.

Ironically, the new profitability and lucrative northern markets also extended the life of archaic systems in some areas. The more conservative old Pacific-slope hacienda owners, who still used Criollo cattle and practiced extensive grazing, expanded their acreage into marginal and untitled lands, at the expense of campesinos and their food crops.[83] As the cattle economy expanded, so did social conflict on the land. Ranching involves extensive land use and campesinos often have ill-defined land titles. By the early 1970s class competition became more violent as campesinos were expropriated, their ancestral food-growing lands stripped from them by aggressive ranchers. Alternatively, landlords used tenant farmers for clearing the forest fringe. Wherever smallholders survived, they kept a few head of cattle for their own purposes of draught power, meat, and milk.

Costa Rica is a vivid example of the process and its linkage with the U.S. convenience-food trade. In 1950 cattle-raising lands of Costa Rica accounted for only one-eighth of the country's area; they expanded to more than one-third by the early 1980s. In 1960 the country's cattle herds totaled around 950,000 head, but by 1980 they had reached 2.3 million. Between 1960 and 1980, beef production more than tripled.[84] Costa Rica's beef exports, all of which went to the United States, steadily increased from a 1959–63 average of 17.5 million pounds to 50 million pounds in 1972.[85]

In contrast, Nicaragua, under the dictator Anastasio Somoza, was much slower to modernize its ranching. Most Nicaraguan cattle were grown on Pacific coastal lands, close to population centers, on flat or rolling terrain and rich volcanic soils. The Somoza family itself controlled approximately half of the country's ranch lands. What pasture remained was largely small ranches; commercial operations were mostly 100–500 head apiece, hardly enough to encourage innovation. Somoza did some upgrading of Criollo stock with American Brahman sires for the export market; a two-tier industry emerged. Improved transportation on new all-weather roads and processing in U.S.-designed slaughterhouses allowed the ruling family and a few other ranchers to expand their operations, penetrating into formerly remote areas. Exports went 98 percent to the United States; in 1959–63 the annual average was 20.7 million pounds; it then rose steeply to 65.9 million in 1972.[86]

In the early 1980s this region-wide export trend finally began to reverse, reducing the force of the hamburger connection, as U.S. consumption of beef began to fall. Though total American beef consumption fell only slightly, this was enough to cause major cuts in imports from the south. Beef exports from Central America peaked at 162,000 metric tons in 1979, representing 40 percent of the region's total production. By 1980 the total dropped to 110,000 (31 percent), and by 1985 to an estimated 61,000 tons (19 percent). Production totals fell from 400,000 tons in 1979 to 318,000 tons in 1985.[87] But by then severe damage had been done. While the connection between North American hamburgers and Central American forest felling was greatly reduced after 1980, its thirty-five year history had produced permanent changes in the equation of social power that determined the fate of the forest. Large amounts of forest were now ragged at best.

In all of Latin America only Amazonia underwent more massive expansion of rainforest ranching in those years. The American presence in Amazonia, though significant, was more limited, a minor force on the forest frontier. It centered in Brazil, where U.S. industrial interests had long been familiar with operating conditions. Brazil's massive cattle population provided beef almost exclusively for its growing domestic market. In colonial Brazil the Portuguese variant on the Iberian cattle culture had been an adjunct of sugar plantations along the northeast coast. Farther inland, in the arid Sertão plateau, vast sprawling ranches evolved in the 1600s. Then, in the eighteenth century, cattle surged into Minas Gerais following the gold rush and slave raids. Cattle were a phenomenon of the moving frontier, providing animal traction and processing scrub vegetation into animal protein for the settlers, while degrading newly cleared lands. Ranchers formed a powerful political elite in the countryside, ruling over a poverty-stricken peasantry.

In the nineteenth and early twentieth centuries, the urban centers of Brazil, primarily Rio de Janeiro and São Paulo, generated a steadily expanding market for beef. This provided some opportunity for American meat packers. After World War I, Americans began investing in Brazilian packing plants but on a smaller scale than in Argentina. By 1929 the three major U.S. meat packers—Wilson, Swift, and Armour—constructed and operated packing plants at the ports of Rio Grande, Rosario, and Rio de Janeiro.[88] This was a tiny fragment of the national picture; it enhanced Brazil's industry but did not shape it. Until after World War II Americans played no significant role in assisting cattle to penetrate the mighty Amazonian rainforest because commercial cattle ranching in the Amazon lowlands began on a significant scale only after 1950.

In the 1950s it was a very different matter, as the Brazilian government and its associated oligarchy of coffee magnates and cattle ranchers turned its interest toward Amazonia as the next frontier of national greatness. Brazil's cattle herd doubled between 1945 and 1968, when it reached 90 million. By then only two commercial beef producing countries had larger herds: the United States, with somewhat over 100 million, and the USSR, with slightly under 100 million.[89] Moreover, Brazil's herds were still mostly in older ranch areas south of Amazonia, the Criollo cattle ranging widely across unimproved pasture. Almost none of the ranching complex was geared to the capital-intensive export market and its modern methods. In 1970 Brazil exported only 2 percent of its total beef production, and this figure was about to reverse. The country was heading toward importing beef for its burgeoning market, as the United States had done earlier.[90]

When Brazil launched its Amazonia development program in full scale in 1966, American companies quickly entered that riskier arena farther north, including Swift, Armour, United Brands, and International Foods.[91] In Brazilian ranching and marketing, the new American ventures clustered at the top end of the corporate scale, often linked with Brazilian partners. The King Ranch of Texas was in the forefront of corporate cattle breeding, veterinary medicine, and pasture management. Though a minor element in Brazil's overall cattle complex, the Texan ranch was in the forefront of expansion, eating the rainforest in the most scientific way.

The King Ranch was the largest and most technically advanced in the continental United States. By that time the ranch was known internationally for its huge capital resources, efficient corporate structure, powerful land-clearing machinery, and careful range management. Its fame was, above all, based on its work in cattle genetics, searching to produce a new breed that combined the rapid beef production of Europe's finest breeds (Aberdeen Angus, Shorthorn, and Hereford) with the Criollo's hardiness and Zebu's resistance to diseases of hot climates, both arid and moist. This was a long and expensive process, but it was successful when, in 1940, the Department of Agriculture officially accepted the Santa Gertrudis cross as the only new American breed of the twentieth century.

By the early 1950s the owner, Bob Kleberg, grandson of the founder of King Ranch, began looking internationally for grazing lands and economies that could help him break out of the increasing cost crunch of the American cattle economy. He was ready to challenge the tropics, to increase his fortune by showing the world that it was possible to intensify beef production in both the arid and the humid tropics. Kleberg was a distinctively American sort of technocratic idealist: he was confident that a large enough scale of Yankee (in this case Texan) energy and know-how could solve any of the world's problems, and do it profitably. As a writer for *Fortune* magazine quoted Kleberg's view of the tropics in 1969, "In these parts of the earth are to be found the last immense reserves of cheap undeveloped or underdeveloped land capable of sustaining livestock in numbers large enough to provide whole populations with beef . . . the hot climates where much of the human race lives on the rim of famine."[92]

Kleberg was looking for properties in the traditional ranching countries of Latin America. In 1952 he began purchasing old ranch land in Cuba. By 1959 he was running 7,600 cattle there, a modest number in itself, but he used that herd for breeding Santa Gertrudis bulls to cows elsewhere around the country. This experiment ended in 1960, when Fidel Castro expropriated the King estancia as a vivid symbol of gringo imperialism, and Kleberg lost $2 million on the venture.[93] In retrospect, he mused,

After my experiences in Cuba I had this clear idea: that I would take the King Ranch into the tropics, both wet and dry, with a straightforward commitment to show the less developed countries how to create a profitable supply of cheap animal proteins. My aim is to promote the mass production of tropical beef protein at low cost. Tropical agricultural economies are mostly weak, in part because what they have to sell—coffee, sugar, cotton, rice—is in oversupply. Beef, however, is not in oversupply. It can be produced indefinitely, moreover, without exhausting the land, provided one takes care of the grass cover.[94]

He was surely right about the dilemma of monocrop export economies and agroecosystems, but it was too early to tell whether the beef industry was as sustainable in the tropics as he believed.

Simultaneously, Kleberg was moving into the more modernized ranching system of Argentina but there, too, in an innovative way that only his scale of operations could achieve. In the early 1950s President Juan Peron, in his distinctive brand of populism, set out to curb the power of the cattle barons of the pampas. He placed price ceilings on domestic beef, a popular move with his voters, and sharply raised beef export taxes. By 1955, when the oligarchy forced him out of office, Argentina's beef exports (still largely to Europe) had fallen by half, leaving new market openings for other countries' beef. The King Ranch decided to enter Argentine beef production and pasture management, which the Chicago meat packers had always avoided. Kleberg was a friend of Juan Reynal, scion of one of the old ranching families, through international polo circles. Incorporating together as King Ranch Argentina, they bought two old estancias totaling forty-three thousand acres in Santa Fe state, the heart of the pampas, where Argentine ranchers already grew the highest quality, most productive beef in the world, using European stock of Aberdeen Angus and Shorthorn. This was a Texas cattleman's pride at work: to show that he could mix competitively with the best in the world. But Kleberg had more in mind than that.

Several hundred miles farther north, in Corrientes state on the Paraguay border, was the Gran Chaco, a region of oppressive summer heat, ticks and cattle disease, and annual winter flooding, where poor back-country ranchers had run lean Criollo stock since early colonial days, and a few ranchers had recently introduced the meatier Herefords. The productivity of the Chaco was far lower than the pampas and the obstacles to profitable grazing far greater, but the land was also far cheaper. Kleberg was convinced that with the scale of investment funds and modern machinery at his command, he could make this area of the dry subtropics productive too, for the beckoning international market. Around 1960 he bought Aguay, a 36,000-acre tract where "the flat grayish land is undergirded three feet down by basaltic rock and, in the brittle shadeless brush, ostrich mingle with the cattle and sheep."[95]

Six years later he consolidated his position in Corrientes by buying a second ranch, Oscuro, 85,000 acres of scrub forest. Year-round water was the key. His team drilled deep wells, put up windmills to power them, bulldozed ponds, and built a dam to create a new reservoir. Enough money and machinery could accomplish anything, it seemed. Kleberg's team quickly cleared 15,000 acres of the partially degraded Chaco woodland, replacing it with exotic grasses, and— this was the real innovation in Argentina—used King's pampas ranches as a breeding base for the Santa Gertrudis cross, which they trucked north to Aguay and Oscuro for fattening on the less expensive range. By 1970, 5,000 steers were sent to market annually. In cattle management they proved their methods to be better than anything Brazil had achieved before, giving King and Swift a great competitive advantage on that front. But could they clear the magnificent forest quickly and cheaply? This had traditionally been done by frontier squatter families, who could clear a maximum of five acres per year. Pairs of fifty-ton tractors could do the same work in an hour. Here too high technology could attack the forest much more efficiently, leaving the squatters with no role at all to play, at least on the corporate frontier.

The greatest challenge of all rainforest frontiers, the Amazon basin, stretched from southern Venezuela into Brazil. Brazil was opening to a new round of foreign investment possibilities. Swift was already long active there, but only in meat processing. By the early 1950s Swift was increasingly interested in raising cattle as well, to assure a steady supply to the slaughterhouses; and in inflationary times, owning land was a safe investment. So Swift organized International Packers Ltd. (IPL) as its Latin American subsidiary, and then merged with Deltec International, a large South American financial house, adding politically influential Brazilian partners and their capital. But they still needed a corporate partner for ranch management. IPL's head, Thomas Taylor, was a friend of Kleberg. Kleberg in his survey of Latin American possibilities in 1952, liked the looks of Amazonia's reliable rains and cheap land, as well as the steadily growing domestic beef demand in Brazil's cities. So he and Deltec joined in a 50/50 partnership, to buy old estates and manage them on more competitive modern lines.

Kleberg began farther south, to the old coffee lands of São Paulo, where he separately bought two tracts, called Mosquito and Formosa, near the Paraguay border, and 71,000 additional acres jointly with IPL farther northeast, closer to Rio. On the new pastures the Santa Gertrudis cattle reached marketing weight of 1,000–1,200 pounds in two and a half years, in contrast to three and a half to five years for their more traditional competition. And by artificial insemination, the King combine achieved a calving percentage of over 90 percent, in contrast to less than 70 percent with older stock.

By the late 1960s Kleberg dreamed even bigger ambitions in Amazonia itself. He bought 180,000 acres in Pará state in the eastern Amazon rainforest, 300 miles south of Belem, and began negotiating with the government of Pará for 120,000 more. He calculated he could clear 100,000 acres and plant them with African grasses in twelve years. This would revolutionize ranching in the wet tropics, and make it abundantly clear that the only limit to clearing the rainforest would be the amount of corporate capital mobilized. Kleberg saw a certain nobility in this, contrasting his system of corporate sustainability with his vague understanding of traditional methods. He warned, "The forest is not eternally fertile. Where the Indians had farmed the land, without replenishing the soil with fertilizers, the humus was exhausted and legumes must be introduced to restore the nitrogen to the soil; it is the right combination of perennial grasses and legumes that makes cattle pastures productive."[96] The thought that centuries-old methods of agroforestry might be sustainable did not cross his mind; he might have observed that the ancient system could not provide for the massive protein requirements of a growing population, or the profitability of modern corporate technology.

In the same years, the Rockefeller family was moving into Amazonia. Like the King Ranch, the New Yorker Nelson Rockefeller began his tropical beef ranching first in Venezuela, in conjunction with his oil interests. He took the plunge into Amazonia in 1956, buying a major share in the Brazilian-owned Bodoqueña Ranch, a virtual territory of its own, more than one million acres in Mato Grosso state on the Brazil-Bolivia border, where 50,000 Criollo cattle grazed, extremely inefficiently. Rockefeller planned to replace them gradually with 250,000 Santa Gertrudis from his brother Winthrop's ranch in Arkansas. He also set up a new company called IBEC Research, Inc., which would conduct research on intensive rainforest ranching and hold training seminars and extension services for Brazilian ranchers. His beef would not be for export, but for urban markets like Rio and São Paulo in eastern Brazil. For an operation on that scale he would need to build a slaughterhouse, which would compete with the four existing major packers, Swift, Armour, Wilson, and Anglo. But they all were entering the era of corporate mergers: old American adversaries were beginning to be partners overseas, buying major holdings in each other's operations. In 1968, when Swift and Armour merged their Brazilian interests, Rockefeller invested jointly with them in purchasing an 180,000-acre ranch in the older ranching territory of Lower Amazonia, near Paragominas in Pará state.[97] Like Kleberg's King Ranch, Rockefeller's personal corporation played an important role in the intensification of cattle ranching in the wet tropics, in counterpoint with their local partners and rivals.

CONCLUSION: THE ECOLOGICAL COST OF TROPICAL RANCHING

The web of circumstances that have linked North American cattle interests to the depletion of Latin America's forests and domestication of its natural grass-lands has been spun for half a millennium. More than most domestic animals that Europeans took with them to the Americas, cattle moved the agricultural frontier of modern capitalism onward, and determined that frontier's social and environmental impacts. For four centuries they were a crucial component of settlement in tandem with crops, especially on forest frontiers, helping squatters survive and establishing landlords' ownership claims.[98] Then, in the twentieth century, modern crossbreeds, the product of the scientific revolu-tion in cattle management, were adapted to a wide range of tropical ecological settings, both arid and moist.

Until the mid-twentieth century the presence of cattle in the moist tropical forest was limited by disease and the lack of appropriate pasture. But a host of changes, in both the livestock industry and the wider economy, accelerated the reduction of the forest belt. Ranchers benefited financially from rising international markets and used their profits to consolidate their hold on polit-ical power and the land. Subsistence farmers were displaced into cities or onto marginal (usually forest) lands, causing further environmental damage in their daily struggle for survival.

The new capabilities accelerated into the rainforest from the 1950s onward, propelled by technologies, capital and markets, much of which were provided by the United States. In the era of industrial ranching and processing, as North American pasture lands and production costs rose inexorably above those of Southern lands, it became convenient to use Latin American lands—whether arid savanna or moist forest—as a less expensive adjunct to the American beef industry. Chicago was a pivot of the global beef system, which transformed the natural rhythms of grassland and forest into the economic rhythms of the international marketing system. This provided new goods for those people anywhere who had purchasing power, but it destroyed or digested rural pre-industrial cultures, and replaced or degraded natural environments.

In the semi-arid grasslands, from the Great Basin of the United States southward as far as the Argentine pampas, people who ate cattle that ate grass replaced native species with more aggressive African species, and severely reduced grasslands' carrying capacities to relatively stable but lower levels. Then improvements to pasture and breeds appeared, but with rising social and ecological costs of monopolized water and land.

The sharpest irony of the new cattle breeding was that for adaptation to dry land climate and vegetation, the old Criollo breed was most viable. Its relegation nearly to extinction by the faster nutrient cycling of the hybrids, was the mark that modernization and specialization of the ranching tradition was nearly complete.[99] But before that happened, the Criollo itself had contributed to increasing scarcities or extinctions of wildlife in Mexico and Argentina. This aspect of ranching history is rarely considered in the literature, but it was a major consequence of the domestication of natural grasslands.

The invasion of corporate cattle ranching into the moist lowland forests of tropical America has been a different and more recent chapter in the environmental history of ranching. Massive rainforest clearances for cattle production began only in the 1950s. But the entire development of industrial and scientific ranching, including increasingly cost-pressured, large-scale, centralized operations, prepared the tropical New World rainforest for that more recent onslaught.

Unsustainable Yield: American Loggers and Foresters in the Tropics

TROPICAL TIMBER EXPLOITATION IN THE TWENTIETH CENTURY

The global loss of tropical forests mounted slowly for centuries, increased under the colonial regimes of the early industrial era, and then accelerated exponentially from the 1940s onward. The increase occurred for many reasons; the most important, undoubtedly, was the expansion of agriculture in all of its forms. Export crops and beef production degraded or replaced incalculable extents of tropical forest and wetland and savanna, as if they had no biological or even economic value. But the money value of the forest itself has also risen, primarily in the form of timber products. As the tropical timber industry developed, wood products joined foods as major commodities that Northern economies could harvest from tropical lands. Native forests retreated before the loggers, as light railways, heavy-wheeled vehicles for grading roads and hauling timber, and more efficient multipurpose sawmills became available to meet rapidly increasing global demand.

The United States provided markets for tropical hardwoods beginning in the eighteenth century but, as a portion of total American hardwood consumption, tropical imports were always minute. Domestic hardwoods like oak, maple, and walnut provided as much as 99 percent of each year's consumption. But in terms of harvests in some tropical countries, the American market for tropical hardwood produced major ecological impacts.

Americans Claim to be environmentally friendly & aware yet why they chose to ignore what we are doing to other countries

...ns played four major roles in tropical forest exploitation, not only ...rs and consumers but also as loggers and forest managers. Logging companies measured their success largely in terms of the scale, efficiency, and profitability of the timber harvest. In contrast, professional foresters saw their effectiveness in terms of managing the forests for a sustainable yield. But it was a thin line between loggers and foresters. Although foresters and forest ecologists studied the complexity, fragility, and extent of tropical forests, most of their time was spent studying and managing commercially important species, since no species had any "value" unless it was recognized by the buyers of finished products. More than agronomists and ranch managers, they struggled to understand how to maintain the forest for future human use. And by the 1950s some had begun to wrestle with the social, as well as ecological, issues that are imbedded in forest use.

These foresters faced a profound dilemma, which today remains unresolved. Was it possible, by introducing more systematic management of timber resources, to establish sustainable forestry in the tropics and contribute to social welfare into the future? Or would modern timber technology be yet another power in the hands of those who wanted quick profits at the expense of entire ecosystems? Through the work of pioneering American tropical foresters, we can glimpse what the forests of Latin America and Southeast Asia were like, how the patterns of human pressure on them escalated, and how these ecological technicians envisioned the future of domesticated tropical ecosystems.

AMERICAN MAHOGANY LOGGERS IN THE CARIBBEAN BASIN

Tropical hardwoods were a profitable export from Caribbean islands and mainland lowlands from the time of the first Spanish settlements. High-grading— felling only the finest trees—was practiced by the first Portuguese to intrude on the Bahia coast of Brazil in the early sixteenth century.[1] These loggers were interested only in brazilwood, which they exported to Europe as a source of red dye. The dye was highly valued in the clothing industry, which was expanding to meet the demand generated by a rising and prospering population. Constrained by the only timber transport method then available, a team of oxen, loggers rarely penetrated far from waterways or into steep hilly areas. The full diversity of the deeper forest remained. But by 1600, high-grading reduced the forest along the coasts and riverways to economic insignificance.

As Portuguese power declined and Europe's colonial initiatives migrated to the Caribbean, dyewood hunters discovered logwood, another source of red dye. A hardwood of the lowland moist forest, logwood grew prolifically from Campeche and Yucatan in Mexico through coastal Belize to Honduras and Nicaragua. In the 1600s, despite the Spanish navy's attempts to suppress them, British pirates generated a large-scale export of logwood for the cloth mills of northern Europe. This trade lasted for over three hundred years.[2] The anarchic ways of these loggers, or Baymen, served them well in the turbulent political conditions that prevailed until 1670, when Spain and Britain agreed by treaty that Belize would become the British possession of British Honduras. Even thereafter political instability was so severe and working conditions were so harsh that the loggers took what they could easily find and sailed away. Logs had to be floated to the coast in the rainy season. One early traveler observed,

> During the wet season, the land where the logwood grows is so overflowed, that they step from their beds into water perhaps two feet deep, and continue standing in the wet all day, till they go to bed again; but nevertheless account it the best season in the year for doing a good day's labour in. . . . When a tree is so thick that after it is logged, it remains still too great a burthen for one man, we blow it up with gunpowder.[3]

The size of the logwood tree did not affect the extraction of dye, so the loggers took all available trees, large and small; modern ideals of sustained-yield forestry were beyond imagining. As easily accessible stands of logwood declined, the Baymen moved farther inland, using oxen for hauling and Garifunas (escaped African slaves from the British Caribbean islands) as laborers. Exports to Europe rose from 700 tons in 1800 to 35,000 tons in 1896.

The era of logwood exports to Europe ended suddenly in the late 1890s when chemical dyes suddenly replaced dyewoods throughout Europe. Only 3,600 tons of logwood were exported from British Honduras in 1913.[4] This was just one of numerous examples of industrial products replacing depleted tropical resources on international markets.

In the first century of the colonial enterprise, dyewoods were almost the only timbers exploited for European use. European navies changed that in the seventeenth century, as they began using mahogany in European and Caribbean shipyards. Havana was the major shipyard for the Spanish fleet; in the 1600s Cubans began to comb their forests for mahogany. A major increase in the demand for mahogany occurred in the mid-eighteenth century, when it became the most fashionable furniture wood in Europe. Chippendale and other styles, whose elegant lines and elaborate detail required a fine-grained, easily tooled wood were perfected by craftsmen working with mahogany.[5]

Like most tropical hardwoods, mahogany grows scattered in mixed-species forests, not in easily accessible single-species stands. Mahogany logging inevitably was a matter of high-grading. Sawyers with their oxen searched the forest for single large trees of high commercial value, carving out logging trails as they went. Each great tree that fell shattered numerous smaller trees in its path. After the woodsmen left a logged mahogany forest, many other species remained standing, as did young, twisted, or old mahogany trunks. The best seed trees of mahogany were felled, and as the oxen dragged them to a nearby river for floating away, they damaged still more trees and tore the soil along the paths and riverbanks. Mahogany does not regenerate easily or grow rapidly; it can take up to one hundred years for a tree to mature. Thus, although a degraded mahogany forest was still ecologically stable, its quality as a sylvan community of species was damaged.

British loggers led the way in this phase of forest exploitation, searching the entire Caribbean coast for mahogany, Spanish cedar, and other cabinet woods. By the late 1700s, mahogany extraction surpassed the dyewood trade. The logging was carried on in a setting of legal confusion; titles to land were cloudy and contract systems were rudimentary. Quarrels were frequent among the mahogany cutters, most of whom worked the forests without bothering to establish formal rights.

During the late 1800s, Yankee loggers became a major force around the Caribbean. Their operations became the major pressure on the mahogany forests, intricately interweaving the U.S. forest economy with that of the Caribbean basin. The first Americans to appear were not lumbermen but shippers, middlemen between the loggers and the manufacturers of fine furniture in American cities from New Orleans to Boston. As urban affluence expanded in the United States during the nineteenth century, an increasingly prosperous middle class demanded more tropical hardwoods for furniture, paneling, and other uses. Craftsmen used several rainforest species in their fine cabinetry, but mahogany dominated the market. In the first decades of U.S. independence, they imported mahogany mostly from Cuba, by way of their commercial offices in Havana, but also from Honduras and British Honduras. The east-coast markets thus provided profits for Cuban and Spanish speculators who cleared mahogany forests in central Cuba to grow the white gold of sugar.

The early Yankee entrepreneurs and speculators were a motley lot who made short-term investments in small concessions and organized the logging themselves. Representative of them was Walter Wilcox, best known as a writer of wilderness camping books, who operated in the rainforest of Cuba. Shortly after Cuban independence, Wilcox bought a timber concession on the Bay of Pigs on the south coast, in an area of mangrove swamps and hardwood forests where a few scattered local farmers scratched out a minimal subsistence. Wilcox saw himself as a resourceful frontiersman: a year after his first reconnaissance visit, he returned "with a force of carpenters and laborers and a cargo of lumber and tools. A place was cleared in the forest for a house, docks were built, gardens laid out, wells dug." He added parenthetically, "In all that time we were not molested by the natives."[6] Other early operators worked along the Caribbean coast of Mexico; they included the first long-term operation by a firm specializing in tropical hardwood imports. The Ichabod Williams family firm of New York, whose lumber operations specialized in tropical hardwoods throughout the company's long life from 1838 to 1966, became specialists in negotiations with local authorities, contracts with local labor, and shipment of logs to their sawmill in Bayonne, New Jersey.[7]

When easily accessible supplies in Mexico were depleted and the first series of land concessions ran out toward the end of the nineteenth century, several American companies began searching the Central American rainforests, starting across the border in Guatemala. The region was crudely cosmopolitan. Mexican businessmen from Tabasco, as well as Englishmen and Lebanese from British Honduras, competed with the Yankees as investors. The loggers they hired were an itinerant collection of men far from home for long periods of time. Many were working off debt peonage incurred in other parts of Central America and Mexico. On their occasional recreational forays into muddy frontier towns, they drank, brawled, and whored. Like the rootless loggers in the commercially penetrated forests of many countries, they had no stake in the health of the forest, which they attacked like commercial game hunters. In that turbulent setting the largest of the Yankee firms, the American-Guatemalan Mahogany Company, founded in 1907, cut over sixteen million board feet of mahogany in twenty-three years, mostly in the Usumacinta River basin.[8] Companies like this enabled U.S. mahogany imports to double between 1900 and the late 1920s.[9]

Farther around the Caribbean coast, into Nicaragua, the George D. Emery Company of Boston was the most important producer of timber products. The company experienced initial success but ultimate frustration. Its history illustrates the formidable difficulties that affected profit-making in the timber industry. In 1894 Emery negotiated two leases with the Nicaraguan government that gave him the timber rights in previously untouched forests along rivers flowing into the Caribbean. Casa Emery was soon exporting about one thousand mahogany and Spanish cedar logs monthly to Boston, an unprecedented scale of operations. Its workforce of 1,300 included local Miskito Indians and other minorities, but 100 Americans were imported for the more highly skilled jobs.[10] In 1905, using newly available dynamite, Emery began deepening river channels to smooth travel and log floating.[11] Emery's competitors began using dynamite in the same way. The channel blasting and the logging operations along the riverbanks had downstream effects: siltation and the disrupted flow of water damaged lowland riverine systems near the coast by increasing flooding and damaging fisheries.

The tangles of tropical forests were matched by the tangles of tropical politics. No timber concession was ever granted except through political maneuvering, and none was secure against changing political winds. Casa Emery's concessions had been granted by a friendly regime in Managua, but Central American governments were unpredictable and faction-ridden. Timber operators, in contrast to banana growers, could easily be replaced; high-grading for maximum short-term profits was the inevitable result. In 1909 Emery became entangled in a Nicaraguan presidential campaign, one in which the U.S. government was enmeshed, as well. Emery backed the losing candidate, and the new government retaliated by revoking his concession, ending his fifteen years of logging on the Miskito coast. Washington attempted to intervene through diplomatic channels, on the usual principle of defending the sanctity of American investments abroad, but this time it did no good. Finally, Emery sold out in 1911 to Ichabod Williams, whose sources of supply were diverse, enabling him to continue his business for a full century.

Casa Emery initiated a far higher level of capital and milling technology into mahogany extraction than the rainforest had ever experienced. As in many other fields of resource extraction, the scale of American capitalism shaped major changes. The aftermath of World War I brought a momentous change to the forests. After a severe but brief postwar depression in the timber industry, mahogany investments expanded in the 1920s, into ever more remote forests. Motor-driven tractors appeared, along with large skidders and log-wagons, equipment that far surpassed oxen. Tractors could operate with ease on hilly terrain and could haul logs several miles from the cutting site to the river.

The new scale of investment and technology was evident downriver as well. At log collection points near the mouths of rivers, more sophisticated sawmills appeared that were capable of milling a wider variety of species and utilizing a higher percentage of each log. The situation was parallel to expanded-scale technology in the sugar refineries. The imported sawmills were too expensive and too efficient for local millers; they could neither afford them nor compete with them. Ladinos were beginning to produce mahogany furniture but their efforts were largely stymied by the financial and organizational power of United States and European industry. Local operators could function only on the fringes of the Northerners' corporate power. The semi-anarchic life of mahogany logging companies in the region contrasted sharply with the other tropical location where Americans worked, the Southeast Asian country where the United States had its most important experience of direct colonial rule.

AMERICAN TIMBERMEN IN THE COLONIAL PHILIPPINES

American forestry operations in Southeast Asia before World War II presented a striking contrast to events in the Caribbean basin, for two reasons. First, a complex trade in tropical hardwoods controlled by the Chinese and Europeans had existed throughout the region for centuries before the Americans arrived. Second, in 1904 American foresters were given the direct responsibility of constructing a forestry service for the islands; in the Caribbean, Americans had similar control only in Puerto Rico. The Philippine islands played a pivotal role in the history of tropical logging and silviculture in the United States and Southeast Asia, for it was there that U.S. foresters and timber firms learned the methods of systematic tropical logging.

By the 1920s the alliance forged between American foresters and loggers and their Filipino counterparts and protégés produced a forest economy that was as modern as any in tropical Asia. The Philippines became a stage that showcased the tropical foresters' great gamble with technological and political power. The advanced technology of timber extraction that was developed in the Philippines turned the islands into one of the first great tropical timber exporters, but it also prepared the way for the tragic devastation of the islands' vast forest cover that began after 1946, the year of Philippine independence. The interplay of American rule and Filipino society resulted in reckless and often illegal deforestation after 1950. In recent years, the natural wealth of these forests has been squandered and the biotic treasures of the islands have been decimated.[12]

Export markets drove the exploitation of the Philippines' lowland forests. Although the islands were net importers of timber in 1900, by the 1920s that trend had been reversed. Hardwood timber was shipped to many markets, primarily in the United States. By 1960 the Philippines was the single largest forest products exporter in Southeast Asia. Little of the forest being cut was growing back as a timber resource; the nation was steadily borrowing from the future, with sobering consequences. The roots of the disaster lay in the power of the country's landowning elite, which controlled the export of timber as well as sugar and other plantation crops.

When the Philippine islands fell to the United States in 1898, America inherited one of the great treasures on the planet. Much of lowland Southeast Asia is covered by a richly diverse rainforest dominated by the *Dipterocarpaceae* family of giant hardwoods. In other areas are seasonally dry monsoon forests, which have a different biological composition dominated either by deciduous species or by extensive stands of pine. In brackish coastal lowlands are some of the most extensive mangrove forests in the world. The evergreen dipterocarp rainforest represents a species composition that is almost entirely different from that found in the humid tropics of Latin America and Africa, but both types of rainforest contain several hundred tree species in a small acreage.[13] Its exquisite biotic complexity dazzled early Western observers, who saw it as both intimidating and a challenge to conquer.

For centuries, Southeast Asia had carried on international trade of tropical timber products that far exceeded the trade in either Latin America or Africa. Hardwoods and aromatic species such as sandalwood and sappanwood had their major market in the regionally powerful markets of China. *Lauan*, or Philippine mahogany, had been exported from the Philippines for centuries before the Spanish conquerors arrived in the 1570s. In a pattern typical of many parts of Southeast Asia, local men cut the trees and Chinese merchants exported the timber, much of it heading to markets in southern China. The immensity of the forest resources on the Philippine islands was evident to the Spanish colonial rulers, but they were able to exploit only a fragment of that wealth. At the end of the Spanish era in 1898, primary forests covered fully two-thirds of the islands' territory, and three-quarters of that were diptero-carp forests.[14] Mature lauan trees are the great commercial timber wealth of the Philippines, but once logged they regenerate very slowly. Hence, loggers operated largely in the shrinking virgin forests.

The Spanish regime placed most of its attention on Manila's hinterland. European officials frequently struck up alliances with men they called *caciques*, or local overlords. Many of the other islands retained much of their forest cover through the 1800s. By 1898 logging was still primitive and localized. Trees were cut by light, blunt axes, then hauled by *carabao* (water buffalo) to rivers; then the logs were floated to sawmills downstream. There were only five or six power-driven sawmills in the country, all of them in the environs of Manila.

The first U.S. link to the islands' timber wealth appeared in the 1890s, when American companies began importing redwood and Douglas fir for their building projects in Manila.[15] Like much of the international trade of the southwest Pacific at the height of the imperialist scramble, this was a high-risk business. No American company or logger survived for long until U.S. rule was formally established in the Philippines after 1898. American control brought the stability that timber operators needed if they were to profit from their investments. Thereafter, the exploitation of forest wealth in the Philippines was distinctively shaped by American logging and forestry practices and by the ways the U.S. regime's Bureau of Forestry functioned as an arm of the American colonial system.

American foresters knew little about the forest ecosystems that they were about to manage and exploit. Even in the United States professional forestry was still in its infancy, but it was being rapidly shaped by Gifford Pinchot, head of the forest service in Washington. In the Philippines, his protégé, George P. Ahern, became the creator of modern forestry management and timber exploitation in the Philippines.[16] The Americans now controlled one of the great rainforests of the planet, and they had much to learn about it. Pinchot assigned Ahern the job of creating a forestry bureau in the new colony. His task was to learn as rapidly as possible the rudiments of Southeast Asian forest biology, assemble a team to work with him, and design a system of forestry laws.

In 1901 Ahern wrote to Pinchot, urging him to visit the islands and tour their forest resources with him. Pinchot was delighted to have his first view of the tropical abundance, because, as he later wrote, "of experience in tropical Forestry I had exactly none. But I had learned something about Forestry in Burma and in British India." Pinchot arrived in Manila that October; he and Ahern set out immediately to explore their new biological cornucopia. On their first stop, Mindoro Island, where U.S. timber operations would soon begin, they walked for a day "through almost distressingly interesting tropical forest, where every tree was new and strange." The two men visited every major island, taking copious notes on the forests, the local economy, and the people.

Their fascination focused on scores of tree species that they had never seen before. They delighted in the beauty and grandeur of the trees; yet at the same time they were calculating their potential value as timber. In Negros, south of the region of new sugar plantations, they hiked into a forest that Pinchot called "the most luxuriant I have yet seen, and in by far the best silvicultural condition. On the lower slopes it consisted of old trees from 130 to 150 feet in height, frequently with from 90 to 100 feet of clear trunk, standing in a selection forest in which all age classes were represented." The two men began to design a system of sustainable timber exploitation. Existing logging operations in the rainforest could not have been further from sustainable. Pinchot recorded in his diary that on the southernmost island, Mindanao, they sought out one well-known sawmill, owned by the Philippine Lumber and Development Company. "We expected to find bad work, and we found it. Everywhere we went the untouched forest was in a superb condition. [Yet] I have never seen a more complete slash. . . . Everything was destroyed as far as logging had gone. Unquestionably the kind of logging now going on will lead to erosion of the most serious character on a surface so steep as to be totally unfit for agriculture."[17]

It was urgently important to stop such logging operations, and the only way to do that was to design strict forest laws and train a generation of foresters who would have the authority to control both the ravaging work and the corrupt influence in Manila that protected it. Pinchot and Ahern designed a set of laws that were adopted in 1904. This was the fulfillment of the Progressive dream: full authority placed in the hands of those who knew best what was necessary to meet human and biological needs. From then until his retirement in 1914,

Ahern was committed equally to rapidly modernizing the timber industry of the country and making the forest wealth serve the long-term needs of the Filipino people. Both ambitions were, at best, only partially fulfilled.

Ahern was confident that modern scientific forestry and the rapid expansion of timber exports could overcome the pervasive poverty of the islands. One urgent priority was to modernize timber operations so that the islands would no longer have to rely on imported lumber for domestic needs. The Philippines had been importing building timber since the nineteenth century despite the great riches of its forests. Like many of the rapidly expanding ports of the southern Pacific rim, Manila was being built with redwood and Douglas fir from the U.S. Pacific Northwest.[18] Ahern and his team saw that their great challenge of reversing that pattern was a matter of establishing competent laws, organizing their effective administration and linking that system to the most up-to-date, large-scale logging technology.

The Bureau of Forestry forged close working relations with American logging firms that were interested in expanding their operations into the tropics. Often the bureau carried out detailed field studies for these firms. The results were impressive: major American firms began operating in the islands almost as soon as the forestry laws were in place. Ahern and Pinchot knew their commercial counterparts well. Their contacts with the timber industry in the American northwest immediately yielded fruit when the Insular Lumber Company, the first modern lumber company in the Philippines, was launched in 1904. Headed by W. P. Clark, a leading manufacturer of sawmill equipment in Seattle, Insular took advantage of the new law to gain a 300-square-kilometer timber concession in the lauan forests of Negros, where intensive forest clearing for sugar plantations had begun.

Thereafter, sugar expansion and lumber operations were closely linked, and their alliance was far more efficient than were those anywhere in Latin America. As one forester observed with pride six years later, "The operations are an exact copy of the lumbering operations of a large company in Seattle, Washington, and the sawmill, of 100,000 board-feet daily capacity, is as thoroughly fitted up with up-to-date appliances and as well run as almost any mill in America. . . . All this is a new venture, believed to be utterly impossible a few years ago."[19]

The technological transformation was dramatic. On tour several years later, the leading American forester and ecologist Barrington Moore, although skeptical of some of the aspects of forest management that he saw, wrote, "In utilizing the forests the most astounding progress has been made from a lumbering point of view."[20] American supervisors controlled every aspect of logging operations as foremen, superintendents of logging railways, sawyers, and yard managers. All other workers were local, including those trained for various semiskilled jobs. By 1911, Insular employed eight hundred Filipino and Chinese laborers, who worked under only eighteen American supervisors.

Under Ahern's direction, the bureau also cultivated close relations with Filipino loggers, teaching them to expand and modernize their operations. In this work, the foresters were entirely in tune with the general tenor of American colonialism in Manila, where entrepreneurs from the United States and their local counterparts evolved much closer working relationships than those that developed in most other colonial systems. In forestry as in plantation agriculture, one broad consequence of these ties was the strengthening of Manila's elite, allowing them to dominate land use after independence.

Nonetheless, conflicts between the Bureau of Forestry and Filipino commercial interests soon became evident. The landed and commercial elite resisted any system of sustained-yield logging, and their opposition quickly found a political voice in the national legislature. The lower house, which was made up entirely of elected Filipinos, annually opposed any additions to the bureau's budget. Dean Worcester, secretary of the interior for the colonial government, criticized local lumbermen for wanting only quick profits and resisting restraints on their access to the forest.[21] Worcester knew that they had power as a lobby, and he worried—prophetically—about their capacity to circumvent the bureau's regulatory powers.

Until the 1920s, Philippine timber primarily supplied domestic markets. Ahern's ambition was to make the Philippines an exporter of timber and the timber industry an important contributor to the islands' net balance of trade by marketing Philippine timbers to the burgeoning ports of Hong Kong, Nagasaki, Shanghai, Sydney, and Singapore. Insular Lumber successfully introduced lauan timber to international markets, under the name of Philippine mahogany, to exploit the popularity of true mahogany from the American tropics. By 1920 lauan began to replace redwood in the ports of the western Pacific. Yet most Philippine mahogany exports were destined for the western United States, to be used as paneling, doors, and furniture. A less extensive trade developed with businesses in the northeastern states, including furniture makers in Michigan who began purchasing red lauan from New York importers in the 1920s.

The ultimate issue was whether the expansion of production in the dipterocarp forests could be sustained. For many years, foresters, in their enthusiasm for the challenge, tended to estimate that fellings could be greatly accelerated without permanent damage to local soil and vegetation patterns. This was a dangerous stance, for these foresters knew little about the biotic cycles of the rainforest. Only a few were alert to the danger. As early as 1910 Moore warned of the danger of rapid cutting when loggers knew so little about the forests' rate of regeneration. He challenged the government's habit of putting pressure on the Bureau of Forestry to maximize production and revenue while minimizing its management and research budget. Unfortunately, voices such as this were rarely heard in the general enthusiasm for the new wealth.

The harvesting of the Philippine forests took more than one form. Government policy encouraged clear-cutting of lowland forests on land that seemed flat enough to warrant conversion to rice production. Moore argued that it was foolish to destroy any forest if its land was not needed for crops. In forests on steep slopes or higher elevations, which were not marked for conversion to rice, foresters used a selection system to harvest the timber, marking each mature tree for cutting. Because the bureau had a severely limited staff, this system was too slow to satisfy the market for timber.

Soon the system was changed to diameter-limit cutting, which allowed loggers to take every commercially useful tree that was over forty centimeters in diameter. The system was extremely wasteful, because in areas without sawmills loggers left behind everything felled except the main trunks of large trees. Foresters gradually learned that the diameter-limit system led to severe forest depletion and little regrowth because smaller trees were burnt by the sun when the upper canopy was disrupted. The number of new seedlings in clearings was reduced to an estimated one-eighth of the natural rate in undisturbed forest. The foresters' early optimism that dipterocarp forests would respond to cutting just as temperate forests did was being eroded.

These political, economic, social, and ecological trends were all tied to the global economy, the relative prosperity of which, during most of the 1920s, encouraged export production of plantation crops and timber. The following decade brought a severe downturn in the Philippine export economy and, with it, a change in the pattern of pressures on the land. By the 1930s forestry policy and management were no longer the exclusive preserve of the Americans. The colonial administration emphasized educating and training Filipinos and turning actual planning and administration over to them as rapidly as possible. Americans rarely questioned the character of the power structure that they were both creating and reinforcing in the dependent country. They built the colonial administration and the transition to self-rule on an alliance with the landed and commercial elite—the sugar barons and others. The forestry profession reflected this reality and adjusted to it.

In 1910 Ahern had founded a college of forestry at Los Baños, not far outside Manila, where his team began training Filipino foresters. Some of the first graduates of the basic course there were sent on to Yale Forestry School, the alma mater of Pinchot, for advanced training in American forestry management. By the mid-1920s nearly all foresters in the islands were Filipino; the entire five-hundred-man hierarchy of guards, rangers, and foresters was made up of nationals, except for five Americans at the top. In 1936 Arthur Fischer, the last American chief of the bureau, turned his office over to his Yale-seasoned protégé, Florencio Tamesis. From that time forward Americans were only consultants. No other tropical colony moved local men into authority over forest resources so fast.

Internationally, forestry was a profession with high social prestige. In tropical countries especially, foresters were recruited almost exclusively from high status backgrounds; the social perspectives of their class fit well with the profession's belief in the prerogatives of expertise. Filipino foresters were almost exclusively recruited from the landed class, with its links to Manila society. These young men understood the realities of urban and international markets and assumed that urbanization and rising standards of consumption were the pattern of progress. Except for those who specialized in laboratory analysis or sawmill technology, they loved being in the deep forest, discovering new species of trees, shrubs, and vines. They were paternalistic or hostile to the agrarian poor and at best condescending to the tribal cultures of the mountain forests.

When the global economy contracted sharply in 1930, markets for tropical primary products went into a state of collapse. The economy of the Philippines was no exception, and timber exports declined with other commodities. The worldwide Depression did not affect the overall pattern of ownership in the timber industry. The political setting did change significantly in 1935, when a new constitution brought the islands commonwealth status and internal autonomy, one step short of total independence. The new government, dominated by the landlords, set about legislating to defend Filipino commercial interests against foreign competition, especially the Chinese. The special ties with U.S. lumber interests were carefully preserved, however; under the new legislation, only Filipino or American firms could be given long timber leases. Investment by other foreigners was limited to 40 percent of a firm's capital.

By that time, the logging industry stood fifth in capital investment in the country, fourth in the value of its production, and second in the size of its labor force. It had become a major force in the national economy. The United States remained the largest single market, one the bureau continued to cultivate. A booklet issued by the bureau in 1939 reminded its potential buyers that when Americans bought Philippine lumber, they were "helping not only the Filipinos, but also the American lumbermen in the Philippines and the American machine manufacturers in the United States."[22]

The symbiosis between American and Philippine lumber industries was shattered by World War II. During the Japanese occupation of the islands, forestry was totally disrupted. Many Filipino foresters joined the resistance against the Japanese occupation, and forest administration and control dissolved. The last year of the war was the most destructive. As the Japanese forces retreated, they destroyed nearly all the sawmill machinery in the country. They left Manila and other cities badly battered. In the process of withdrawing from the Manila area, the Japanese burned the records of the Bureau of Forestry and leveled the college of forestry at Los Baños.

The war left a legacy of severe social disruption on forested land. The upheavals of the war dispossessed masses of peasant squatters, who searched for new land after the war was over. In 1948 Tamesis summarized the dilemma of social policy that the foresters faced: "Forest destruction increased after the liberation. Illegal clearings to alleviate the food shortage destroyed valuable forests. On account of the tremendous demand for timber, illegal cutting and timber smuggling became widespread. The great number of unlicensed firearms left over from guerrilla warfare makes enforcement of forest law difficult, especially in the more remote regions."[23]

The most pressing task after the end of the war was the islands' final transition to independence, which was accomplished in 1946. The rebuilding of the country and its economy began simultaneously, starting with ravaged Manila. The devastated timber industry revived rapidly. Approximately one hundred cast-off U.S. military sawmills were installed, old lumber was recycled, and new supplies were milled.

As the political system and economy stabilized, the forest wealth of the Philippines was tapped again. The islands became the great supplier of timber products throughout Southeast Asia. Timber products became a leading source of export earnings and enormous wealth and power for individuals with political influence, many of whom began logging illegally. Market demand rapidly outstripped administrative control in the forests, for the forestry administration could not be reestablished in the countryside until the early 1950s.

The 1950s saw a sharp decline in production costs of lauan plywood and veneer, and Philippine lauan exports dominated the Southeast Asian industry through the 1960s. The Bureau of Forestry recovered very slowly from its wartime decimation and it had little power to control the issuance or management of timber concessions. The College of Forestry at Los Baños was slow to recover after the war. Although a new generation of forestry recruits went to Yale for training, especially in wood technology, from 1946 on the college itself was effectively revived only in 1957, with major assistance from the Division of Forestry and Forest Products of the United Nation's Food and Agriculture Organization (FAO) and the U.S. International Cooperation Agency.

In the 1960s the timber supply in Philippine forests began to decline precipitously as its virgin forests disappeared. The gamble taken by the American foresters in the previous generation—that more efficient, larger-scale logging technology and controlled management could both utilize and sustain the Philippine forests—had apparently failed. Timber merchants with powerful political leverage in Manila and a burgeoning squatter population with political patrons in the countryside were the twin forces driving disastrously rapid deforestation. In 1959 Nicolas Lansigan, head of the Society of Filipino Foresters, attacked the lumber barons publicly, concluding, "While some lumbermen are decidedly of the desirable type who are frankly worried about the fate of the forests and the future of their investments . . . many are plain timber miners of the cut-and-get-out variety."[24]

Of the few American foresters who visited the country in the 1950s, the most prestigious was Tom Gill. The Philippine government and the U.S.

International Cooperation Agency co-sponsored Gill's tour of the islands in 1959. He was commissioned to assess the quality of logging and forestry operations throughout the islands and he was appalled at what he saw. Addressing the Philippine Lumber Producers Association in Manila at the end of his tour, Gill reported, "Some weeks ago I flew over and visited Cebu, Bohol and Negros. Parts of these islands made me think I was back again in Korea, North China, or the man-made deserts of Mexico. For I saw thousands upon thousands of hectares of cut-over, burned-over and abandoned land, pock-marked with red and yellow scars of bare earth at the mercy of sun, wind and rain."[25]

When Ferdinand Marcos was elected president in 1965, the race to cut the last easily accessible lauan forests accelerated rapidly. Marcos's rule was effectively a dictatorship, and his policy of "crony capitalism" bled the country dry: he rewarded his friends with vast short-term timber concessions.[26] Trade statistics from these years dramatically register the shrinkage of timber supplies. By 1985, purchasing power from earnings had fallen to 13 percent of the 1970 level. By the mid-1970s, 5.3 million hectares of the Philippines were listed as treeless ex-forest land; much of this was critical watershed. Moreover, logging roads led to the destruction of far more than just trees: they allowed squatters to penetrate the region. Squatters slashed and burned patches of forest, planted survival crops that they tended for a brief time, and then turned the degraded land over to cattle. The nation's forest cover shrank from 50 percent of its total surface in 1950 to a mere 24 percent in 1987.

The Marcos regime made it extremely difficult for foreign corporations to operate legally and competitively in the Philippines. In the 1970s a few multinational companies operated there, including Georgia-Pacific, Boise-Cascade, International Paper, Weyerhaeuser, and the largest Japanese competitor, a subsidiary of Mitsubishi.[27] But by the 1980s direct U.S. investment in the Philippine timber economy was minimal. The major American connection with deforestation there in recent years has been indirect, taking the form of markets for forest products harvested by Japanese firms in Mindanao and elsewhere and manufactured in Asia for the American market. The connection between the world economy and deforestation in the Philippines remains vital, but it is by no means a simple one.[28] In Latin America and the Caribbean the involvement of Americans in forest management developed in rather different ways.

THE ROOTS OF SUSTAINABLE FORESTRY IN TROPICAL AMERICA

Latin America experienced a similar postwar acceleration in the timber industry, although it was slower and more tentative than the postwar growth in the
Philippine islands. Slower growth was a reflection of the region's corporate
technology, forestry administration, and government support for forest
exploitation, which was less developed there than it was in the Philippines.
Although World War II was not fought on New World soil, the timber
resources of all the Americas were mobilized for the war effort. The American
military sponsored a search in tropical woodlands for strategic timber species
such as exceptionally light balsa, which was used for airplane parts, and
mahogany, which was transformed into boats and gliders.[29] The number of
tropical species used in Northern markets increased, adding another element
to the complex ecological legacy of global warfare.[30]

Probably most fundamental for the long term, World War II brought further acceleration of technological scale. Between 1943 and 1945 three U.S.
firms—Ichabod Williams from New York, Freiberg Mahogany of Cincinnati
and New Orleans, and Weis Fricker of New Orleans—introduced trucks and
other mechanized equipment for hauling timber in the Guatemalan Petén and
in British Honduras, hauling out millions of board feet of hardwood. This was
a clear example of how urgent wartime priorities, and their associated profits,
increased corporate capability to extract natural resources in peacetime.

As the war ended in 1945, Allied planners knew that Europe and East Asia
faced a monumental task of rebuilding that would continue to place heavy
demands on the planet's natural resources. Northern Europe's conifer forests
could not provide for all of Europe's timber needs, and the Soviet Union,
home of the world's greatest conifer forests, was crippled. Canada and the
United States had only a limited capacity to expand their harvest of yellow
pine, Douglas fir, and other conifers. High consumption levels in the United
States were also driving the timber cutting: per capita timber consumption
there was five times that of Europe, and its 8 percent of the world's population
was using two-thirds of global wood pulp. South America, where consumption was very low and the timber industry was underdeveloped, had the
largest reserve of unexploited forest.

The United States still imported far more timber from the Philippines than
from Latin America. The entire U.S. market for tropical hardwoods was modest from the American perspective: tropical species were less than 1 percent of

U.S. consumption. American timber imports from Latin America rose from 974,000 cubic feet in 1948 to 1,291,000 cubic feet in 1956, only a gradual increase. But, just as in earlier years, the U.S. demand for specialty hardwoods was very significant for the tropical exporters themselves, and thus for the tracts that they harvested.[31]

There was obviously major potential for increased timber production throughout the forest region of Latin America, but there were many hindrances to the expansion of the industry. Old mahogany firms, both American and European, continued to provide specialty hardwoods, yet they faced familiar difficulties in dealing with local authorities. An FAO study in 1959 concluded that although Latin America had ample resources, the unattractiveness of investment in an unprofitable industry had resulted in a severe shortage of development capital.

The forest products industry in North America began to respond to this opportunity. Major Northern timber corporations had accumulated the scale of investment capital and the technical and managerial capacity needed to begin risking major investments in the tropics. They also had achieved greater efficiency, extracting a wider range of forest species and processing a higher percentage of each tree. Because Yankee companies were able to use more of the harvested trees, they could out-compete local operators. Local firms exported only the best logs, wasting most of the rest of the cut.

Waste on such a scale was intolerable to the generation of foresters working in Latin America in the 1950s, led by Leslie Holdridge, the most experienced American expert in Central America, who observed,

> Only a small part of the potential productivity of the land is being utilized by the present wood-working industries of the country. Increased use depends on many factors, such as the improvement of transportation facilities, management of forest lands to reduce loss from fire, control of utilization practices that destroy the productive capacity of the forests, the establishment of more efficient manufacturing methods, and the development of marketing organizations to promote the sale of manufactured products.[32]

Holdridge and his colleagues urged local mill owners to build modern sawmills that were designed to make fuller use of the harvested trees than hand axes and saws could. They also promoted the manufacture of plywood and veneer, made possible by sophisticated new machinery, which would not only raise efficiency but also increase the variety of species that could be milled. In the years that followed, their more professional approach was adopted slowly by the logging industry.

Politics continued to make systematic forest management a difficult science to practice. Throughout Central America small Yankee expatriate firms competed with the local sawmill operators. Like the individual Americans who had migrated to warmer climates for small-scale farming or trade, their numbers and cumulative impact are difficult to trace. Tom Gill did not overlook them, though. Toward the end of his long career, he described them with fervor:

> Ever since forestry graduates first emerged from our colleges, men have been going out to work for foreign powers or private companies, or to teach or, precariously, to start enterprises of their own. Outgrowth of conditions where not only their work but life itself was often a gamble, the stories of these men are among the most stirring sagas in American forestry. . . . They left behind something that has come to be recognized as inherent in the American forestry tradition—a willingness to try anything once, and a positive genius for dealing with the unexpected.[33]

Gill could not resist the indulgence of praising this national myth: that the dynamic, resourceful Yankee had introduced a valuable quality into the saga of resource exploitation in the tropics.

A half-century of beginnings in tropical forestry was starting to bear fruit. American foresters had first turned their professional interest south into the Caribbean (in parallel to their work in the Philippines) in the aftermath of the Spanish-American War. When the United States permanently took over Puerto Rico in 1898, the island's forests were the only tropical forests in Latin America or the Caribbean directly administered by the United States. The U.S. Forest Service was almost totally ignorant of the physical and biological properties of Caribbean forests, and in 1911 it established the U.S. Tropical Forest Experiment Station, a research station in Río Piedras, just outside San Juan, to carry out research in the Luquillo Forest Reserve.

Substantial research on sustained-yield forestry management began in the 1920s. It had to begin with taxonomic studies to identify and catalog the vast variety of tree and shrub species in the exotic woodlands. Research was designed to broaden the range of marketable species, and for that it was important to understand life cycles and regeneration conditions. This was the beginning of the study of rainforest ecology; it was centered in the wood technology laboratory at Yale Forestry School. Samuel Record, the leading tropical wood technologist in the Americas, directed the agenda there, and published the research results in the journal *Tropical Timbers*, which served the needs of tropical biological science and the timber trade alike.

Through the fledgling institute in Puerto Rico, American foresters developed connections to the emerging international forestry network. A British research institute, the Imperial Forest Research Institute, was founded in Trinidad in the 1920s as the empire's American research base for tropical forest science.[34] The center in Trinidad was linked to the Empire Forestry Association, a worldwide network established by the British in 1921.

In the 1930s the small group of Americans at Río Piedras also began to develop liaisons with foresters working in the independent countries of Latin America. No formal international organization yet existed to facilitate those contacts—such organizations developed more readily in parts of the tropics that were still under colonial rule. Because the foresters at Río Piedras were employees of the U.S. Forest Service, however, they were not bound by the fiscal constraints of private companies. In addition to their research on forest biology and timber products, they could address the broader issues of forestry law and administration in each country and promote the training of competent forest managers. Their agenda was therefore far broader and more ambitious than that of their counterparts who worked in private industry

Contacts with Mexico led the way, aided by long-established connections with the father of Mexican natural resources management, Miguel de Quevedo. Thirty years of his work finally resulted in the Mexican government passing forest laws in 1936 (which were based on American law) and establishing its first forestry training program.[35] Aside from this, Latin American countries had no real administrative or technical capacity to design or enforce forestry laws before the 1950s.[36] Government timber inspectors were usually untrained and often corrupt.

By the early 1940s the British and American scientists working together carried out some detailed ecological studies, which led to experiments in which exotic tree species were planted and assessed for their possible commercial value. But the researchers were not given even minimal resources to enable them to study such basic matters as tropical soils, watershed protection or the impact of forest fire. Surprisingly, they were not even able to initiate studies of forest economics.[37]

The efforts of forest scientists and administrators had little impact against the increasing incidence of high-grading and the expansion of croplands before World War II. Nevertheless, the groundwork was being laid for what would emerge with postwar peace. Until Latin American countries could train their own cadres of foresters—and that did not happen until the 1960s and beyond—North Americans played a dominant role as their mentors and exemplars. Hence, the significance of a small group of Yankee foresters who became absorbed with the challenges of tropical timber management and the biology of tropical forests that were strikingly different from the temperate forests where they had learned their trade.

Foresters had to work within the institutional and social frameworks of tropical countries. After 1945, as tropical governments became more assertive, foresters tried to channel national development policies toward sustainable timber management, integrated with agriculture. All too often political, economic, and demographic pressures were far stronger than foresters' ecological knowledge of the tropics. They gambled with a stake that many now regret: the tools of timber extraction raced far ahead of the wisdom to use them with restraint.

Moreover, most foresters understood little about rural tropical populations and their traditional ways of living with forests. Whether implicit or explicit, the social policy embraced by professional foresters was only rudimentary. It began with a genuine concern to provide for local consumption needs, primarily in terms of meeting construction timber requirements. Foresters believed that settled farming was the best method of sustenance agriculture. Until at least the 1960s foresters were nearly unanimous in condemning all forms of shifting agriculture. They failed to distinguish between ancient tribal agriculture and the damage caused by dispossessed lowland peasants forced into mountain forest watersheds.

Most foresters did not trace the dilemma of the dispossessed peasants back to its source, in the politics of plantation monocropping. Only an occasional forester ever pointed to the system of land tenure, in which a few powerful people controlled most of the land, as a primary impetus of forest degradation. Neither was there much mention at all of this class hierarchy as a major source of high birth rates among the rural poor, the population pressure that foresters and wildlife conservationists routinely agreed was becoming a major pressure on forest resources.

Foresters were trained to study tree communities, not human communities. Here, as in all other areas of tropical resource utilization, specialization, although necessary, promoted a separation of technical from social and political understanding. Thus they unwittingly contributed to accelerating the transformation of tropical Nature into commodity patterns, biologically simplified, ecologically unstable, socially polarized, and culturally degraded.

But that was not the whole story. By the 1950s a few tropical foresters who had the requisite combination of biological knowledge plus social awareness began warning that the forest resources of the tropics could not be indefinitely preserved unless the whole range of social factors could be integrated in management strategies. These foresighted individuals understood local subsistence as well as tree growth and distant markets, but they had little political voice until a groundswell of change in political consciousness began to appear internationally in the late 1960s.

After the United Nations was founded in 1945, it became a major pathway for American influence in tropical forestry, specifically through the FAO, which worked urgently to provide food for a war-worn world. Forestry was added to its portfolio at the urging of a small group that included Pinchot's American protégés, Tom Gill and others.[38] The FAO forestry division was born with a sense of urgency to use all forest products to maximum efficiency, especially to rebuild a war-torn world. Little additional lumber supply was available from the United States and Canada, so American foresters saw that tropical regions could play a greatly expanded role in international trade and thus economic development, and that tropical countries could not afford to leave their forest resources "underutilized" while draining foreign exchange to pay for imports.

The fledgling state of professional forestry in Latin America was indicated by the fact that when the FAO's forestry division was founded, Gill and Watts, not Ladinos, represented the region. FAO launched its forestry consultations in Latin America in 1948 at a conference in Teresopolis, Brazil. The emphasis of the conference was entirely on productive utilization of resources. The idea that some natural regions should be preserved in their original character was still beyond the ideological horizon. Participants agreed that many forests were badly depleted and poorly managed, with a resulting "havoc" of erosion;

they also agreed that other vast areas of forest were virtually untouched and should be brought under active management for socioeconomic development. As one conference resolution put it, "Latin-American forests should be utilized in accordance with modern scientific and mechanical concepts, and in such ways as to raise the standards of living of local populations to a level compatible with human dignity." The resolutions went on to propose "rational expansion of forest products industries drawing on the long accumulated wealth of virgin forest tracts, so as to take the utmost advantage of present export possibilities," and "increased efficiency at all stages of production."[39]

American technical assistance for forest management spread throughout Latin America, not only through FAO channels but also through the International Cooperation Agency (ICA), the forerunner of the Agency for International Development, in which forestry aid played a major role.[40] The pattern of American influence in forestry aid was set in 1946, when a team of U.S. foresters who had been sent to Chile by the ICA submitted a report that became a model for subsequent U.S. assessments.[41] Chile, twice the size of California and 2,650 miles long from the deserts of its northern border with Peru to the icy south of Tierra del Fuego, had sixteen million hectares of forests, which constituted 22 percent of Chile's land. Most of the forest cover was in the cool, moist south. The American team reported that much of it had already been degraded to varying degrees, primarily by ill-advised clearing for agriculture. In the optimistic vein that characterized American development aid, they reported that production could easily and sustainably be tripled in those already damaged forests.

However, no one yet understood much about how to manage rainforests sustainably. Their great variety of tree species, most of which could not be identified by anyone except the tribal inhabitants of the forests, defeated any attempt to extract the value of more than a few timber species in any area. But foresters were optimistic about the possibilities for the "rational exploitation" of the rainforest along "scientific" lines. The images of rationality and science were compelling when juxtaposed with their converse: the wastefulness, inefficiency, political corruption, and administrative weakness that existed throughout the region. Unfortunately, tropical foresters had not accumulated enough experience to anticipate the silvicultural complexities and social pressures that continue even today to make their goal elusive.

Reforestation was also a vital element of the tropical foresters' vision of development, but the tree planting they had in mind was single-species groves of fast-growing softwoods, usually Caribbean pine or eucalyptus, that would provide commercial lumber and paper pulp. The American team that visited Chile in 1946 reported that replanting of logged forests in Chile had already reached 143,000 hectares, of which pine accounted for 58 percent and eucalyptus 31 percent. These efforts did not establish a true forest with varied species of flora and fauna but a one-species crop: any species that was plantation-grown displaced natural forests. The trend began to accelerate rapidly in the 1950s and became dominant throughout the tropics in the 1960s.

Experiments with tree replanting had begun in the early 1900s, when U.S. timber firms and banana corporations in Central America experimented with planting several commercially valuable hardwood species. The earliest efforts at reforestation were made by the Emery Company on its Nicaraguan concession. To comply with a clause in Nicaragua's forestry law (one that was usually ignored), Emery established experimental mahogany stands. The abrupt end of its concession in 1909 ended that effort.

In the late 1920s the United Fruit Company's research center at Tela, Honduras, took up experiments with hardwood reforestation under its first director, Wilson Popenoe. Popenoe made similar sustained efforts at Antigua, Guatemala. By 1960 mature cypress plantations were established on various sites.[42] In the 1950s United Fruit Company also put over two thousand acres in teak, which had been experimentally introduced from Southeast Asia early in the century. Teak did exceptionally well on its banana plantations near Quepos and Golfito, on Costa Rica's Pacific coast, where the seasonally dry climate was similar to that of teak's homeland in southern India and Southeast Asia. The company also experimented with more than twenty other species, including hardwoods from central Africa and India.[43]

United's experiments were the work of its director of tropical research, Vining Dunlap, who like his mentor and predecessor, Popenoe, took a biologist's interest in tree plantations that went beyond immediate corporate calculations of profitable trade possibilities. The work was centered at Lancetilla, near Tela, where an old-growth forest had been long protected because it was the watershed for the town of Tela. Dunlap's research team had fifty-four species of seedlings under trial, led by mahogany, primavera, cedar, and 6,300 acres of teak, a hardwood of tropical Asia that (unique among tropical hard-woods) grows in dense natural stands.

Working with the sugar company's researchers, in 1960 a team of forest biol-ogists from the research center in Puerto Rico carried out a survey of reforesta-tion work throughout Latin America. The team, headed by Bruce Lamb, found a wide variety of multispecies trials that supported efforts to repair or enrich existing forests. In some, foresters and agronomists were encouraging natural regeneration of selectively felled hardwoods like mahogany and Spanish cedar, although little was yet known about the soil and light conditions needed by the hardwood seedlings. The report highlighted the United Fruit Company, whose work it termed the most extensive experimental reforestation in Central Amer-ica. But investors at company headquarters in Boston, where a rapid return on capital was the standard of value, did not share the interests of the agronomists and foresters. In the 1950s the policymakers for United Fruit ordered the forestry work at Tela to be gradually phased out. Once again corporate priori-ties, in research as well as marketing, were narrow and shortsighted.

The insatiable demand for profits on international markets continued to grow, and the trend inevitably forced forest managers and development plan-ners to raise fundamental questions. Was the future of tropical forests to be dominated by one-species tree farms, or was the vast diversity of plant and animal species in the rainforest a fundamental value in itself? What role should be given to tropical silviculture? For whose benefit should the forests be managed?

The term *sustained yield* meant many things to many people, and the debate over sustained yield of tropical forests was highly contentious. The ecologists' meaning, preservation of rainforest ecosystems in all their diversity, was not even a common goal in the first two postwar decades. Crucial research on ecosystem management, to say nothing of the social aspects of forest protection, had barely begun. The fledgling research institutes struggled with miniscule budgets, and rainforest ecosystems were so exquisitely complex that it would take years of additional work by forest biologists and ecologists just to develop an adequate taxonomy, or even to standardize terminology for the research, to say nothing of understanding how entire interlocking life systems function.

Until the late 1960s few people, even the best informed, felt any sense of urgency about the threat to the diversity of life in the wet tropics. The natural forest regions of the tropical Americas were still vast, and nearly all development specialists except for a few foresters saw them as the adversary to be conquered. Even in Central America, where U.S. fruit growers had made heavy inroads into the forests for commercial cropping and transport infrastructure, the forest zone beyond the plantations was still nearly impenetrable in the 1950s. Leslie Holdridge first explored the Sarapiquí rainforest region between Costa Rica's central valley and the banana zone in the early 1950s. He found no paved roads; transport was possible only by small boats along a few rivers. Only a few peasant huts and clearings along the streams interrupted the majestic forest.[44]

In his later years, Holdridge insisted that his generation of foresters was too sanguine in their expectation that the forests of Latin America could easily be made to produce abundantly forever. His younger colleague, Gerardo Budowski, put it more bluntly in 1970, when he looked back on his early years around 1950: "As a University student in Caracas, I believed, like everyone else—in fact I may even say today that I was 'obsessed'—that the greatest potential of my country was in those vast areas of "virgin forests" mapped in solid green that were sparsely settled and just awaited the drive of ambitious government planners to be opened to civilization."[45]

As a young forest biologist in 1940, Holdridge had sketched what was then a novel approach to sustainable rainforest management: he argued that sustainability would be possible only if the fixation on single-species plantations were replaced by locally varied systems of mixed farming and agriculture, taken in part from traditional subsistence farming. In characterizing the vast zone that lay between fertile alluvial lowlands and high mountain slopes, he repeated conventional wisdom: "This is the zone where land-use evils first come into focus, where the farmers recall the 'good old days' of fertile soils, the soil expert frowns at the soil erosion in progress, the forester points out the felling of the forests as the source of the evil, and most all unite in pointing at the system of 'conuco' or shifting agriculture as a prime evil which must be abolished at all costs." A change of far-reaching social and biological priorities required many steps, however. As an alternative approach Holdridge presented the case for what later came to be known as agroforestry or agroecology. He argued that intercropping of trees and food crops was "the most practical and least expensive of methods for establishing forest plantations."[46]

Both European and American agronomists and foresters in the Caribbean basin had begun to introduce the Burmese system of *taungya* in the 1930s, which British foresters in India had been adapting for many years. In the taungya system, which evolved in teak forests, local tribals or peasants planted the commercial species, and for the first two to four years they planted their food crops between the rows of teak seedlings. When the tree canopy was dense enough to suppress the understory crops, the workers moved to a new location and repeated the process. Until the 1960s there were only a tiny number of forestry plantations of this sort in tropical America.

The work of the experiment station in Puerto Rico was the key to the development of forest management strategies that could protect biological diversity. In Puerto Rico itself the foresters' strategy was to work within the biological structure of existing forests, in part because local markets had always used a wide variety of wood species on a small scale for housing construction, furniture, wagons, boats, and many other purposes. In 1947 Frank Wadsworth, the future director of the experiment station, surveyed the impact of silviculture in the region. He stressed the need to maintain forests until they could be studied, pointing out that in the rainforest "perpetual cover, mixed composition, and all-aged structure" should be protected. Wadsworth insisted that a complete understanding of the region, including "knowledge of local environments, forest structure and composition, qualities of tree species, and social and economic factors" was essential for silviculture.[47] He charged foresters to encourage the use of all species with any market demand for local and urban use—the article went on to enumerate ninety-eight species.

Wadsworth knew enough about rainforest silviculture to understand its difficulties. He pointed out that there were many problems in this approach: each species was widely dispersed through the forest; it was difficult to supervise cutting; the regeneration of fast-growing light-loving species was rarely successful in shady areas. Moreover, the practice of silviculture was a process of mediation: "Silvicultural practice is a compromise between the biological requirements for optimum future wood production and the economic requirements of the logging industry. This compromise must provide a present yield as well as an improved resource for the future."[48]

A debate had begun in international forestry circles over the relation between tropical forestry and local subsistence. Those who took the issue most seriously saw great virtue in the oldest, least highly monetized and modernized farming systems, those of Indian shifting agriculturists. Forest biologists who were challenging the prevailing assumptions of their profession had some important support from other conservationists from the late 1940s on. In 1947 William Vogt wrote an article in *Unasylva*, FAO's forestry journal, which in both tone and substance was startlingly at odds with most of what was being written by foresters at the time. Entitled "Latin-American Timber, Ltd.," a deliberately indignant pun, Vogt's article began, "Every sector of the human race enjoys—or suffers from—its own superstitions. There are few superstitions as deeply grounded as the belief that Latin America is rich in timber resources." Vogt, who knew the region from Mexico to northern South America as well as any North American of his time, granted that "the region between the Rio Grande and Cape Horn includes one of the greatest remaining extensions of forest," but he reminded his readers that most of that forest grew on steeply sloping lands that were highly susceptible to erosion, had nutrient-deficient soils, or suffered harsh aridity.[49] He calculated that only about 5 percent of Latin America's soils could support intensive agriculture, and most of that was river-bottom alluvium.

Vogt argued that between twenty and forty million Latin Americans were already displaced from their lands, not because of political conflicts but because of terminal land degradation, dating back as far as the early days of the Spanish conquest. He proceeded to describe highland forests that had been stripped to serve the silver mines of colonial Mexico, the woodlands of densely populated El Salvador that had been chopped away for firewood, the highland oak forests of Costa Rica that were being degraded as the new Pan American Highway was being built, the Andean hill forests of Venezuela that had given way to agriculture under Spanish rule. In each case he pointed to the disruption of hydrological systems. Irrigation water in upland Mexico was increasingly scarce. Manmade erosion was crippling the capacity of the Lempa River in Guatemala and El Salvador to provide hydropower. Floods in the Venezuelan Andes were exacerbating the annual flooding of the llanos. And agricultural expansion at the expense of forests on the Andean slopes of southern Chile had led to such soil loss that plans for reforestation were jeopardized.

No other writer of the late 1940s sounded such an urgent alarm. An outsider to the forestry profession, Vogt raised a broad conservation perspective. In the immediate postwar years he was the most trenchant critic of forestry management as well as governmental development policies generally.[50] His writings only obliquely suggested that the political factor of landownership was a source of massive landlessness, but few other North American writers at the time even hinted that tensions between rich and poor were causing eco-logical stress in Latin America. By and large, Yankee commentators and resource managers simply took for granted the power structures of Latin America—and the ways that North Americans reinforced them—until the late 1960s.

Forestry planners were caught in the intensifying tensions among three goals: short-run acceleration of timber yields, sustained-yield timber manage-ment, and conserving rainforest ecosystems as a biologically diverse whole. The mainstream of American forestry practice had not prepared its men ade-quately the meet this challenge. The consensus was beginning to be chal-lenged in an intensifying debate within international forestry circles over the ultimate goals of their work. Gill and other American foresters working in the tropics after the war were among the first to raise the issues of the debate. They charged that the Forest Service as a whole, and the higher authorities in Washington whom it served, had been unwilling to pay much attention to tropical forestry and resource management. Gill had been frustrated for many years about the general indifference of American foresters working in the United States to developments in the rest of the world, especially the tropics. In 1948 he launched the International Society of Tropical Foresters, running it virtually single-handedly from his home in Washington. By 1960 its mem-bership had passed three hundred and included nearly every name of any importance in tropical forestry. Several American members in Latin America represented U.S. corporations, including United Fruit in Honduras and Champion Paper in southern Brazil. A large number of Latin Americans were also members by that time, as were many nationals of India and Southeast Asia. The list included officers of private-sector corporations and foresters in the employ of governments and international agencies.

In 1960 the U.S. government and the U.S. timber industry offered for the first time to host the World Forestry Congress, inviting the world's foresters to Seattle for the organization's fifth meeting. Several American members of the International Society of Tropical Foresters had lobbied hard for this sup-port. Gill chaired the planning subcommittee on problems of tropical forestry. In a plenary address to the Congress, he commented that for American forestry, this was the belated end of a "trail of indecisive detours and bewil-dering back-trackings." By hosting the conference, the U.S. forestry community had set "the official seal of approval" on "America's participation in international forestry."[51]

In the Pacific, the international network of foresters had been institutionalized through the forestry division of the Pacific Science Association. The association, which had been founded in Honolulu in 1920, held triennial conferences in cities around the Pacific, giving scientists in many fields the opportunity to develop together international agendas of research and policy planning. The forestry division was established almost immediately after 1920. Its agenda covered the laws and technology of tropical timber extraction, concern about sustained-yield timber management, and concern about the damage to watersheds caused by prevailing logging technology.

This pattern was equally evident at the Tenth Pacific Science Congress in 1961 in Honolulu. Revived in 1949 after a wartime paralysis, the congresses continued the prewar tradition of comparing the latest technology of tropical timber management and debating the development priorities of government policies. At the Honolulu congress the Standing Committee on Forestry described its broadening research agenda for tropical forests, which included strategies of natural regeneration of tropical forests and the particularly difficult challenge of reforesting logged areas that had become dominated by cogon grass.[52] This agenda did not address the preservation of tropical forest ecosystems for their biodiversity or their contribution to controlling global atmospheric warming—these overarching issues began to be of concern to specialists and the public only in the early 1970s. The agenda of the science congress was however moving toward that more inclusive scope.

Together, concerned foresters and their conservationist allies in other fields faced an enormous task of slowing down the attack on the world's tropical forests. On one front was the steady incursion of subsistence farming and local agricultural industry, which supplied crops and meat to a rapidly expanding population in tropical countries. On the other front was the aggressive corporate agricultural industry, which exported monocrops to markets in ever more affluent North America.

By 1970 the record of tropical forestry represented seven decades of work by a tiny handful of men who had produced only a deeply ambiguous achievement. They had created a system of science and management dedicated in principle to the sustained yield of forest resources, but, in so doing, they had participated in a wider process that unleashed the forces of technological and corporate power in the rainforest, power that was backed by a development ideology that saw the exploitation of tropical resources largely in terms of short-range payoffs. The science of tropical timber management had grown out of experience in relatively simple temperate forest ecosystems. Sustaining the yield of marketable commodities from the fragile cornucopia of the tropical forest was far harder to achieve.

Conclusion: Consuming Appetites

Historians of modern American society have shown that the nation's search for democracy and general affluence, "the good life," led to a great surge of consumption spending in the aftermath of World War II. For fifteen years, the American Dream of material security and prosperity had been throttled, first by the Great Depression and then by the forced austerity of wartime. After 1945, the urge to buy and consume fueled a booming economy. America's industry, strengthened by the war, was ready to provide the goods that strong consumer savings and rising incomes made available for a broadened middle class. The world's greatest consumer economy has reached far beyond its own geographical boundaries to create its wealth, stretching nearly around the world for valuable natural resources. It transformed not only American life and landscapes but distant places and societies, as well.

By the 1960s the American system of global domination was largely in place. Based firmly on a booming consumer economy at home its affluence was built on oil, the automobile, and the highway system. The petroleum industry had developed a formidable capacity to provide for American consumers' energy needs from sources around the Caribbean basin and the Middle East, as well as domestic wells. The automobile industry gave millions the mobility and status they demanded, rapidly expanding the ranks of the middle class. The nation's highways were improved, and the interstate highway system was nearing completion by the end of the decade. The car culture, America on wheels, brought a steadily rising demand for rubber, from both international petroleum and tropical plantations. The family car made possible the great suburban housing boom, and with it shopping malls and megastores to supply mass consumption.

This unprecedented, broadly based prosperity was intimately connected to the global reach of American political, military, and industrial power. During the Cold War, American hegemony had accelerating impacts everywhere that American resource extraction had previously penetrated. The outward expansion of America's economy into the tropics was rationalized by an ideology of egalitarian democracy and affluence: the belief that the Third World could follow the United States into democracies of political freedom and purchasing power. Corporate investors moved ahead confidently. American consumption of tropical agricultural and forest products flourished.

But Americans were largely unaware of the ecological consequences of their prosperity. The great distance between corporate policymaking and consumers on the one hand, and the social and environmental impacts in production locations on the other, meant that the impacts of investment and consumption were (and remain today) mostly beyond the horizon of consumers' awareness.[1] In the vacuum of information, the advertising industry romanticized the tropical producers as Chiquita Banana and Juan Valdez and gave no hint of the environmental price paid for our satisfactions.

Many of these trends have been maintained with little fundamental change of character in recent years. Yet, in other ways, the world has shifted dramatically since the 1960s. While the global American economic web was largely spun by the late 1960s, a number of broad changes were also falling into place that brought greater complexity to North-South economic relations and their resulting ecological trends. This story would require another long volume; it can only be suggested here.

For one, the consolidation of U.S. tropical agrobusiness was accelerating; by 1970 there were only three American multinational fruit firms left. The fruit companies were also diversifying their products, adding citrus plantations to their range of production strategies. Further, the fruit companies, like the cane sugar importers, were diversifying their source locations as a hedge against political instability and crop diseases. At the same time, they were no longer merely expanding into primary forests and virgin soils; instead, they were entering a period of consolidation and intensification. In existing locations, agronomic research laboratories and experimental farms were able to overcome some long-standing obstacles to sustained production. They were creating more productive or disease-resistant varieties and using better tillage methods to reduce erosion.

However—and this is a major qualification—much of this stabilization and increased production was ultimately illusory, for it was bought by the new era of agrochemicals. American agrochemical giants such as Monsanto and Dow Chemical began massive export of petroleum-based fertilizers and pesticides that had been banned in the United States for their excessive toxicity. All these changes were happening in a setting of heightened competition in a globalizing economy, rapidly becoming more complex and competitive than in the half century when U.S. companies largely had their own way. The exploitation of the tropics was accelerated by revived economies in Western Europe and Japan, in an era of unbridled economic growth and consumption of global resources, plus a global population boom.

In addition, tropical governments and societies were changing. Nationalism and populism strengthened as governments grew more assertive against the foreign corporations, regarding profits but not yet regarding the environmental costs of their operations. In the same countries, especially in Latin America, labor movements were becoming more aggressively organized, especially on foreign-owned plantations where workers were concentrated and could be rallied against the gringo managers. These movements were concerned primarily with wages, benefits, and working conditions. Only in the 1980s did they begin to address environmental concerns, when they began to focus on chemical pollution and its health effects.

Indeed, until the late 1960s there was little concern anywhere for environmental impacts or limits of resources in the tropics. In previous years the ground had been laid for that awareness by tropical agronomists and foresters, professionals in resource management. By about 1970 the tropical forest conservation movement was born, emphasizing "sustainable management" and adding preservation of the remaining natural ecosystems to the agenda. The International Society of Tropical Foresters, founded by the American Tom Gill, created a new network of professional concern for the difficult task of environmentally sustainable production in tropical forests. Others challenged this understanding of conservation. Led by the International Union for the

Conservation of Nature, a network of wildlife biologists worked for the preservation first of endangered wildlife, and then entire natural systems.[2]

Environmental awareness was beginning to be global in its horizons. The United Nations conference on the global environment, held in Stockholm in 1972, brought international institutions into play to provide a global forum for the new debate. In the United States, the late 1960s belatedly saw a dawning recognition that vast ecological transformations had occurred since the late nineteenth century, not only at home but in the tropical world too, and that the trend was accelerating. Limits—of both natural resources and the biosphere's capacity to absorb pollution—were beginning to be ominously visible.

Older conservation organizations such as the Audubon Society and the Sierra Club began to highlight tropical issues more clearly; previously their agendas had been largely domestic. Newer organizations, led by the World Wildlife Fund and then Friends of the Earth, placed major emphasis on saving tropical wildlife and their habitats, building alliances with fledgling activist groups in tropical countries. But though these American non-governmental organizations began advocating tropical forest protection, they largely ignored consumerism and crop imports, the embarrassing home-grown causes of tropical decline. And even their limited agenda was largely ignored by the national government, the producers and marketers of tropical products, and the consumers.

The controversy over "globalization" and its social and environmental costs is a relatively new debate, but the phenomenon itself has a five-hundred-year history, the history of intercontinental trade networks. Perhaps we should see this in the even longer perspective of the global transformation from natural ecosystems to managed landscapes, in which the changing frontier between forest and agriculture has been central. In the era of industrial technology, characterized by larger scales of capital investment and tighter links to affluent consumer societies, the global system escalated in the nineteenth and twentieth centuries.

Since the 1960s there has been a related debate over whether rising global population or escalating consumption has been the chief engine of global ecological degradation. In the first years of this debate, many writers blamed rapid increases in rural poor populations for most loss of forest to farmland. More recently, other voices have asserted that affluent consumers in capitalist economies have taken far more than their share of the tropics' agricultural production, often for products of little or no nutritional value, such as sugar and coffee. The debate is still unresolved.

The globalization of American firms has been central to the development of tropical agriculture. That international reach—from home base in temperate North American climates to production sites in the tropics—took many forms. Some firms expanded internationally from beginnings in the domestic American economy, such as beef processing and tropical timber importers. Other firms were international from the start. Commodity traders who bought sugar and coffee at tropical ports evolved into the banana and rubber companies that integrated operations from the lands where the trees grew to the stores where American consumers bought their products. Some, such as sugar importers, competed with domestic production; others did not. Some managed tropical lands directly; others only bought the products of local plantations, keeping a wary distance from responsibility for managing the land. In every case, both commercial and agroindustrial capitalists went wherever prospects for profits led to new source areas and were largely able to dictate terms to local governments.

Capitalist agriculture for export to the North meant specialization on single products, monocrops chosen for their profitability on the international market. Varied crops grown by small-scale farmers for local consumption were displaced by less nutritional products selected for distant consumers. In the process, plant and animal species introduced from one continent into another displaced far more diverse communities of indigenous species. The benefits of the domestication of the biosphere have been many and obvious. But the underlying cost of the transformation has been the dislocation of tropical flora and fauna, the impoverishment of soils, and the disruption of water resources.

Even now our knowledge of the losses of biodiversity is only fragmentary. Since the acceleration of scientific concern in the 1960s, there has been growing understanding of what is required for sustainability of tropical forest flora and fauna and soils. But much of the new science and policy planning has not been implemented by the private sector, or required by governments, despite many warnings and slowly increasing public awareness.

In an insecure world, we are increasingly aware that security must be ecological as well as political. The debate over Americans' secure access to tropical resources, which began with concern over strategic metals and oil after

World War I, has broadened to a realization that we must assure sustained production of natural resources and entire ecosystems, and that this requires greater global social justice as well. Ultimately, our history must be understood in the broader perspective of humanity's relation to the entire living biosphere. As this study exemplifies, the depletion of tropical life systems is now finally becoming more clear, as global climate change brings us all—governments, investors, workers and consumers, rich and middle class and poor alike—fatefully together.

Notes

INTRODUCTION: AMERICA'S GLOBAL ENVIRONMENTAL REACH

1. Global environmental trends are being played out not only in terms of natural resources, of course, but also in the other fundamental dimension of environmental change, the rise in pollution of land, water, and air. This book rarely discusses pollution issues but concentrates on the reduction (and beginnings of better management) of natural resources. For an entry into the modern history of global pollution, see John H. McNeill, *Something New Under the Sun: An Environmental History of the Twentieth-Century World* (New York: W. W. Norton, 2000).

2. See Michael Williams, *Americans and Their Forests: A Historical Geography* (Cambridge: Cambridge University Press, 1989).

3. This book uses the term "tropics" broadly, equating it with the Cold War term "the Third World," i.e., formerly colonial countries, or with the global South, the more current term. The value of using "tropical" is that it reminds us to keep ecosystems in mind, as each chapter defines the natural setting more specifically.

4. This study does not attempt to include the global environmental histories of oil and minerals, which have not yet been written in any integrated way. For a global history of the petroleum industry, see Daniel Yergin, *The Prize* (New York: Simon and Schuster, 1991).

CHAPTER 1: AMERICA'S SWEET TOOTH

1. For the key role of cane sugar in the rise of the modern world system, see Sidney W. Mintz, *Sweetness and Power* (New York: Viking, 1985).

2. G. C. Stevenson, *Genetics and Breeding of Sugar Cane* (London: Longmans Green, 1965).

3. Anthony Reid, "Humans and Forests in Pre-Colonial Southeast Asia," *Environment and History* 1 (1995): 93–110.

4. Fernand Braudel, *The Structures of Everyday Life: The Limits of the Possible* (New York: Harper and Row, 1981), 224–27; Mintz, *Sweetness and Power*, 74–138.

5. Noel Deerr, *The History of Sugar*, 2 vols. (London: Chapman and Hall, 1949–50); J. H. Galloway, *The Sugar Cane Industry* (Cambridge: Cambridge University Press, 1989), chaps. 3–7.

6. W. R. Aykroyd, *Sweet Malefactor: Sugar, Slavery and Human Society* (London: Heinemann, 1967).

7. Robert G. Albion, *Forests and Sea Power* (Cambridge, Mass.: Harvard University Press, 1926); Graeme Wynn, *Timber Colony* (Toronto: University of Toronto Press, 1981); Richard W. Judd, *Maine, the Pine Tree State* (Orono: University of Maine Press, 1995).

8. John H. McNeill, *Atlantic Empires of France and Spain: Louisbourg and Havana, 1700–1763* (Chapel Hill: University of North Carolina Press, 1985), 15–16, 106–13. For the staggering depletion of the North Atlantic's fishing resources, see Farley Mowat, *Sea of Slaughter* (Boston: Atlantic Monthly Press, 1984).

9. Richard W. Van Alstyne, *The Rising American Empire* (New York: Norton, 1974), 147–48.

10. Basil Rauch, *The American Interest in Cuba, 1848–1855* (Cambridge: Cambridge University Press, 1948).

11. Laird W. Bergad, *Cuban Rural Society in the Nineteenth Century* (Princeton: Princeton University Press, 1990).

12. Rebecca J. Scott, *Slave Emancipation in Cuba: The Transition to Free Labor, 1860–1899* (Princeton: Princeton University Press, 1985).

13. Esteban Montejo, *The Autobiography of a Runaway Slave* (Harmondsworth: Penguin, 1970).

14. Edwin F. Atkins, *Sixty Years in Cuba* (New York: Arno Press, 1980), 67.

15. Atkins, *Sixty Years*, 105.

16. Thomas Barbour, *A Naturalist in Cuba* (Boston: Little Brown, 1945), 15.

17. Bergad, *Cuban Rural Society*, 306–7.

18. Quoted in Van Alstyne, *Rising Empire*, 167.

19. Earl E. Smith, *The Forests of Cuba* (Petersham, Mass.: Harvard Forest Publication, 1954), 13, 34–35.

20. Leland H. Jenks, *Our Cuban Colony: A Study in Sugar* (New York: Vanguard, 1928), 153.

21. Jenks, *Our Cuban Colony,* 207.

22. Tom Gill, *Tropical Forests of the Caribbean* (Washington, D.C.: Randolph Lathrop Pack Foundation, 1931), 90–91, 159–63.

23. Harry A. Franck, *Roaming Through the West Indies* (London: T. Fisher Unwin, 1921), 76–78.

24. Franck, *Roaming,* 78.

25. Donald R. Dyer, "Sugar Regions of Cuba," *Economic Geography* 32 (1956): 179; Reinaldo Funes Monzote, "Deforestation and Sugar in Cuba's Centre-East: The Case of Camaguey, 1898–1926," in *Territories, Commodities and Knowledges: Latin American Environmental History in the Nineteenth and Twentieth Centuries,* ed. Christian Brannstrom (London: Institute for the Study of the Americas, 2004), 148–70.

26. Mark Smith, "The Political Economy of Sugar Production and the Environment of Eastern Cuba, 1898–1923," *Environmental History Review* 19, no. 4 (Winter 1995): 31–48.

27. J. Fred Rippy, *Globe and Hemisphere* (Chicago: Regnery, 1958), 155.

28. J. H. Parry and Philip Sherlock, *A Short History of the West Indies,* 3d ed. (London: Macmillan, 1971), 258–59.

29. Dana Munro, *The United States and the Caribbean Republics, 1921–1933* (Princeton: Princeton University Press, 1974); Bryce Wood, *The Making of the Good Neighbor Policy* (New York: Columbia University Press, 1961); Irwin F. Gellman, *Good Neighbor Diplomacy, 1933–1945* (Baltimore: Johns Hopkins University Press, 1979).

30. Samuel Farber, *The Origins of the Cuban Revolution Reconsidered* (Chapel Hill: University of North Carolina Press, 2006), 72.

31. Eric Williams, *From Columbus to Castro: The History of the Caribbean, 1492–1969* (New York: Harper and Row, 1970), 479.

32. Edward Boorstein, *The Economic Transformation of Cuba* (New York: Monthly Review Press, 1968), 181–212.

33. Medea Benjamin, Joseph Collins, and Michael Scott, *No Free Lunch: Food and Revolution in Cuba Today* (San Francisco: Institute for Food and Development Policy, 1984), 123–24.

34. Sergio Diaz-Briquets and Jorge Perez-Lopez, *Conquering Nature: The Environmental Legacy of Socialism in Cuba* (Pittsburgh: University of Pittsburgh Press, 2000), chap. 4; José Alvarez and Lazaro Pena Castellanos, *Cuba's Sugar Industry* (Gainesville: University of Florida Press, 2001).

35. John Vandermeer and Ivette Perfecto, *Breakfast of Biodiversity* (Oakland, Calif.: Institute for Food and Development Policy, 1995), 120–25.

36. Lawrence Mosher, "At Sea in the Caribbean," and Walter LaFeber, "The Alliances in Retrospect," in *Bordering on Trouble: Resources and Politics in Latin America,* ed. Andrew Maguire and Janet Welsh Brown (Bethesda, Md.: Adler and Adler, 1986), 235–69, 337–88.

37. The sugar planters developed sophisticated agronomic science for increasing productivity of the varieties they planted, and resistance to plant diseases. For this important work, see Stuart McCook, *States of Nature: Science, Agriculture, and Environment in the Spanish Caribbean, 1760–1940* (Austin: University of Texas Press, 2002), chaps. 3–4.

38. For a considerably more detailed and nuanced discussion of sugar in Hawaii, see the first edition of my *Insatiable Appetite* (Berkeley and Los Angeles: University of California, 2000).

39. Gavan Daws, *Shoal of Time: A History of the Hawaiian Islands* (Honolulu: University of Hawaii Press, 1968), 226.

40. For Spreckels and other San Francisco connections to Hawaii and the Philippines, see Gray Brechin, *Imperial San Francisco: Urban Power, Earthly Ruin* (Berkeley and Los Angeles: University of California Press, 1999).

41. Benito F. Legarda Jr., *Foreign Trade, Economic Change and Entrepreneurship in Nineteenth Century Philippines* (Ph.D. diss., Economics Department, Harvard University, 1955), chaps. 4, 7; Norman Owen, *The Philippine Economy and the United States* (Ann Arbor: University of Michigan Papers on South and Southeast Asia, No. 22, 1983).

42. John A. Larkin, *Sugar and the Origins of Modern Philippine Society* (Berkeley and Los Angeles: University of California Press, 1993), 49–50; Dennis Roth, *The Friar Estates of the Philippines* (Albuquerque: University of New Mexico Press, 1977).

43. Dennis Roth, "Philippine Forests and Forestry: 1565–1920," in *Global Deforestation and the Nineteenth-Century World Economy,* ed. Richard P. Tucker and J. F. Richards (Durham: Duke University Press, 1983), 30–49.

44. Harold Conklin, *Hanunoo Agriculture* (Rome: Food and Agriculture Organization, 1955).

45. Quoted in Alfred W. McCoy, "A Queen Dies Slowly: The Rise and Decline of Iloilo City," in *Philippine Social History: Global Trade and Local Transformations,* ed. Alfred W. McCoy and Ed. C. de Jesus (Quezon City: Ateneo de Manila University Press, 1982), 323.

46. Dean Worcester, *The Philippines, Past and Present* (New York: Macmillan, 1914), II: 897–99; Carlos Quirino, *History of the Philippine Sugar Industry* (Manila: Kalayaan Publishing Co., 1974); Larkin, *Sugar,* chaps. 2–3.

47. Herbert S. Walker, *The Sugar Industry in the Island of Negros* (Manila: Bureau of Science, 1910), 16; Robert E. Huke, *Shadows on the Land: An Economic Geography of the Philippines* (Manila: Bookmark, 1963), 311.

48. McCoy, "A Queen Dies," 317–26.

49. Luzviminda Bartolome Francisco and Jonathan S. Fast, *Conspiracy for Empire: Big Business, Corruption and the Politics of Imperialism in America, 1876–1907* (Quezon City: Foundation for Nationalist Studies, 1985), chaps. 17, 24, 29.

50. Quoted in Francisco and Fast, *Conspiracy,* 225.

51. Frank Golay, "Taming the American Multinationals," in *The Philippine Economy and the United States: Studies in Past and Present Interactions,* ed. Norman G. Owen (Ann Arbor: University of Michigan Center for South and Southeast Asian Studies, 1983), 160.

52. Norman G. Owen, "Philippine-American Economic Interactions: A Matter of Magnitude," in Owen, *Philippine Economy,* 177–98.

53. This and following material are taken from Herbert S. Walker, *The Sugar Industry in the Island of Negros* (Manila: Bureau of Science, 1910).

54. Walker, *Sugar Industry,* 14–21, 133–36.

55. Quirino, *History,* 53, 61; Golay, "Taming," 157.

56. Quoted in Larkin, *Sugar,* 170–71.

57. Gary Hawes, *The Philippine State and the Marcos Regime: The Politics of Export* (Ithaca: Cornell University Press, 1987), 83; Larkin, *Sugar,* 175–76.

58. Larkin, *Sugar,* 150, 203, 239.

59. Frank H. Golay, "Economic Collaboration: The Role of American Investment," in Frank H. Golay, ed., *The United States and the Philippines* (Englewood Cliffs, N.J.: Spectrum, 1966), 102–20.

60. Hawes, *Philippine State,* chap. 3; Robert Pringle, *Indonesia and the Philippines: American Interests in Island Southeast Asia* (New York: Columbia University Press, 1980).

61. Anonymous, *Draft Environmental Report on the Philippines* (Washington, D.C.: Department of State and U.S. Man and the Biosphere Secretariat, January 1980), 67.

62. Violeta Lopez-Gonzaga, *Voluntary Land-Sharing and Transfer Scheme in Negros* (Bacolod: Social Research Center, La Salle College, 1986); Frank Lynch, *A Bittersweet Taste of Sugar* (Quezon City: Ateneo de Manila University Press, 1970).

63. McCoy, *Priests,* 160.

CHAPTER 2: BANANA REPUBLICS

1. Joseph Grunwald and Philip Musgrove, *Natural Resources in Latin American Development* (Baltimore: Johns Hopkins University Press, 1970), 364.

2. Robert C. West and John P. Augelli, *Middle America: Its Lands and Peoples,* 2d ed. (Englewood Cliffs, N.J.: Prentice-Hall, 1976), 388.

3. Herbert Feis, *Europe: The World's Banker, 1870–1914* (New Haven: Yale University Press, 1930).

4. See the first edition of *Insatiable Appetite* (Berkeley and Los Angeles: University of California Press, 2000) for the story of bananas in Jamaica, including a century of British corporate competition for banana exports to Europe.

5. Leo Marx, *The Machine in the Garden: Technology and the Pastoral Ideal in America* (Oxford: Oxford University Press, 1964).

6. Watt Stewart, *Henry Meiggs: Yankee Pizarro* (Durham: Duke University Press, 1946); Charles D. Kepner Jr., *Social Aspects of the Banana Industry* (New York: Columbia University Press, 1936; reprint, New York: AMS Press, 1967).

7. Pierre Stouse, "The Instability of Tropical Agriculture: The Atlantic Lowlands of Costa Rica," *Economic Geography* 46 (1970): 78–97.

8. Frederick Upham Adams, *Conquest of the Tropics* (Garden City: Doubleday Page, 1914), 152–62.

9. Kepner, *Social Aspects,* 17–18.

10. Aviva Chomsky, *West Indian Workers and the United Fruit Company in Costa Rica, 1870–1940* (Baton Rouge: Louisiana State University Press, 1996).

11. Thomas L. Karnes, *Tropical Enterprise: The Standard Fruit and Steamship Company in Latin America* (Baton Rouge: Louisiana State University Press, 1978), 102–8.

12. Mary W. Helms, *Middle America: A Cultural History of Heartland and Frontier* (Englewood Cliffs, N.J.: Prentice-Hall, 1975); Bernard Nietschmann, *Between Land and Water: The Subsistence Ecology of the Miskito Indians, Eastern Nicaragua* (New York and London: Seminar Press, 1973); Craig L. Dozier, *Nicaragua's Mosquito Shore: The Years of British and American Presence* (Tuscaloosa: University of Alabama Press, 1985).

13. Philippe Bourgois, *Ethnicity at Work: Divided Labor on a Central American Banana Plantation* (Baltimore: Johns Hopkins University Press, 1989), 27–28.

14. O. Henry, *Cabbages and Kings* (New York: Doubleday, Page, 1912), 21.

15. John Soluri, *Banana Cultures: Agriculture, Consumption, and Environmental Change in Honduras and the United States* (Austin: University of Texas Press, 2005), chaps. 1–3.

16. Walter LaFeber, *Inevitable Revolutions: The United States and Central America* (New York: Norton, 1983), 44–45.

17. Dozier, *Nicaragua's Mosquito Shore*, chap. 9.

18. Harold M. Denny, *Dollars for Bullets: The Story of American Rule in Nicaragua* (Westport, Conn.: Greenwood Press, 1980), 142.

19. Paul Standley, "The Flora of Lancetilla," *Bulletin of the Field Museum of Natural History—Botany* 5, no. 10 (1931): 8–49.

20. Quoted in Soluri, *Banana Cultures*, 48.

21. William Durham, *The Soccer War: Scarcity and Survival in Central America* (Stanford: Stanford University Press, 1979).

22. Wilson Popenoe, *Manual of Tropical and Subtropical Fruits* (New York: Hafner Press, 1920).

23. Stuart McCook, *States of Nature: Science, Agriculture, and Environment in the Spanish Caribbean, 1760–1940* (Austin: University of Texas Press, 2002), chaps. 2, 5, 6.

24. Karnes, *Tropical Enterprise*, 84.

25. Samuel Crowther, *The Romance and Rise of the American Tropics* (Garden City, N.Y.: Doubleday Doran, 1929), 318–19.

26. Dana G. Munro, *The United States and the Caribbean Republics, 1921–1933* (Princeton: Princeton University Press, 1974), 380; Herbert Feis, *The Diplomacy of the Dollar, 1919–1932* (New York: Norton, 1950).

27. Grunwald and Musgrove, *Natural Resources,* 371.

28. Steve Striffler, *In the Shadows of State and Capital* (Durham: Duke University Press, 2002).

29. James J. Parsons, "Bananas in Ecuador: A New Chapter in the History of Tropical Agriculture," *Economic Geography* 33 (July 1957): 201–16.

30. Parsons, "Bananas in Ecuador," 206.

31. Paul J. Dosal, *Doing Business with Dictators: A Political History of United Fruit in Guatemala, 1899–1944* (Wilmington, Del.: Scholarly Resources Books, 1993), chap. 9.

32. Juan José Arevalo, *The Shark and the Sardines* (New York: Lyle Stuart, 1961).

33. LaFeber, *Inevitable Revolutions,* 111–26.

34. Robert G. Williams, *Export Agriculture and the Crisis in Central America* (Chapel Hill: University of North Carolina Press, 1986).

35. Edmund P. Russell, *War and Nature: Fighting Humans and Insects with Chemicals from World War I to Silent Spring* (Cambridge: Cambridge University Press, 2001).

36. John Vandermeer and Ivette Perfecto, *Breakfast of Biodiversity* (San Francisco: Institute for Food and Development Policy, 1996).

37. Grunwald and Musgrove, *Natural Resources,* 374–76.

38. LaFeber, *Inevitable Revolutions,* 100.

39. LaFeber, *Inevitable Revolutions,* 99–105.

40. Stouse, "Instability of Tropical Agriculture," 91–95.

41. Tom Barry, Beth Wood, and Deb Preusch, *Dollars and Dictators* (New York: Grove Press, 1983), 15–31.

42. Barry, Wood, and Preusch, *Dollars and Dictators,* 17.

43. Murdo J. MacLeod, *Spanish Central America: A Socioeconomic History, 1520–1720* (Berkeley and Los Angeles: University of California Press, 1973), chaps. 1–2.

44. V. D. Wickizer, *Coffee, Tea and Cocoa* (Baltimore: Johns Hopkins University Press, 1977).

45. Lori Ann Thrupp, "Pesticides and Policies: Approaches to Pest-Control Dilemmas in Nicaragua and Costa Rica," *Latin American Perspectives* 15, no. 4 (Fall 1988): 37–70; Lori Ann Thrupp, "Sterilization of Workers from Pesticide Exposure: The Causes and Consequences of DBCP-induced Damage in Costa Rica and Beyond," *International Journal of Health Services* 21, no. 4 (1991): 731–57.

46. *The World Banana Economy, 1970–1984: Structure, Performance and Prospects* (Rome: Food and Agriculture Organization of the United Nations, 1986), 8.

47. For the fascinating story of the banana advertising campaign in the United States (without which more natural forest would still remain in the American tropics), see Soluri, *Banana Cultures,* and Virginia Scott Jenkins, *Bananas: An American History* (Washington, D.C.: Smithsonian Institution Press, 2000).

48. *World Banana Economy,* 40–42.

49. Daniel Faber, *Environment under Fire* (New York: Monthly Review Press, 1993).

CHAPTER 3: THE LAST DROP

1. Fernand Braudel, *Civilization and Capitalism, 15th—18th Century,* vol. 1, *The Structures of Everyday Life: The Limits of the Possible* (New York: Harper and Row, 1979), 249–60.

2. William G. Clarence-Smith and Steven Topik, eds., *The Global Coffee Economy in Africa, Asia, and Latin America, 1500–1989* (Cambridge: Cambridge University Press, 2003).

3. Michael F. Jimenez, "'From Plantation to Cup': Coffee and Capitalism in the United States, 1830–1930," in *Coffee, Society, and Power in Latin America,* ed. William Roseberry, Lowell Gudmundson, and Mario Samper Kutschbach (Baltimore: Johns Hopkins University Press, 1995), 38–64.

4. Joseph Grunwald and Philip Musgrove, *Natural Resources in Latin American Development* (Baltimore: Johns Hopkins University Press, 1970), 320–30.

5. Stanley J. Stein, *Vassouras: A Brazilian Coffee County, 1850–1900* (Cambridge, Mass.: Harvard University Press, 1957).

6. Mary Karasch, *Slave Life in Rio de Janeiro, 1808–1850* (Princeton: Princeton University Press, 1987).

7. Warren Dean, *With Broadax and Firebrand: The Destruction of the Brazilian Atlantic Forest* (Berkeley and Los Angeles: University of California Press, 1995), 178–90.

8. Stein, *Vassouras*, 217.

9. Stein, *Vassouras*, 221.

10. This section is derived from Warren Dean, *Rio Claro: A Brazilian Plantation System, 1820–1920* (Stanford: Stanford University Press, 1976); quotation is on p. 2.

11. Dean, *Rio Claro*, 2.

12. Dean, *Rio Claro*, 3.

13. Joseph E. Sweigart, *Coffee Factorage and the Emergence of a Brazilian Capital Market, 1850–1888* (New York and London: Garland Publishing, 1987), 12–16.

14. William H. Ukers, *All About Coffee* (New York: Tea and Coffee Trade Journal Company, 1922), 484.

15. Stein, *Vassouras*, 58 n. 21.

16. Sweigart, *Coffee Factorage*, 37.

17. Ukers, *All About Coffee*, 527–29.

18. Ukers, *All About Coffee*, 484.

19. Stein, *Vassouras*, "Epilogue."

20. Joseph L. Love, *São Paulo in the Brazilian Federation, 1889–1937* (Stanford: Stanford University Press, 1980), 42–50.

21. Joseph Brandes, *Herbert Hoover and Economic Diplomacy: Department of Commerce Policy, 1921–1928* (Pittsburgh: University of Pittsburgh Press, 1962), 130–35.

22. Ukers, *All About Coffee*, 530–34.

23. Warren Dean, "Forest Conservation in Southeastern Brazil, 1900–1955," *Environmental Review* 9, no. 1 (Spring 1985): 55–69.

24. Don D. Humphrey, *American Imports* (New York: Twentieth Century Fund, 1955), 278, table 42.

25. Verena Stolcke, *Coffee Planters, Workers and Wives* (Oxford: Macmillan, 1988), 43–57.

26. Love, *São Paulo* (Stanford: Stanford University Press, 1980), 52.

27. For samples of the wide literature on the culture and economics of this era that is relevant, see Richard Wightman Fox and T. J. Jackson Lears, eds., *The Culture of Consumption: Critical Essays in American History, 1880–1980* (New York: Pantheon Books, 1983); Neva R. Goodwin, Frank Ackerman, and David Kiron, eds., *The Consumer Society* (Washington, D.C.: Island Press, 1997); Kenneth T. Jackson, *Crabgrass Frontier: The Suburbanization of the United States* (Oxford: Oxford University Press, 1985); William E. Leuchtenburg, *Paradox of Plenty: American Society Since 1945* (Boston: Little Brown, 1975); Paul Wachtel, *The Poverty of Affluence: A Psychological Portrait of the American Way of Life* (New York: Free Press, 1983).

28. James J. Flink, *The Automobile Age* (Cambridge, Mass.: MIT Press, 1988).

29. Harvey Levenstein, *Paradox of Plenty: A Social History of Eating in Modern America* (Oxford: Oxford University Press, 1983); Harvey Levenstein, *Revolution at the Table: The Transformation of the American Diet* (Oxford: Oxford University Press, 1988).

30. United Nations Food and Agriculture Organization (UNFAO), *World Coffee Trade 1963* (New York: United Nations, 1963), 7.

31. For fine-grained analysis of the transformation of the Paulista West, see Christian Brannstrom, "Coffee Labor Regimes and Deforestation on a Brazilian Frontier, 1915–1965," *Economic Geography* 76 (2000): 326–46; Christian Brannstrom, "Rethinking the 'Atlantic Forest' of Brazil: New Evidence for Land Cover and Land Value in Western São Paulo, 1900–1930," *Journal of Historical Geography* 28, no. 3 (2002): 420–39.

32. John McNeill, "Deforestation in the Araucaria Zone of Southern Brazil, 1900–1983," in *World Deforestation in the Twentieth Century,* ed. J. F. Richards and Richard Tucker (Durham, N.C.: Duke University Press, 1987), 15–32.

33. *Annual Coffee Statistics: 1958* (Washington, D.C.: Pan American Coffee Bureau, 1958), 14, 18–20, 27.

34. Walter LaFeber, *Inevitable Revolutions: The United States in Central America* (New York: Norton, 1983). LaFeber spells out some of the environmental implications more explicitly in "The Alliances for Progress," in Janet W. Brown and Andrew Maguire, *Bordering on Trouble: Resources and Politics in Latin America* (Bethesda, Md.: Adler and Adler, 1986), 337–88.

35. J. W. F. Rowe, *The World's Coffee* (London: Her Majesty's Stationery Office, 1963), chap. 9, "The 1962 International Coffee Agreement," 190.

36. United States Government, *The International Coffee Agreement* (Washington, D.C.: Government Printing Office, 1963).

37. UNFAO, *World Coffee Trade 1963*, 39–40, 77.

38. Stolcke, *Coffee Planters*, 242–46; Preston E. James, "Trends in Brazilian Agricultural Development," *Geographical Review* 43, no. 3 (July 1953): 302–27.

39. Dean, *Rio Claro*, 49.

40. For the northern Andes as an ecological region, see Dennis V. Johnson, ed., "The Northern Andes: Environmental and Cultural Change," *Mountain Research and Development* 2, no. 3 (August 1982): 253–336.

41. John V. Lombardi and James A. Hanson, "The First Venezuelan Coffee Cycle, 1830–1855," *Agricultural History* 44, no. 4 (1970): 355–68; Doug Yarrington, *A Coffee Frontier: Land, Society, and Politics in Duaca, Venezuela, 1830–1936* (Pittsburgh: University of Pittsburgh Press, 1997).

42. Lombardi and Hanson, "First Venezuelan Coffee Cycle," 365–68.

43. Carl Sauer, *The Early Spanish Main* (Berkeley and Los Angeles: University of California Press, 1966).

44. Catherine LeGrand, *Frontier Expansion and Peasant Protest in Colombia, 1850–1936* (Albuquerque: University of New Mexico Press, 1986), chap. 1.

45. Marco Palacios, *Coffee in Colombia, 1850–1970: An Economic, Social and Political History* (Cambridge: Cambridge University Press, 1980), 63. The material that follows is derived largely from LeGrand and Palacios.

46. James D. Henderson, *Modernization in Colombia: The Laureano Gomez Years, 1889–1965* (Gainesville: University of Florida Press, 2001).

47. Gabriel Garcia Marquez gives a vivid account of the devastation to the riverside forests, which was caused by the steamers' appetite for fuelwood, in the final chapter of his novel, *One Hundred Years of Solitude* (New York: Avon Books, 1970).

48. James J. Parsons, *Antioqueño Colonization in Western Colombia*, rev. ed. (Berkeley and Los Angeles: University of California Press, 1968).

49. David Bushnell, *The Making of Modern Colombia: A Nation in Spite of Itself* (Berkeley and Los Angeles: University of California Press, 1993), 169.

50. Palacios, *Coffee in Colombia*, 23.

51. Palacios, *Coffee in Colombia*, 227–42.

52. Palacios, *Coffee in Colombia*, 212.

53. J. Fred Rippy, *The Capitalists and Colombia* (New York: Vanguard Press, 1931), 152–76.

54. Bushnell, *Making of Modern Colombia*, 173.

55. Bushnell, *Making of Modern Colombia*, 201–22.

56. T. Lynn Smith, "Land Tenure and Soil Erosion in Colombia," in *Proceedings of the Inter-American Conference on Conservation of Renewable Natural Resources* (Washington, D.C.: Department of State, 1948), 155–60. Nearly twenty years later Smith expanded this analysis at length in *Colombia: Social Structure and the Process of Development* (Gainesville: University of Florida Press, 1967); quotations are on p. 155.

57. Grunwald and Musgrove, *Natural Resources*, 326.

58. Bushnell, *Making of Modern Colombia*, 223–35.

59. Other variations were played out closer to American homes, that is, in Central America. See the first edition of *Insatiable Appetite* for this discussion (Berkeley and Los Angeles: University of California Press, 2000).

60. For an analytic overview, see Steven C. Topik, "Coffee Anyone? Recent Research on Latin American Coffee Societies," *Hispanic American Historical Review* 80, no. 2 (2000): 225–66.

61. Timothy C. Weiskel, "Toward an Archaeology of Colonialism: Elements in the Ecological Transformation of the Ivory Coast," in *The Ends of the Earth: Perspectives on Modern Environmental History*, ed. Donald Worster (Cambridge: Cambridge University Press, 1988), 162–69.

CHAPTER 4: THE TROPICAL COST OF THE AUTOMOTIVE AGE

1. Susanna Hecht and Alexander Cockburn, *The Fate of the Forest: Developers, Destroyers and Defenders of the Amazon* (New York: Harper Perennial Books, 1989), 75.

2. Barbara Weinstein, *The Amazon Rubber Boom, 1850–1920* (Stanford: Stanford University Press, 1983), 177, 206; Hecht and Cockburn, *Fate of the Forest*, chap. 5.

3. Warren Dean, *Brazil and the Struggle for Rubber: A Study in Environmental History* (Cambridge: Cambridge University Press, 1987), chap. 3.

4. Wolf Donner, *Land Use and Environment in Indonesia* (Honolulu: University of Hawaii Press, 1987), 10–15; Anthony J. Whitten et al., *The Ecology of Sumatra* (Yokyakarta: UGM Press, 1984), chap. 1.

5. James W. Gould, *Americans in Sumatra* (The Hague: Martinus Nijhoff, 1961), 28–30.

6. Tys Volker, *From Primeval Forest to Cultivation* (Medan: Deli Planters Association, 1924), 87.

7. Volker, *From Primeval Forest,* 7.

8. Clark E. Cunningham, *The Postwar Migration of the Toba-Bataks to East Sumatra* (New Haven: Yale University Press, 1958), 11.

9. For the corporation's activities, see Glenn D. Babcock, *History of the United States Rubber Company* (Bloomington: Bureau of Business Research, Indiana University, 1966).

10. Volker, *From Primeval Forest,* 77; Gould, *Americans in Sumatra,* chap. 3.

11. Cunningham, *Postwar Migration,* 12.

12. H. Stuart Hotchkiss, "Operations of an American Rubber Company in Sumatra and the Malay Peninsula," *Annals of the American Academy* 112 (March 1924): 154.

13. Ladislao Szekely, *Tropic Fever* (Kuala Lumpur: Oxford University Press, 1979).

14. Ann Laura Stoler, *Capitalism and Confrontation in Sumatra's Plantation Belt, 1870–1979* (New Haven: Yale University Press, 1985).

15. Babcock, *History of United States Rubber,* 176–79.

16. T. A. Tengwall, "History of Rubber Cultivation and Research in the Netherlands Indies," in *Science and Scientists in the Netherlands Indies,* ed. P. Honig and F. Verdoorn (New York: Board for the Netherlands Indies, Surinam and Curacao, 1945), 349–50.

17. Alfred E. Eckes Jr., *The United States and the Global Struggle for Minerals* (Austin: University of Texas Press, 1979), 46.

18. Joseph Brandes, *Herbert Hoover and Economic Diplomacy: Department of Commerce Policy, 1921–1928* (Pittsburgh: University of Pittsburgh Press, 1962), 106–28.

19. Harvey S. Firestone, *Men and Rubber: The Story of Business* (Garden City: Doubleday, Page, 1926), 258–59.

20. Firestone, *Men and Rubber*, 253.

21. Firestone, *Men and Rubber*, 262–63.

22. Stephen D. Krasner, *Defending the National Interest: Raw Materials Investments and U.S. Foreign Policy* (Princeton: Princeton University Press, 1978), 101–3.

23. Torkel Holsoe, *Third Report on Forestry Progress in Liberia, 1951–1959* (Washington, D.C.: International Cooperation Administration, 1961), 1–10.

24. Yekutiel Gershoni, *Black Colonialism: The Americo-Liberian Scramble for the Hinterland* (Boulder: Westview, 1985), 1–6, 67–95.

25. Robert Clower et al., *Growth Without Development: An Economic Survey of Liberia* (Evanston: Northwestern University Press, 1966), 159–64.

26. Quoted in Firestone, *Men and Rubber*, 264.

27. W. W. Schmokel, "Settler and Tribes: Origins of the Liberian Dilemma," in *Western African History*, ed. Daniel F. McCall, Norman R. Bennett, and Jeffrey Butler (New York: Praeger, 1969), 174.

28. Firestone, *Men and Rubber*, 267.

29. Krasner, *Defending the National Interest,* 104–5.

30. Clower, *Growth Without Development,* 157.

31. Charles M. Wilson, *Liberia: Black Africa in Microcosm* (New York: Harper and Row, 1971), 132–34.

32. Wilson, *Liberia,* 133.

33. Clower, *Growth Without Development,* 158.

34. Eckes, *United States,* 80–83, 93–102; Alfred Lief, *The Firestone Story* (New York: McGraw Hill, 1951), 250–51.

35. W. J. S. Naunton, "Synthetic Rubber," *History of the Rubber Industry,* ed. P. Schidrowitz and T. R. Dawson (Cambridge: Heffer, 1952), 100–109.

36. Naunton, "Synthetic Rubber," 104.

37. Jonathan Marshall, *To Have and Have Not: Southeast Asian Raw Materials and the Origins of the Pacific War* (Berkeley and Los Angeles: University of California Press, 1995), 33–53.

38. Lief, *Firestone Story,* 251–52.

39. S. A. Brazier, "The Rubber Industry in the 1939–1945 War," in Schidrowitz and Dawson, *History of Rubber,* 316–26.

40. Colin Barlow, *The Natural Rubber Industry: Its Development, Technology and Economy in Malaysia* (Kuala Lumpur: Oxford University Press, 1978), 408.

41. Enzo R. Grilli, Barbara Bennett Agostini, and Maria J. 't Hooft-Welvaars, *The World Rubber Economy: Structure, Changes and Prospects* (Baltimore: Johns Hopkins University Press, 1980), 21.

42. Barlow, *Natural Rubber Industry,* 408; Grilli, Agostini, and 't Hooft-Welvaars, *World Rubber Economy,* 186–87; Harold J. Stern, *Rubber, Natural and Synthetic* (London: Maclaren, 1954).

43. Karl Pelzer, "The Agrarian Conflict in East Sumatra," *Pacific Affairs* 30 (1957): 152.

44. Richard Robison, *Indonesia: The Rise of Capital* (Sydney: Allen and Unwin, 1986).

45. Pelzer, "Agrarian Conflict," 159.

46. Charles A. Fisher, *South-East Asia: A Social, Economic and Political Geography* (London: Methuen, 1964), 319–21.

47. Lesley Potter, "Indigenes and Colonisers: Dutch Forest Policy in South and East Borneo (Kalimantan), 1900 to 1950," in *Changing Tropical Forests,* ed. John Dargavel et al., (Durham, N.C.: Forest History Society, 1988), 127–54.

48. Clower, *Growth Without Development,* 156.

49. Clower, *Growth Without Development,* 156. The company's sawmill at Harbel produced about 720,000 board feet of lumber in 1961, all for the plantation's use.

50. Clower, *Growth Without Development,* 150.

51. J. Gus Liebenow, *Liberia: The Evolution of Privilege* (Ithaca: Cornell University Press, 1969), 71–84.

52. Wilson, *Liberia,* 137.

53. Liebenow, *Liberia,* 216–17.

54. Grilli, Agostini, and 't Hooft-Welvaars, *World Rubber Economy,* 7.

55. Wade Davis, *One River: Explorations and Discoveries in the Amazon Rain Forest* (New York: Simon and Schuster, 1996), 370.

CHAPTER 5: THE CROP ON HOOVES

1. Alfred W. Crosby, *The Columbian Exchange: Biological and Cultural Consequences of 1492* (Westport: Greenwood Press, 1972), chap. 3; Alfred W. Crosby, *Ecological Imperialism: The Biological Expansion of Europe, 900–1900* (Cambridge: Cambridge University Press, 1986), chap. 8.

2. Robert Orr Whyte, *Tropical Grazing Lands: Communities and Constituent Species* (The Hague: Junk, 1974).

3. C. J. Bishko, "The Peninsular Background of Latin American Cattle Ranching," *Hispanic American Historical Review* 32 (November 1952): 491–515; Karl W. Butzer, "Cattle from Old to New Spain: Historical Antecedents," Paper at Latin American Geographers' Meeting, Merida, Mexico, January 1987; David E. Vassberg, *Land and Society in Golden Age Castile* (Cambridge: Cambridge University Press, 1984); Julius Klein, *The Mesta* (Cambridge, Mass.: Harvard University Press, 1920).

4. Richard W. Slatta, *Cowboys of the Americas* (New Haven: Yale University Press, 1990), chap. 2.

5. John R. McNeill, *Atlantic Empires of France and Spain: Louisbourg and Havana, 1700–1763* (Chapel Hill: University of North Carolina Press, 1985), 170; Allan J. Kuethe, "Havana in the Eighteenth Century," in *Atlantic Port Cities: Economy, Culture, and Society in the Atlantic World, 1650,* ed. Franklin W. Knight and Peggy K. Liss (Knoxville: University of Tennessee Press, 1991), 13.

6. Robert Wasserstrom, *Class and Society in Central Chipas* (Berkeley and Los Angeles: University of California Press, 1983), chap. 6; Murdo MacLeod, *Spanish Central America* (Berkeley and Los Angeles: University of California Press, 1973), chap. 1; Carl L. Johannessen, *Savannas of Interior Honduras* (Berkeley and Los Angeles: University of California Press, 1963), 36–47.

7. John P. Bailey, *Central America: Describing Each of the States of Guatemala, Honduras, Salvador, Nicaragua, and Costa Rica* (London: 1850), 121, quoted in Elbert E. Miller, "The Raising and Marketing of Beef in Central America and Panama," *Journal of Tropical Geography* 41 (1975): 59.

8. Terry G. Jordan, *North American Cattle-Ranching Frontiers: Origins, Diffusion, and Differentiation* (Albuquerque: University of New Mexico Press, 1993), chap. 5.

9. Charles Gibson, *Aztecs under Spanish Rule* (Stanford: Stanford University Press, 1964).

10. MacLeod, *Spanish Central America,* chap. 1.

11. P. J. Bakewell, *Silver Mining and Society in Colonial Mexico: Zacatecas, 1546–1700* (Cambridge: Cambridge University Press, 1971), 68–73. Vast flocks of sheep went through a similar irruption cycle of rapid breeding, with no natural enemies. By the late 1500s, they displaced both indigenous agriculture and its vegetation and moisture base, before declining to long-term steady numbers on degraded lands. Elinor Melville, *A Plague of Sheep* (Cambridge: Cambridge University Press, 1994), chaps. 4–6.

12. Robert C. West, *Sonora: Its Geographical Personality* (Austin: University of Texas Press, 1993), 58–59.

13. Francois Chevalier, *Land and Society in Colonial Mexico: The Great Hacienda,* trans. Alvin Eustis (Berkeley and Los Angeles: University of California Press, 1963).

14. Sandra L. Myres, "The Spanish Cattle Kingdom in the Province of Texas," *Texana* (Fall 1966): 245–46.

15. Jordan, *North American Cattle-Ranching,* 147–58.

16. Paul F. Starrs, *Let the Cowboy Ride: Cattle Ranching in the American West* (Baltimore: Johns Hopkins University Press, 1998), 45–49.

17. Myres, "Spanish Cattle Kingdom," 233–46; Odie B. Faulk, *The Last Years of Spanish Texas, 1778–1821* (London: Mouton, 1964).

18. David J. Weber, *The Spanish Frontier in North America* (New Haven: Yale University Press, 1992), 309–13; quotation is on p. 311.

19. Richard White, *The Roots of Dependency* (Lincoln: University of Nebraska Press, 1983).

20. William Cronon, *Nature's Metropolis: Chicago and the Great West* (New York: Norton, 1991), 82; Arthur M. Johnson and Barry E. Supple, *Boston Capitalists and Western Railroads: A Study in the Nineteenth-Century Railroad Investment Process* (Cambridge, Mass.: Harvard University Press, 1967).

21. Siegfried Giedion, *Mechanization Takes Command* (New York: Oxford University Press, 1948), 218.

22. Giedion, *Mechanization,* 226.

23. Cronon, *Nature's Metropolis,* 248.

24. Cronon, *Nature's Metropolis,* 218.

25. Jeremy Rifkin, *Beyond Beef: The Rise and Fall of the Cattle Culture* (New York: Dutton, 1992), 88.

26. Ralph W. Hidy and Muriel E. Hidy, "Anglo-American Merchant Bankers and the Railroads of the Old Northwest, 1848–1860," *Business History Review* 34 (1960): 150–69; A. W. Currie, "British Attitudes toward Investment in North American Railroads," *Business History Review* 34 (1960): 194–215.

27. Rifkin, *Beyond Beef,* 89–96.

28. Raymond Dasmann, *Environmental Conservation* (New York: Wiley, 1984), 182.

29. Walter P. Webb, *The Great Frontier* (Boston: Houghton Mifflin, 1962).

30. Tom Lea, *The King Ranch,* 2 vols. (Boston: Little Brown, 1957).

31. Tulio Halperin-Donghi, *Economy and Society in Argentina in the Revolutionary Period* (Cambridge: Cambridge University Press, 1975); James Scobie, *Argentina: A City and a Nation* (London: Oxford University Press, 1971), chap. 1; James Scobie, *Revolution on the Pampas: A Social History of Argentine Wheat, 1860–1910* (Austin: University of Texas Press, 1964); Peter Smith, *Politics and Beef in Argentina: Patterns of Conflict and Change* (New York: Columbia University Press, 1969); Oscar Schmieder, "Alteration of the Argentine Pampa in the Colonial Period," *University of California Publications in Geography* 2, no. 10 (September 1927): 303–21.

32. Richard W. Slatta, *Comparing Cowboys and Frontiers* (Norman: University of Oklahoma Press, 1997), chaps. 3, 5, 8.

33. Scobie, *Argentina,* chap. 5.

34. John E. Rouse, *The Criollo: Spanish Cattle in the Americas* (Norman: University of Oklahoma Press, 1977), 94–95, 120–21. These were developed by some of the same breeders who had developed the hybrid sheep that were conquering the colder plains of Patagonia in the same years.

35. Scobie, *Argentina,* 120.

36. Giedion, *Mechanization,* 214–29.

37. Joseph Grunwald and Philip Musgrove, *Natural Resources in Latin American Development* (Baltimore: Johns Hopkins University Press, 1970), 427.

38. J. Fred Rippy, *Globe and Hemisphere: Latin America's Place in the Postwar Foreign Relations of the United States* (Chicago: Regnery, 1958), 41.

39. Alfred Crosby, "Ecological Imperialism: The Overseas Migration of Western Europeans as a Biological Phenomenon," in *The Ends of the Earth,* ed. Donald Worster (Cambridge: Cambridge University Press, 1988), 114.

40. For the limited American involvement in ranching in other South American countries, see details in *Insatiable Appetite*, first edition (Berkeley and Los Angeles: University of California Press, 2000).

41. J. D. Chambers and G. E. Mingay, *The Agricultural Revolution, 1750–1880* (New York: Schocken Books, 1966), chaps. 2–3, 7; Christabel S. Orwin and Edith H. Whetham, *History of British Agriculture, 1846–1914* (London: Longmans, 1964), chap. 5.

42. Cronon, *Nature's Metropolis*, chap. 5; Jordan, *North American Cattle-Ranching*, chap. 2.

43. John E. Rouse, *World Cattle*, 2 vols. (Norman: University of Oklahoma Press, 1970), I: 358–59; Rouse, *Criollo*, 196.

44. Rouse, *Criollo*, 281–83.

45. Scobie, *Revolution on the Pampas*.

46. James J. Parsons, "Spread of African Pasture Grasses to the American Tropics," *Journal of Range Management* 25 (1942): 12.

47. Parsons, "Spread of African Pasture Grasses," 17.

48. Thomas Sheridan, *Where the Dove Calls* (Tucson: University of Arizona Press, 1988); Philip Wagner, "Parras: A Case History in the Depletion of Natural Resources," *Landscape* (Summer 1955): 19–28; A. Starker Leopold, "Vegetation Zones of Mexico," *Ecology* 31 (1950): 512–13.

49. Andrew J. W. Scheffey, *Natural Resources and Government Policy in Coahuila, Mexico* (Ph.D. diss., University of Michigan, 1958), 39–50, 249–60.

50. Miguel Tinker Salas, *In the Shadow of the Eagles: Sonora and the Transformation of the Border during the Porfiriato* (Berkeley and Los Angeles: University of California Press, 1997).

51. John Mason Hart, *Empire and Revolution: The Americans in Mexico since the Civil War* (Berkeley and Los Angeles: University of California Press, 2002).

52. Lindsay Chaney and Michael Cieply, *The Hearsts: Family and Empire* (NewYork: Simon and Schuster, 1981), 40–41; W. A. Swanberg, *Citizen Hearst* (New York: Scribner's, 1961), 29; Oliver Carlson, *Hearst, Lord of San Simeon* (New York: Viking, 1936), 13–14.

53. Carlson, *Hearst*, 117.

54. Swanberg, *Citizen Hearst*, 190.

55. Swanberg, *Citizen Hearst,* 207.

56. Manuel A. Machado Jr., *The North Mexican Cattle Industry, 1910–1975* (College Station: Texas A & M University Press, 1981), 125–26.

57. Max Winkler, *Investments of United States Capital in Latin America* (Boston: World Peace Foundation, 1929), 252–53. See also Robert W. Dunn, *American Foreign Investments* (New York: B. W. Huebsch and Viking Press, 1926), 105–6.

58. Ana Maria Alonso, *Thread of Blood: Colonialism, Revolution, and Gender on Mexico's Northern Frontier* (Tucson: University of Arizona Press, 1995), 166–67.

59. Swanberg, *Citizen Hearst,* 298.

60. Frank Tannenbaum, *The Mexican Agrarian Revolution* (Washington, D.C.: Brookings Institution, 1930), 358–69.

61. Mervin G. Smith, "The Mexican Beef-Cattle Industry," *Foreign Agriculture* 8, no. 11 (November 1944): 256; Machado, *North Mexican Cattle Industry,* 127–35.

62. Don D. Humphrey, *American Imports* (New York: Twentieth Century Fund, 1955), 273.

63. Mark Baldwin, "Soil Erosion Survey of Latin America," *Journal of Soil and Water Conservation* 9, no. 4 (1954): 162.

64. Humphrey, *American Imports,* 274; Machado, *North Mexican Cattle Industry,* 95.

65. Machado, *North Mexican Cattle Industry,* 95–117.

66. E. C. Stakman, Richard Bradfield, and Paul C. Mangelsdorf, *Campaigns against Hunger* (Cambridge, Mass.: Harvard University Press, 1967), 162–76.

67. Sheridan, *Where the Dove Calls.*

68. D. B. Agnew, *The Outlook for Hamburger Livestock and Meat Situation* (Washington, D.C.: U.S. Department of Agriculture, April 1979), 26–28; Douglas R. Shane, *Hoofprints on the Forest* (Philadelphia: Institute for the Study of Human Issues, 1986); James R. Simpson and D. E. Farris, *The World's Beef Business* (Ames: Iowa State University Press, 1982).

69. Grunwald and Musgrove, *Natural Resources,* 428; Lovell S. Jarvis, *Livestock Development in Latin America* (Washington, D.C.: World Bank, 1986), 88.

70. Grunwald and Musgrove, *Natural Resources,* 415–16.

71. For statistics, see Grunwald and Musgrove, *Natural Resources,* 422.

72. J. Fred Rippy, *Latin America in the Industrial Age* (New York: Putnam, 1944).

73. R. C. West, N. P. Psuty, and B. G. Thom, *The Tabasco Lowlands of Southeastern Mexico* (Baton Rouge: Louisiana State University Press, 1969), 118–19, 158–59.

74. Winkler, *Investments of United States Capital,* 51–52.

75. John Thompson, "Production, Marketing and Consumption of Cattle in El Salvador," *The Professional Geographer* 8, no. 5 (September 1961): 20.

76. Robert G. Williams, *Export Agriculture and the Crisis in Central America* (Chapel Hill: University of North Carolina Press, 1986), 78.

77. Billie R. DeWalt, "The Agrarian Bases of Conflict in Central America," in *The Central American Crisis: Sources of Conflict and the Failure of U. S. Policy,* ed. Kenneth Coleman and George Herring (Wilmington, Del.: Scholarly Resources, Inc., 1985), 43–54; Norman Myers, "The Hamburger Connection," *Ambio* 10, no. 1 (1981): 3–8; James Nations and Daniel Komer, "Indians, Immigrants and Beef Exports: Deforestation in Central America," *Cultural Survival Quarterly* (Spring 1982): 8–12; James J. Parsons, "Forest to Pasture: Development or Destruction?" *Revista Biologica Tropicale* 24 (1976): 121–38; Shane, *Hoofprints.*

78. U.S. Department of Agriculture, Foreign Agricultural Service, *World Livestock and Poultry Situation* (Washington, D.C.: April 1985); Williams, *Export Agriculture,* 99, 204, 206.

79. Q. Martin Morgan, *The Beef Cattle Industries of Central America and Panama* (Washington: U.S. Department of Agriculture Foreign Agricultural Service, 1973).

80. Elbert E. Miller, "The Raising and Marketing of Beef in Central America and Panama," *Journal of Tropical Geography* 41 (1975): 64; Williams, *Export Agriculture,* 87–90, 99, 205.

81. J. C. Tanner, "U.S. Cattlemen Buy Spreads in Central America to Exploit Good Grazing, Growing Demand for Beef," *Wall Street Journal,* July 27, 1972, 30.

82. Williams, *Export Agriculture,* 95, 109.

83. Williams, *Export Agriculture,* 106; Miller, "Raising and Marketing," 59–69.

84. P. S. Bartlett, *Agricultural Choice and Change: Decision-Making in a Costa Rican Community* (New Brunswick: Rutgers University Press, 1982); Billie R. DeWalt, "The Cattle Are Eating the Forest," in *Bulletin of the Atomic Scientists* 39, no. 1 (1983): 18–23; George Guess, "Pasture Expansion, Forestry and Development Contradictions: The

Case of Costa Rica," in *Studies in Comparative International Development* 14 (1979): 42–55; Norman Myers, *The Primary Source* (New York: W. W. Norton, 1984); James D. Nations and Daniel Komer, *Tropical Moist Forest Destruction in Middle America: Current Patterns and Alternatives* (Austin: Center for Human Ecology, 1980).

85. Q. Martin Morgan, *The Beef Cattle Industries of Central America and Panama* (Washington: U.S. Department of Agriculture, 1973), 15–18.

86. Morgan, *Beef Cattle Industries*, 8–10.

87. Edward C. Wolf, "Managing Rangelands," in *State of the World 1986*, ed. Lester R. Brown (New York: Norton, 1986), 70–72.

88. Winkler, *Investments of United States Capital*, 88.

89. Grunwald and Musgrove, *Natural Resources*, 410.

90. Rouse, *World Cattle*, 384; Grunwald and Musgrove, *Natural Resources*, 418–26.

91. Myers, *Primary Source*, 138.

92. Charles J. V. Murphy, "The Fabulous House of Kleberg," *Fortune* (June 1969): 112–19, 218–19, 224–25. The quotation is on p. 114.

93. Charles J. V. Murphy, "The King Ranch South of the Border," *Fortune* (July 1969): 132–36, 140, 142, 144.

94. Murphy, "Fabulous House," 134.

95. Murphy, "Fabulous House," 142.

96. Murphy, "King Ranch," 144.

97. Gerard Colby, *Thy Will Be Done* (New York: Harper Collins, 1995), 298–302, 608, 618–21, 632–34, 883.

98. Silvio R. Duncan Baretta and John Markoff, "Civilization and Barbarism: Cattle Frontiers in Latin America," in *The Frontier in History: North America and Southern Africa Compared*, ed. Howard Lamar and Leonard Thompson (New Haven: Yale University Press, 1981), 587–620.

99. Rouse, *Criollo*, 167.

CHAPTER 6: UNSUSTAINABLE YIELD

1. F. W. O. Morton, "The Royal Timber in Late Colonial Bahia," *Hispanic American Historical Review* 58, no. 1 (1978): 41–61.

2. Arthur M. Wilson, "The Logwood Trade in the Seventeenth and Eighteenth Centuries," in *Essays in the History of Modern Europe*, ed. Donald C. McKay (New York: Harper Brothers, 1936).

3. William Dampier, quoted in Narda Dobson, *A History of Belize* (Trinidad and Jamaica: Longman Caribbean, 1973), 55.

4. Stephen L. Caiger, *British Honduras, Past and Present* (London: George Allen and Unwin, 1951), 135, 139.

5. William F. Payson, *Mahogany: Antique and Modern* (New York: E. P. Dutton, 1926).

6. Walter D. Wilcox, "Among the Mahogany Forests of Cuba," *National Geographic* 19 (1908): 485.

7. John C. Callahan, *The Fine Hardwood Veneer Industry in the United States: 1838–1990* (Lake Ann, Mich.: National Woodlands Publishing Company, 1990).

8. Leslie Holdridge, F. Bruce Lamb, and Harold Mason, *Forests of Guatemala* (privately printed, 1950), 60–61.

9. F. Bruce Lamb, *Mahogany of Tropical America: Its Ecology and Management* (Ann Arbor: University of Michigan Press, 1966), 10–21.

10. James J. Parsons, "The Miskito Pine Savanna of Nicaragua and Honduras," *Annals of the Association of American Geographers* 45, no. 1 (1955): 36–63.

11. A. R. Gregg, *British Honduras* (London: Her Majesty's Stationery Office, 1968), 90.

12. Gareth Porter, with Delfin J. Ganapin Jr., *Resources, Population, and the Philippines' Future* (Washington, D.C.: World Resources Institute, 1988); Eric L. Hyman, "Forestry Administration and Policies in the Philippines," *Environmental Management* 7, no. 6 (1983): 511–24.

13. T. C. Whitmore, *Tropical Rain Forests of the Far East*, 2d ed. (Oxford: Clarendon Press, 1984), chaps. 1–4.

14. H. N. Whitford, *The Forests of the Philippines*, Bulletin no. 10 (Manila: Bureau of Forestry, 1911), I: 12–32.

15. David W. John, "The Timber Industry and Forest Administration in Sabah under Chartered Company Rule," *Journal of Southeast Asian Studies* 5 (1984): 55–81.

16. Lawrence Rakestraw, "George Patrick Ahern and the Philippine Bureau of Forestry, 1900–1914," *Pacific Northwest Quarterly* 53 (1967): 142–50.

17. Gifford Pinchot, *Breaking New Ground* (New York: Harcourt Brace, 1947), 224, 226.

18. Thomas Cox, *Mills and Markets: A History of the Pacific Coast Lumber Industry to 1900* (Seattle: University of Washington Press, 1974), chaps. 5, 7.

19. E. E. Schneider, *Commercial Woods of the Philippines: Their Preparation and Uses* (Manila: Bureau of Forestry, 1916), 16.

20. Barrington Moore, "Forest Problems in the Philippines," *American Forestry* 16, no. 2 (1910): 150.

21. Dean Worcester, "Philippine Forest Wealth," *American Forestry* 21, no. 1 (1915): 11.

22. Commonwealth of the Philippines, *Forest Resources of the Philippines* (Manila: Government Printing Press, 1939), 11.

23. Florencio Tamesis, "Philippine Forests and Forestry," *Unasylva* 2, no. 6 (1948): 324–25.

24. Nicolas P. Lansigan, "Our Dwindling Forests," *Forestry Leaves* 11 (1959): 19.

25. Tom Gill, "The Menace of Forest Destruction" (unpublished paper, 1959), 5–6.

26. Robert Repetto, *The Forest for the Trees? Government Policies and the Misuse of Forest Resources* (Washington, D.C.: World Resources Institute, 1988), chap. 3.

27. James K. Boyce, *The Philippines: Political Economy of Growth and Impoverishment in the Marcos Era* (Honolulu: University of Hawaii Press, 1993), 233.

28. Francois Nectoux and Yoichi Kuroda, *Timber from the South Seas* (Tokyo: Tsukiji Shokan, 1989).

29. Callahan, *Fine Hardwood Veneer Industry*, 74–79.

30. For an overview of the environmental impacts of warfare, see Richard P. Tucker and Edmund Russell, eds., *Natural Enemy, Natural Ally: Toward an Environmental History of War* (Corvallis: Oregon State University Press, 2004).

31. John A. Zivnuska, *U.S. Timber Resources in a World Economy* (Baltimore: Johns Hopkins University Press, 1967), 61.

32. Holdridge, Lamb, and Mason, *Forests of Guatemala*.

33. Tom Gill, "America and World Forestry," (unpublished paper, n.d.)

34. Arthur Bevan, "A Forest Policy for the American Tropics," *Caribbean Forester* 4, no. 2 (1943): 49–53.

35. Enrique Beltran, "Forestry and Related Research in Mexico," in *Forestry and Related Research in North America*, ed. Frank H. Kaufert and William H. Cummings (Washington, D.C.: Society of American Foresters, 1955), 254–71; Lane Simonian, *Land of the Jaguar: A History of Conservation in Mexico* (Austin: University of Texas Press, 1995).

36. In South America in the immediate prewar years Brazil and Argentina made similar beginnings. But just as in Mexico, these efforts were frozen by the war and were not revived until about 1950.

37. Caribbean Commission, *Forest Research within the Caribbean Area* (Washington, D.C.: Caribbean Commission, 1947), 5–18.

38. Robert K. Winters, "How Forestry Became a Part of FAO," *Journal of Forestry* 69 (1971): 574–77.

39. United Nations, Food and Agriculture Organization, *Report of the Latin American Conference on Forestry and Forest Products* (Rio de Janeiro: UNFAO, 1948), 8, 13.

40. Gill, "America and World Forestry," 291.

41. Irvine T. Haig et al., *Forest Resources of Chile as a Basis for Industrial Expansion* (Washington, D.C.: U.S. Forest Service, 1946).

42. F. Bruce Lamb, C. B. Briscoe, and G. H. Englerth, "Recent Observations on Forestry in Tropical America," *Caribbean Forester* 21, nos. 1–2 (1960): 47.

43. Hugh M. Raup, "Notes on Reforestation in Tropical America, I" (typescript, 1949).

44. Author interview with Leslie Holdridge, July 1987.

45. Gerardo Budowski, "The Opening of New Areas and Landscape Planning in Tropical Countries" (paper delivered at XII Congress of the International Federation of Landscape Architects, Lisbon, September 1970), 2.

46. Leslie R. Holdridge, "The Possibility of Close Cooperation for Mutual Benefit between Agriculture and Forestry in the American Tropics," *Caribbean Forester* 1, no. 3 (1940): 28.

47. Frank Wadsworth, "An Approach to Silviculture in Tropical America and Its Application in Puerto Rico," *Caribbean Forester* 8, no. 4 (1947): 245–56.

48. Wadsworth, "Approach to Silviculture," 249.

49. William Vogt, "Latin-American Timber, Ltd.," *Unasylva* 1, no. 1 (1947): 19.

50. William Vogt, *Road to Survival* (New York: W. Sloane, 1948).

51. Tom Gill, "America and World Forestry," in *American Forestry: Six Decades of Growth,* ed. Henry Clepper and Arthur B. Meyer (Washington, D.C.: Society of American Foresters, 1960), 282.

52. Norman K. Carlson and L. W. Bryan, "Report of the Standing Committee on Forestry—Tenth Pacific Science Congress, Hawaii," *Malayan Forester* 24, no. 4 (1961): 252–60.

CONCLUSION: CONSUMING APPETITES

1. Thomas Princen, "Distancing: Consumption and the Severing of Feedback," in *Confronting Consumption*, ed. Thomas Princen, Michael Maniates, and Ken Conca (Cambridge, Mass.: MIT Press, 2002), 103–31.

2. Martin Holdgate, *The Green Web: A Union for World Conservation* (London: Earthscan, 1999).

Selected Bibliography

Note to readers: As yet there are few works on world history that seriously consider environmental change. That short list includes both academic studies and surveys by well-informed journalists. I list some of them below. I also list a few recent studies of the social and environmental impacts of tropical export crops, which complement this book.

MODERN WORLD ENVIRONMENTAL HISTORY

Crosby, Alfred W. *Children of the Sun: A History of Humanity's Unappeasable Appetite for Energy.* New York: W. W. Norton, 2006.

———. *The Columbian Exchange: Biological and Cultural Consequences of 1492.* Westport, Conn.: Greenwood Press, 1972.

———. *Ecological Imperialism: The Biological Expansion of Europe, 900–1900.* Cambridge: Cambridge University Press, 1986.

Diamond, Jared. *Guns, Germs and Steel: The Fates of Human Societies.* New York: W. W. Norton, 1997.

Fernandez-Armesto, Felipe. *Civilizations: Culture, Ambition, and the Transformation of Nature.* New York: Free Press, 2001.

Grove, Richard. *Green Imperialism: Colonial Expansion, Tropical Island Edens and the Origins of Environmentalism, 1600–1860.* Cambridge: Cambridge University Press, 1995.

Hughes, J. Donald. *An Environmental History of the World: Humankind's Changing Role in the Community of Life.* London and New York: Routledge, 2001.

Marks, Robert. *The Origins of the Modern World: A Global and Ecological Narrative.* Lanham, Md.: Rowman & Littlefield, 2002.

McNeill, John R. *Something New under the Sun: An Environmental History of the Twentieth Century World.* New York: W. W. Norton, 2000.

McNeill, John R. and William H., *The Human Web: A Bird's-Eye View of World History.* New York: W. W. Norton, 2003.

Perlin, John. *A Forest Journey: The Role of Wood in the Development of Civilization.* New York: W. W. Norton, 1989.

Ponting, Clive. *A Green History of the World: The Environment and the Collapse of Great Civilizations.* London and New York: Penguin Books, 1991.

Pyne, Stephen J. *Fire: A Brief History.* Seattle: University of Washington Press, 2001.

Richards, John F. *The Unending Frontier: An Environmental History of the Early Modern World.* Berkeley and Los Angeles: University of California Press, 2003.

Williams, Michael. *Deforesting the Earth: From Prehistory to Global Crisis.* Chicago: University of Chicago Press, 2003.

ENVIRONMENTAL HISTORY OF WORLD REGIONS

D'Arcy, Paul. *The People of the Sea: Environment, Identity, and History in Oceania.* Honolulu: University of Hawaii Press, 2006.

Elvin, Mark. *The Retreat of the Elephants: An Environmental History of China.* New Haven: Yale University Press, 2004.

Gadgil, Madhav, and Ramachandra Guha. *This Fissured Earth: An Environmental History of India.* Berkeley and Los Angeles: University of California Press, 1992.

Garden, Donald S. *Australia, New Zealand and the Pacific: An Environmental History.* Santa Barbara, Calif.: ABC-CLIO, 2005.

McCann, James C. *Green Land, Brown Land, Black Land: An Environmental History of Africa, 1800–1990.* Portsmouth, N.H.: Heinemann, 1999.

McNeill, John R. *The Mountains of the Mediterranean World: An Environmental History.* Cambridge: Cambridge University Press, 1992.

——, ed. *Environmental History in the Pacific World.* Aldershot: Ashgate, 2001.

Peluso, Nancy. *Rich Forests, Poor People: Resource Control and Resistance in Java.* Berkeley and Los Angeles: University of California Press, 1991.

Totman, Conrad. *The Green Archipelago: Forestry in Preindustrial Japan.* Berkeley and Los Angeles: University of California Press, 1989.

TROPICAL EXPORT CROPS

Dean, Warren. *Brazil and the Struggle for Rubber.* Cambridge: Cambridge University Press, 1987.

———. *With Broadax and Firebrand: The Destruction of the Brazilian Atlantic Forest.* Berkeley and Los Angeles: University of California Press, 1995.

Hobhouse, Henry. *Seeds of Change: Five Plants That Transformed Mankind.* New York: Harper and Row, 1985.

McCook, Stuart. *States of Nature: Science, Agriculture, and Environment in the Spanish Caribbean, 1760–1940.* Austin: University of Texas Press, 2002.

Melville, Elinor. *A Plague of Sheep: Environmental Consequences of the Conquest of Mexico.* Cambridge: Cambridge University Press, 1994.

Mintz, Sidney. *Sweetness and Power: The Place of Sugar in Modern History.* New York: Viking, 1985.

Pendergrast, Mark. *Uncommon Grounds: The History of Coffee and How It Transformed Our World.* New York: Basic Books, 1999.

Soluri, John. *Banana Cultures: Agriculture, Consumption, and Environmental Change in Honduras and the United States.* Austin: University of Texas Press, 2005.

Viola, Herman J., and Carolyn Margolis, eds. *Seeds of Change: Five Hundred Years since Columbus.* Washington, D.C.: Smithsonian, 1991.

Watts, David. *The West Indies: An Environmental History.* Cambridge: Cambridge University Press, 1987.

Index

Adams, Frederick, 48
agronomy, tropical, 4–5; and
  specialization, 221. *See also*
  monocropping; settled farming
Ahern, George P.: and the development
  of forestry laws, 193–97; founding of
  forestry college by, 198
Alliance for Progress, 98
Amazon Steam, 117
American Coffee Company, 107
American Colonization Society, 129–30,
  131
American-Guatemalan Mahogany
  Company, 189–90
American Sugar Refining Company (the
  Sugar Trust), 16, 23, 26, 35; U.S.
  government attempts at controlling,
  16–17
Arbenz, Jacobo, 70–71
Arbuckle, John, 94
Arbuckle Brothers, 91, 92
Arevalo, Juan José, 70
Argentina, 157, 161–63, 171; and the
  American beef industry, 163; beef
  industry of in the Gran Chaco,
  179–80; colonial period of, 161–62;

and the "Conquest of the Desert,"
  162; ecological transformation of due
  to cattle and sheep grazing, 163; labor
  force in, 162–63; transformation of
  the grasslands in, 162–63
Armas, Castillo, 71
Armour, Philip D., 158
Armour Meats, 177, 182
Atkins, Edwin, 14–16, 19, 31–32;
  establishment of Harvard Garden by,
  15
Audubon Society, 220

Baker, Lorenzo Dow, 46, 48
bananas, 113; advertising for, 231n47;
  box shipments of in order to reduce
  bruising, 72; European farming
  techniques for, 52–53; export taxes
  on, 62; exports of from Central
  America, 43, 57, 77; Giant Cavendish
  variety, 60, 65, 69, 72; Gros Michel
  variety, 58, 65, 69, 72; ideal
  conditions for growing, 44–45;
  production of as linked to railroad-
  building, 47–48; small-scale farming
  of, 52; toxification of soils and water

bananas (continued)
  because of banana growing, 78;
  Valery variety, 72. *See also* bananas,
  diseases of
bananas, diseases of: Panama Disease
  (*Fusarium* mold), 58–59, 60, 65, 68,
  69, 70, 72; Sigatoka Disease, 59–60,
  68, 70
Bank of New York, 107
Barbour, Thomas, 15
Barclay, Edwin, 134
Batista, Fulgencio, 22; support of by the
  Truman and Eisenhower
  administrations, 23
Battery Park National Bank, 107
beef: birth of the modern beef industry,
  157–58; and competition between the
  United States and Great Britain, 159;
  development of the beef industry in
  Central American tropical
  rainforests, 171–72, 182–83; exports
  of from Central America to the
  United States, 172–73; exports of
  from the United States to Great
  Britain, 159; importance of
  refrigerated railroad cars to, 158–59;
  mechanization of beef processing in
  the United States, 158; and the rise of
  the hamburger industry, 173; and
  slaughterhouse operations, 173, 174;
  as a symbol of affluence, 170. *See also*
  cattle industry
Belize, 187
Bell Trade Act (1946), 38
Benedicto, Roberto, 39
B. F. Goodrich, 144–45
Blaine, James G., 15
Bolivia (Acre region of), 115–16

"Bolivian Syndicate," 116
Bonilla, Manuel, 55
Borneo, 143
Boston Fruit Company, 46
Brazil, 82, 83, 102, 116, 117; abolishment
  of slavery in, 89; Amazonian
  development program of, 177–78;
  attempts of to restrict new planting of
  coffee, 95–96; beef industry of,
  176–78; and the colonial system of
  crown grants for land, 88; crop
  diversification in, 100; destructive
  effect of coffee plantations (*fazendas*)
  on the ecology of, 84–86, 99–100,
  111–12; development of the Paulista
  West area of, 87–89; effect of World
  War II on coffee production in, 96;
  erosion in, 95; European immigration
  to, 89–90; Paraiba coffee-growing
  area of, 86; Paraná coffee-growing
  area of, 97–98; Portuguese conquest
  of, 87; railroads in, 89; stabilization of
  coffee prices in by international
  investors, 94; Tupi-Guarani farming
  culture of, 87. *See also* Brazil, coffee
  exports of; São Paulo (state)
Brazil, coffee exports of: coffee exporters
  (factors) in, 90; coffee exports to
  Europe, 96; coffee exports to the
  United States, 92–93, 95; total coffee
  exports (1958), 98
Brooklyn Sugar Refining Company, 16
Budowski, Gerardo, 211
Burns, Jabez, 91
Burton, Richard, 86

cacao, 67, 76
Calderon, Rafael, 74

Calles, Plutarco, 167
Canada, 139, 140, 202
Cardenas, Lázaro, 167
Cargill Foods, 175
Carias, Tiburcio, 73
Castro, Fidel, 14, 98, 178; land policies
    of, 23–24
cattle, breeds of: Aberdeen Angus, 164,
    179; American Brahman bulls, 172,
    176; Criollo, 164, 172, 173, 175, 178,
    183; Hereford, 164; Santa Gertrudis,
    161, 174, 180, 181; Shorthorn, 162,
    164, 179; Zebu, 164, 178
cattle industry: and aftosa (hoof and
    mouth) disease, 168–69; and
    competition from settled farming,
    160; and corn-fed hybrid cattle, 152,
    160; in Cuba and the Caribbean, 152;
    destruction of grasslands by cattle
    drives, 160; effect of on Central and
    Latin American ecosystems, 151, 152,
    163, 172–73, 182–83; Hispanic, 152,
    156–57; introduction of cattle into
    Central America and Mexico by the
    Spanish, 152–53, 155; and lowland
    pasture diseases, 172; permanent
    haciendas founded in, 153; products
    for the modernization of, 175;
    relationship of to crop production,
    151–52; relationship of to silver
    mining, 153, 155. See also Argentina;
    beef; cattle, breeds of; grasslands;
    Mexico; Texas
Central America: anti-American
    nationalism in, 62–63; beef exports of
    (1979), 176; crop diversification in,
    76–77, 78; decline in exports of due
    to World War II, 65; development of

the beef industry in moist tropical
    zones of, 171–72; international
    markets for banana exports of, 73;
    labor unrest in, 63–64; major exports
    of (1970s), 174; political conditions in
    after World War II, 69–70. See also
    Central American rainforest,
    conquest of (1872–1945)
Central American rainforest, conquest of
    (1872–1945), 43–44, 69, 77–79;
    banana politics and the control of
    natural resources, 61–65; development
    of the Pacific coastal plain by banana
    companies, 60–61; transformation of
    forest and marshland by banana
    companies, 56–58
Central Intelligence Agency (CIA), 71
Ceylon, rubber production in, 102, 118,
    119, 124, 148
Champion Paper Company, 214
Chicago, 158
Chile, 208; reforestation of, 209
China, 27
Chiquita Banana, 218
Christmas, Lee, 55
Christy Commission, 134
Church, George, 115
Churchill, Winston, 124
Clark, W. P., 195
"Club de la Habana," 14
coffee, 47, 113; and chemical fertilizers,
    100; coffee blight in India and
    Ceylon, 89; Cold War politics of, 98,
    99; colonial trade and consumption
    of in the Americas, 81–83;
    development of instant coffee, 97;
    effect of the Great Depression on
    prices of, 95, 96; effect of

coffee (continued)
"valorization" policy on coffee prices
and production, 93–94; international
markets for, 90–91; market demand
for, 82; markets for in the United
States, 90–96, 112; monopolization of
West Indies coffee exports by Great
Britain, 91; and soil variety, 88;
sustainable coffee production,
110–12; volatility of coffee prices,
98–99; world coffee production levels
(1958), 98; world market for, 99. *See
also* Brazil, coffee exports of; coffee,
types of; New York Coffee Exchange
coffee, types of: Arabica, 91; café suave,
102; Robusta, 91, 97, 144
Coffee Study Group, 98
Cold War, 71, 98, 139
Colombia, 51, 60, 65, 101; American
control of the coffee trade in, 106–7;
Antioquia region of, 106, 109; civil
war (La Violencia) in, 108; climate of
the northern Andes in, 103; coffee
production in, 98, 101–3, 106;
development of infrastructure in,
105; ecological degradation in,
108–10; effect of the Great
Depression on, 108; export economy
of, 106, 107; exports of coffee to
Europe, 105, 109; exports of coffee to
the United States, 105, 109; farming
techniques in, 106; geography and
climate of, 103–4; government
distribution of land in, 110; quinine
production in, 104; settlement of,
104–5; social violence in, 108
Costa Rica, 46–47, 48, 51, 60, 209; beef
industry of, 175; cacao exports of, 76;

Communist Party of, 64, 74; efforts of
to tax banana exports, 62; labor
unrest in, 64; political relations with
American corporations, 73–74. *See
also* Higuerito Project; United Fruit
Company
Cronon, William, 159, 161
Crosby, Alfred, 163
Crowder, Enoch, 19
Crowther, Samuel, 63
Cuba, 7, 51, 178–79, 187–88;
abolishment of slavery in, 14; collapse
of sugar market/prices in
(1930–1932), 21; destruction of
tropical forests in, 19–20;
domestication of nature in, 9–14;
effect of the Great Depression on,
21–22; increase in indigenous
ownership of Cuban sugar mills,
22–23; logging in, 188–89; revolution
in (1868), 12; revolution in (1894),
17; revolution in (1959), 23; strategic
location of, 9–11; sugar production
boom in (1893), 16; sugar production
boom in (pre- and post–World War
I), 18; sugar production in the 1960s,
24–25; workforce of, 14
Cuba, and the United States, 28;
American campaign to annex Cuba,
11; American investment in Cuban
sugar production, 10–11, 12, 18–19;
American investment in Cuban
infrastructure, 12, 17–18; American
military intervention in Cuba, 17;
commercial trade of Cuba with New
England, 9–10
Cuyamel Fruit Company, 54; draining
of marshland by in Nicaragua,

57–58; sale of to United Fruit
Company, 59

"Dance of the Millions," 18, 20, 106–7
Davies, Marion, 167
Davies, Theo H., 35
Davila, Miguel, 55
Davis, Wade, 149–50
Dean, Warren, 87, 100–101
Del Monte, 77, 174
Denman, Leroy, 174
Diaz, Adolfo, 55
Diaz, Porfirio, 165, 166
Doe, Samuel, 146
Dole Fruits, 77
Dulles, Allen, 71
Dulles, John Foster, 71
Dunlap, Vining, 209–10
Dunlop Corporation, 131
Du Pont Corporation, 136, 137
Dutch American Plantation Company
    ("Hoppum"), 122, 124; development
    of the bud-grafting technique for
    rubber trees, 125

East Indies. See Netherlands East Indies
Ecuador, 60, 64–65, 72; acreage of under
    banana cultivation, 68; financing of
    highways in by the United States, 67;
    growth of American banana
    companies in, 66–67; problem of
    sheet erosion in, 67
Eisenhower, Dwight, 23, 71
El Salvador, 62
Emery, George D., 190; and Casa
    Emery's logging techniques, 190–91
Emery Company, 209
Empire Forestry Association, 205

Europe, 138; banana consumption in,
    77–78; chocolate industry in, 76;
    coffee consumption in, 83. See also
    specifically listed European countries
European Economic Community, 140

Federal War (1858), 102–3
Ferrera, Gregorio, 64
Figueres, Pepe, 74
Firestone, Harvey, 3, 128, 148; attempts
    of to establish rubber production in
    the Philippines, 128; capital
    development of the rubber industry
    in Liberia, 132–33; labor recruitment
    policies of in Liberia, 133–34; success
    of his rubber plantations during
    World War II, 143–44; system of
    dividing labor by tribal ethic groups
    in Liberia, 146
Firestone, Harvey, Jr., 137
Firestone Rubber and Tire, 143, 146,
    238n49; lumber operations of, 144
Fischer, Arthur, 198
Follansbee, 166
Ford, Henry, 124
Fort Dodge Laboratories, 175
France, 111; exports of coffee to, 82–83
Franck, Harry, 20
Freiberg Mahogany, 202
Friends of the Earth, 220

Germany (Nazi), 135, 136
Gibbon, Lardner, 115
Gill, Tom, 200–201, 204, 207, 214, 219
globalization, 77, 219; and debates
    concerning population growth and
    consumption, 220–21
Gold Coast, 76

Goodyear, Charles, 114, 116
Goodyear Tire and Rubber, 122, 124,
    141, 148; and the balloon tire, 124;
    and the creation of Wingfoot
    Plantation, 125, 141
grasslands, 183; African (*Gramineaceae*)
    grasses, 164–65; Guinea grasses, 172;
    Old World grasses, 156; Pará grasses,
    172; transformation of the grasslands
    in Latin America, 162–63, 164
Great Atlantic and Pacific Tea
    Company, 107
Great Britain, 51, 63, 76, 82, 118, 121,
    187; beef industry of, 159, 163; cattle
    ranching in its colonies, 157; colonial
    plantations of, 119; domination of
    world rubber markets by, 128;
    monopolization of West Indies coffee
    exports by, 91; need of for synthetic
    rubber, 138
Great Depression, 37, 64, 198–99, 217;
    effect of on coffee prices, 95, 96; effect
    of on sugar prices, 21–22; effect of on
    rubber prices, 126–27
Guatemala, 69–70, 72, 174, 209; exports
    of bananas to Europe, 73; exports of
    bananas to the United States, 70, 72;
    land reforms in (Agrarian Reform
    Law), 70–71; logging in, 189–90;
    malnutrition in, 70

Haiti, 82–83
Hard, Rand & Company, 91
Hearst, George, 166
Havemeyer, Horace, 15–16, 19, 31–32, 35;
    formation of the Sugar Trust by, 16
Hawaii, 33, 40; sugar production in,
    25–27; unionization of sugar workers
    in, 27

Hawaiian-Philippine Company (HPC), 35
Hawaiian Sugar Planters Association
    (HSPA), 27
Hearst, William Randolph, 166; and the
    Babicora hacienda, 166, 167;
    nationalization of Babicora by the
    Mexican government, 167–68
Hevea brasiliensis rubber tree species,
    113, 114, 116; effect of South
    American Leaf Blight on, 117;
    transplantation of seedlings out of
    Brazil to British colonies, 118
Henry, O., 51–52
Herndon, Lewis, 115
Hershey Chocolate Company, 23
Higuerito Project, 75
Holdridge, Leslie, 203–4, 211
Honduras, 44, 51, 77, 174; American
    hegemony in, 72–73; banana
    production in, 73; labor strikes in, 73;
    land sales of by the government,
    54–55; water rights dispute in, 64
Hoover, Herbert, 125
Hoppum. *See* Dutch American
    Plantation Company ("Hoppum")
Hotchkiss, Stuart, 122–23, 125

IBEC Research, Inc., 181–82
Ichabod Williams and Sons, Inc., 189,
    190, 202
I.G. Farben Company (IG), 136, 137
Illinois Central Railroad, 11
Indonesia, 113; American rubber
    corporations in, 118–27; American
    rubber corporations in after World
    War II, 140–43; civil unrest in, 140–41;
    expansion of the rubber industry in,
    142–43; total rubber exports of (1973),
    142. *See also* Java; Sumatra

Insular Lumber Company, 36, 195, 196
Inter-American Coffee Agreement, 96
Inter-American Conference on Natural
    Resources and Conservation, 108–9
International Coffee Agreement, 96,
    98–99
International Coffee Organization, 109
International Cooperation Agency
    (ICA), 208
International Foods, 177
International Packers Ltd. (IPL), 180–81
International Rubber Regulation
    Commission (IRRC), 126
International Society of Tropical
    Foresters, 214, 219
International Sugar Board, 18
International Union for the
    Conservation of Nature, 219–20
Ivory Coast, 111

Jamaica, 46, 48, 51, 101; problem of
    sheet erosion in, 67
Japan, 135, 138, 140; banana
    consumption in, 77–78
Java, 27, 142; cancellation of coffee
    imports from by the New York
    "Syndicate," 91–92
Jenks, Leland, 19
Jones, Jesse, 137
Juarez, Benito, 165

Kahl, E. A., 107
Keith, Minor, 47–48; and the building of
    infrastructure in Panama, 49
Kennedy, John F., 98, 99
Kentucky Blue Grass, 156
King, Charles, 134
King, Richard, 160
King Ranch, 161, 174, 178, 179, 181

Kleberg, Bob, 178–81; purchase of the
    Aguay and Oscuro ranches by, 180;
    purchase of ranch land in Amazonia,
    180–81; views on forest sustainability
    and agroforestry, 181
Knox, Philander, 55
Korean War, 139, 141

Ladinos, 83
LaFeber, Walter, 74
Lansigan, Nicolas, 200
"Latin-American Timber, Ltd." (Vogt),
    213
Laurel-Langley tariff (1956), 38
Law of Forced Rental, 70
League of Nations, 134
Lever Act ([Smith-Lever Act] 1914), 18
Liberalism, 53
Liberia, 113, 135, 143; American
    immigrants to, 130; capital
    development of the rubber industry in
    by Firestone, 132–33; corporate
    infrastructure in, 145–46; division of
    labor by ethnic groups in, 146;
    establishment of, 128–30; labor
    recruitment policies of Firestone in,
    133–34; labor unrest in, 146; land
    concessions of to B. F. Goodrich,
    144–45; land concessions of to
    Firestone, 132, 144; legacy of the
    rubber plantations in, 147; military
    coups in, 146–47; as the Republic of
    Liberia, 130; rivalry between coastal
    and hinterland tribes, 130–31; rubber
    production of the Harbel and Cavalla
    plantations, 143–44; total rubber
    production of (1960), 145; U.S. control
    of the Liberian economy, 131–32
Liberia Company, 144

Liberian Construction Corporation (LCC), 143
Liberian Rubber Corporation, 131
Lowry and Company, 19

Machado, Gerardo, 22
Madeira-Mamore Railway Company, 115
Malaya, rubber production in, 113, 118, 119, 124, 126, 148
Manatí Sugar Company, 21
Marcos, Ferdinand, 38–39, 201
Markgraf, Andreas, 11
Maury, Matthew, 115
McCoy, Joseph G., 159
McHale, Thomas, 36
McKinley, William, 32
Meiggs, Henry, 47
Mexico, 157; beef exports of to the United States, 168–69; economy of after the Mexican revolution, 168; effect of cattle ranching on ecosystem of, 168; effect of the Mexican Revolution on American investments in, 166–67; investment in by American cattle ranchers, 165–66; modernization of the cattle industry in, 168; nationalization of American-owned land by the Mexican government, 167–68; stock and pasture management in, 169; Miskito Coast, 44, 51
Mississippi Delta, 53–54
molasses, 7, 31
monocropping, 147, 206–7, 221; environmental impact of sugar monocropping, 7–8, 19
Moore, Barrington, 195–96, 197
Morgan, J. P., 19, 55
Munro, Dana, 63

National City Bank (New York), 19
National Coffee Federation (FEDECAFE), 107, 109
National Peasant Union Federation, 70
Neoprene, 136, 137
Netherlands, 118–20, 121; crop-growing experiments of in Sumatra, 119; interests of in the East Indies, 118–19; rubber production in Sumatra after World War II, 140–41
Netherlands East Indies, 126, 135
New Asahan Tobacco Company, 122
New York Coffee Exchange, 92–93
Nicaragua, 51, 55–56, 173; banana exports of, 57; beef industry in, 176; transformation of land usage in, 56–58
Noboa consortium, 77
Norris, George, 94

Obregon, Alvaro, 167
Organic Act (1902), 33
Orr, Toby, 175
Oteri and Brothers, 53

Pacific Science Association, 215
Palacios, Marco, 104
Panama, 48, 60, 76, 175; infrastructure in, 48–49
Panama Canal, 33, 50, 105
Parsons, James, 165
Pelzer, Karl, 142
Peron, Juan, 179
Peterson, Rudolph, 174–75
Philippine Lumber and Development Company, 194
Philippine National Bank, 33
Philippines, 113, 128; American investments in, 33–34; conflicts

among mill owners and sugar planters, 36; and the deforestation of Negros Island, 30, 39; effect of World War II on sugar production in, 37–38; hardwood timber harvesting on Negros Island, 36; impact of American capital on, 27–28, 38; independence of (1946), 38; monastic estates in, 28, 31, 33; and the New People's Army, 39; pacification campaign against natives in, 31; Papa Isio's revolt in, 31; plantation communities in, 30–31; polarization between laborers and plantation owners in, 36; politics of sugar under Marcos, 38–39; proposed annexation of by the American sugar cartel, 31–32; and the "quota race" following the 1934 tariff, 37; rebuilding of after World War II, 199–200; seizure of by the United States from Spain, 28; social chaos in, 39; Spanish conquest of, 28; sugar exports of, 31, 37; sugar production in, 25, 28, 32–33, 35–36; technical modernization of the sugar industry in, 34–35. *See also* Philippines, colonial logging industry of

Philippines, colonial logging industry of, 191–92; American control of, 193–94; American logging of redwood and Douglas fir in, 193; and deforestation, 201; development of laws to control logging operations, 193–97; different forms of logging, 197; effect of the Great Depression on, 198–99; effect of World War II on, 199; exploitation of lowland forests in, 192; exports of *Lauan* (Philippine mahogany) before 1570, 192–93, 196, 200; and the

global economy, 197–98; international exports of lumber from, 196–97; modernization of timber operations, 195; relationship between Filipino loggers and American logging interests, 196; relationship between sugar plantation clear cutting and logging, 195; richness of tropical hardwoods in, 192

Pinchot, Gifford, 193–94, 195

Platt Amendment (1903), 17

pollution, 223n1

Popenoe, Wilson, 59, 209

Puerto Limon, 47

Puerto Rico, 28, 101, 212

Quevedo, Miguel de, 205

Reconstruction Finance Corporation, 135, 137

Reynal, Juan, 179

Rio de Janeiro, 90

Rionda y Polledo, Manuel, 21

Rockefeller, Nelson, 181–82

Rockefeller, Winthrop, 181

Roosevelt, Franklin, 22, 135, 137

Roosevelt, Theodore, 32, 131

Root, Elihu, 32, 131

Rowe, J.W.F., 99

rubber, 147–50; American rubber corporations in Indonesia, 118–27; American rubber speculators in Amazonia, 114–18; Buna-S rubber, 136, 137; Chinese laborers in the rubber industry, 123–24; collapse of the world rubber market (1912), 118; collapse of the world rubber market (1921), 124; devastation of rubber trees by parasites, 89; effect of the

rubber (continued)
   Great Depression on rubber prices,
   126–27; effect of oil prices on
   synthetic rubber, 149; environmental
   effect of the rubber plantations, 121,
   134, 148–49; and the era of industrial
   rubber, 113–14; global production of
   (1946, 1950, 1973), 139–40; labor
   conditions in the rubber industry,
   123–24; and latex extraction, 116;
   natural rubber plantations after 1945,
   139–43; Pará rubber, 117; production
   of in the Amazon basin, 117; rise in
   prices of (1923–1925), 124–25; as a
   strategic war materiel, 128, 135;
   synthetic rubber, 135–39, 149; use of
   by the automobile industry, 124–25,
   139, 140, 147; and the vulcanization
   process, 114, 116. See also Ceylon;
   Firestone, Harvey; Goodyear Tire
   and Rubber; Hevea brasiliensis rubber
   tree species; Liberia; Malaya; United
   States Rubber
Rubber Association of America, 128
Rubber Regulation Committee, 135
Rubber Reserve Company, 135, 137
Russell and Sturgis Company, 30

Sandino, Augusto, 63–64
San Pedro Sula, 52, 53, 54
Santo Domingo, 51
Santos, 90, 91, 101, 105
São Paulo (city), 86
São Paulo (state), 86–87; overproduction
   of coffee in, 93; "valorization" policy
   of for coffee prices, 93–94
settled farming, 160, 161
sheep ranching, 163, 240n11, 241n34
Sielcken, Herman, 93–94

Sierra Club, 220
slavery/slaves, 82, 87; abolishment of
   slavery in Brazil, 89; abolishment of
   slavery in Cuba, 14; slave revolts in
   Haiti, 83; slavery and slave estates
   (fazendas) in Brazil, 83, 84–85, 88.
   See also sugar (cane sugar), and the
   slave trade
Smith, T. Lynn, 108–9
Smithfield Market, 159, 163
Smoot-Hawley Tariff (1930), 21
Soledad Estate, 15
Soviet Union, 24–25, 177, 202
Spain, 10, 17, 31, 187; abolishment of
   slavery in Cuba by, 14; Spanish rule
   of Central America, 45–46
Spreckles, Claus, 16, 27–28, 35
Standard Brands, 174; Standard Fruit
   Company (later Dole Fruits), 44, 49,
   65, 73; founding of, 54
Standard Oil of New Jersey, 136, 137
Standard Steam Navigation Company,
   46
Standley, Paul, 57
Stettinius, Edward, 144
Stevenson, James, 124
Stevenson Plan (1922), 124, 125
Stouse, Pierre, 75
sugar (beet sugar), 2, 11–12, 16, 33, 37;
   cultivation of in Europe, 11;
   cultivation of in the United States,
   11–12; effect of on cane sugar prices,
   12; effect of World War I on, 18
sugar (cane sugar), 25, 40–41, 88, 113,
   226n37; collapse of the world sugar
   market (1975–1985), 39;
   consumption of in England, 8;
   consumption of in Europe, 7, 8–9;
   consumption of in the United States,

2, 7; environmental impact of sugar monocropping, 7–8, 19; history of, 8; hybridization of, 8; muscovado sugar, 12, 31; prices of, 12; refined white sugar, 12; refineries (centrals), 13, 17; refining processes of, 12–13; and the slave trade, 7, 9, 11; tariffs on, 16–17, 18, 37

Sugar Trust. *See* American Sugar Refining Company (the Sugar Trust)

Suharto, Mohammed, 141–42

Sukarno, 141

Sumatra, 119–20; civil unrest in after World War II, 140; deforestation of, 125; effect of deforestation on watersheds in, 125–26; effect of World War II on, 127; pacification of indigenous peoples in, 120; tobacco exports of, 119; use of fertilizers in, 125. *See also* Dutch American Plantation Company ("Hoppum")

Surleaf, Ellen Johnson, 147

sustainable growth/management. *See* tropical rainforests, sustainable forestry in

Swift, Gustavus F., 158

Swift and Company, 177, 180, 182

Taft, William Howard, 32, 56

Tamesis, Florencio, 198

Tannenbaum, Frank, 168

Taylor, Charles, 146–47

Taylor, Thomas, 180

Tenth Pacific Science Congress (1961), 215

Texas: and cattle drives on the Chisholm Trail, 160; cattle ranching in colonial Texas, 155–57; consolidation and modernization of ranches in, 160–61; investment of Texas ranchers in northern Mexico, 165–66; number of cattle in (1860), 159; tobacco, 25, 104, 119, 120; overplanting of, 121

Treaty of Ayacucho, 116

Triangular Trade, 9

Trinidad, 205

Tripp, Juan, 144

tropical fruits, 76–77, 97. *See also* bananas

tropical hardwoods, 4, 36, 187–88; brazilwood, 186; *Dipterocarpaceae* hardwood family, 192, 193; effect of World War I on, 191; exports of to Europe (1800, 1896), 187; mahogany loggers in the Caribbean basin, 186–91; market for in the United States, 202–3; sustainable harvesting of, 4, 185; teak, 209, 210, 212; tree plantations for, 209. *See also* Philippines, colonial logging industry of

tropical rainforests, 223n2; aromatic species of wood in, 192; damage to ecosystem of caused by logging, 188; damage to hydrological systems caused by logging, 213, 234n37; declining forest cover in the tropics, 2; diseases of, 44; dyewood, 187; exploitation of for timber, 185–86; "slash and burn" technique used to destroy, 19–20. *See also* Central American rainforest, conquest of (1872–1945); tropical hardwoods; tropical rainforests, sustainable forestry in tropical rainforests, sustainable forestry in, 202–3, 215–16, 219–20; and debates over "sustained yield," 210; development

tropical rainforests (conintued)
    of sustainable forestry techniques,
    204–5; ecological research on exotic
    tree species, 205–6; goals of forest
    management, 214; increased
    efficiency of saw mills and logging
    machinery, 203–4; organization
    formed to support, 214–15; and
    reforestation, 209–10; and the
    relation between forestry and local
    subsistence, 212–14; and social policy
    toward native tropical populations,
    206–7; and the taungya system,
    211–12
Truman, Harry S., 23
Tubman, William, 144, 146
Turbana, 77

UNIBAN consortium, 77
United Brands, 174, 177
United Fruit Company, 4, 44, 55, 59, 65,
    172, 214; acreage controlled by in
    Costa Rica, 76; acreage controlled by
    in Honduras, 59; acreage controlled
    by in Panama, 48, 76; associate
    producer system of, 75–76; banana
    exports of to the United States from
    Honduras, 49; banana production of
    in Costa Rica, 74–75; clearing of
    forests by, 50–51; competition of with
    Standard Fruit Company, 68;
    contract of with the Costa Rican
    government, 62; and crop
    diversification, 76–77; founding of,
    48; and its "Great White Fleet" of
    banana boats, 49, 65; and the
    overthrow of Arbenz government in
    Guatemala, 71; presence of in
Ecuador, 67–68; presence of in
    Guatemala, 70–72; presence of in
    Panama, 48–49; purchase of the
    Cuyamel Fruit Company by, 59, 64;
    and railroad-building in Costa Rica,
    47; rainforest land owned by, 51;
    reforestation efforts of, 209–10;
    rivalry of with Costa Rican
    government, 60–61; workforce of,
    49–50
United Nations Food and Agricultural
    Association (FAO), 200, 207–8
United States, 46, 54, 90, 138, 220; access
    of to tropical resources, 221–22;
    agrochemical exports of, 219; banana
    consumption in, 3–4, 43, 77–78; beef
    consumption in, 4, 168–69, 171; beef
    industry of, 177; coffee consumption
    in, 3, 83, 95, 97; and the consolidation
    of tropical agrobusiness, 218–19;
    decline in per capita consumption of
    during baby boom years, 65; demand
    for tropical hardwoods in, 4;
    ecological empire of, 1–5, 79, 217–18;
    growth of the middle class in, 188;
    post–World War II economy of,
    96–97; rubber consumption in, 3–4,
    125; stockpiling of rubber supplies
    by, 139; support of for the overthrow
    of Arbenz in Guatemala, 71; timber
    consumption of, 202–3; vulnerability
    of to loss of rubber supplies in World
    War II, 136–37. See also Cuba, and
    the United States
United States Rubber Company, 117,
    121–22, 141, 148; acreage controlled
    by in Sumatra, 122; losses of, 125
Uruguay, 161, 164, 171

U.S. International Cooperation Agency, 200–201

Vaccaro brothers (Joseph, Luca, and Felix), 54, 56
Valdez, Juan, 112, 218
Van Alstyne, Richard, 10
Van Horne, William, 17–18
Venezuela, 101, 102, 181; coffee planters' rebellion in, 102; and the Federal War (1858), 102–3
Villa, Pancho, 167
Vogt, William, 213–14
Volker, Tys, 120

Wadsworth, Frank, 212
Walker, Herbert, 34–35
Wallace, Henry, 21, 135
Washington, Booker T., 131
Weber, David, 156
Weis Fricker Company, 202

West Indies, 82–83; commercial trade of with North America, 9–11; monopolization of West Indies coffee exports by Great Britain, 91
Wilcox, Walter, 189
Williams, Eric, 23
Wilson Meats, 177, 182
Wilson Tariff (1894), 16
Worcester, Dean, 35, 196
World Forestry Congress (1960), 214–15
World Wildlife Fund, 220
W. R. Grace Company, 175

Zelaya, José Santos, 55
Zemurray, Samuel, 54, 55, 56, 57; cattle ranching activities of, 172; establishment of the Lancetilla experimental farm, 59; sale of Cuyamel Fruit Company by, 59, 64
Zetas, Alfredo, 19

About the Author

Richard Tucker is Adjunct Professor of Natural Resources at the University of Michigan. An environmental historian, he has published on the history of deforestation in India and other colonial and tropical countries. He is co-editor of *Global Deforestation and the Nineteenth-Century World Economy* (1983) and *World Deforestation in the Twentieth Century* (1987). He is presently working on the environmental impacts of warfare; he has co-edited Natural Enemy, *Natural Ally: Toward an Environmental History of War* (2005).